Patriotism and Citizenship

Sean Richey

Patriotism and Citizenship

A Contractual Theory of the Impact of Patriotism

palgrave
macmillan

Sean Richey
Atlanta, GA, USA

ISBN 978-3-031-89884-6 ISBN 978-3-031-89885-3 (eBook)
https://doi.org/10.1007/978-3-031-89885-3

This Palgrave Macmillan imprint is published by the registered company Springer Nature Switzerland AG
The registered company address is: Gewerbestrasse 11, 6330 Cham, Switzerland

For Masako

Contents

1 **Introduction** 1
Findings on the Impact of Patriotism 6
Prior Understandings of the Impact of Patriotism 8
Annotated Table of Contents and Detailed Chapter Outline 9
Chapter Two: A Contractual Theory of Patriotism 9
Chapter Three: Who is Patriotic and Who is Not 9
Chapter Four: What Patriotism Means to People 10
Chapter Five: Patriotism and Collective Action 10
Chapter Six: Patriotism and Voter Turnout and Political Participation 11
Chapter Seven: Patriotism and Diffuse Support 11
Chapter Eight: Patriotism and Political Judgment 12
Chapter Nine: Patriotism and Authoritarianism, Racism, Bigotry, and Xenophobia 12
Chapter Ten: Local Patriotism 13
Chapter Eleven: Conclusion 13
References 13

2 **A Contractual Theory of Patriotism** 17
Prior Theories of Patriotism 19
A Contractual Theory of Patriotism 23
A Contractual Theory of Patriotism 24

A Model of the Contractual Theory of Patriotism 26
Model of Collective Action and Patriotism 27
Model of Decision-Making and Patriotism 30
Empirical Predictions Derived from the Theories of Patriotism 32
Voter Turnout and Political Participation 32
Civic Participation 33
Political Judgement 33
Diffuse Support 34
Xenophobia 35
Empirical Predictions Derived from the Collective Action Theory of Local Patriotism 36
Conclusion 36
References 37

3 Who Is Patriotic And Who Is Not 41
General Levels of Patriotism 42
The Unpatriotic are a Real, But Small Group in America 47
Patriotism and Demographics 49
Patriotism and Ideology and Partisan Identification 55
Conclusion 60
References 61

4 What Patriotism Means to Americans 63
What Patriotism Means to Americans 64
List 1: How Americans Show Patriotism 64
Qualitative Text Analysis 67
Quantitative Text Analysis 69
Sentiment Analysis 70
Sentiment Analysis by Subgroups 72
Conclusion 74
References 75

5 Patriotism and Collective Action 77
Collective Action and Civic Engagement 78
Benefits of Civic Engagement 79
Experimental Results 80
Survey Results 83
Conclusion 91
References 92

6 **Patriotism and Voter Turnout and Political Participation** 95
Voter Turnout as a Civic Duty 97
Results for Voter Turnout 100
Results for Political Participation 105
Conclusion 108
References 110

7 **Patriotism and Diffuse Support** 111
Importance of Diffuse Support 112
Measuring Diffuse Support 113
Political Trust 115
Political Efficacy 116
Satisfaction with Democracy 117
Conclusion 121
References 122

8 **Patriotism and Political Judgment** 123
Democracy and Political Judgment 125
Patriotism and Discerning Problems with America 126
Results for Conspiracy Theories 128
Results for Economic Outcomes 131
Conclusion 138
References 139

9 **Patriotism and Authoritarianism, Racism, Bigotry, and Xenophobia** 141
Patriotism and Authoritarianism, Racism, Bigotry, and Xenophobia 142
Data 143
Measuring the Authoritarian Personality with SCA 143
Measuring Racism with the Symbolic Racism Scale 145
Measuring Bigotry with Attitudes Toward Gays and Lesbians 145
Measuring Xenophobia with Attitudes Toward Muslims and Immigration 146
Results 147
Conclusion 153
References 154

10 Local Patriotism 157
Conceptualizing Local Patriotism 160
Patriotism at the National Level 161
Local Patriotism and Citizens' Attitudes and Behaviors 162
Experimental Procedures 164
Data and Methods 166
Dependent Variables 166
Local Patriotism Variable 168
Control Variables 170
Methods 172
Results 172
Prediction 1 172
Prediction 2 174
Prediction 3 175
Prediction 4 175
Conclusion 179
References 180

11 Conclusion 185
Future Areas of Research on Patriotism 187
Impact of Nationalism on Citizenship 187
Unpatriotic Americans: Causes and Impacts 188
Patriotism and Cognition 189
Potential Ways to Increase Patriotism Through Civic Participation 190
Conclusion 192
References 192

Appendix 195

Index 203

List of Figures

Fig. 3.1	Patriotism data from a 2021 online survey showing the percentage that said they like or love America	43
Fig. 3.2	A histogram of patriotism data from the 2012 ANES, shown as the percent who say they hate, dislike, neither dislike nor hate, like, or love America	44
Fig. 3.3	This graph shows the percentage who are extremely proud to be an American. Data from the Gallup Poll Social Survey	46
Fig. 3.4	This bar graph shows the mean of those who feel mostly proud, both proud and ashamed, and mostly ashamed of their country. Data from nationally representative samples in France, Germany, the United Kingdom, and the United States from Pew (2020)	47
Fig. 3.5	A boxplot of patriotism data from 2021, shown as the mean with 95% confidence intervals of those who say they hate, dislike, neither dislike nor hate, like, or love America, separated by age groups	51
Fig. 3.6	This histogram shows the percentage expressing different feelings toward America, differentiated by race and ethnicity. Data from ANES 2012	52
Fig. 3.7	This graph shows the percentage and 95% confidence intervals expressing different feelings toward America, differentiated by parental nativity—data from ANES 2012	53

Fig. 3.8	This histogram shows the mean with 95% confidence intervals of Americans who feel mostly proud, both proud and ashamed, and mostly ashamed of America, differentiated by gender. Data from Pew 2020	54
Fig. 3.9	This bar graph shows the mean of Americans who feel patriotic, differentiated by ideology	56
Fig. 3.10	This histogram shows the mean with 95% confidence intervals of Americans who feel mostly proud, both proud and ashamed, and mostly ashamed of America, differentiated by ideology. Data from Pew 2020	57
Fig. 3.11	This histogram shows the mean with 95% confidence intervals of Americans who feel mostly proud, both proud and ashamed, and mostly ashamed of America, differentiated by partisan identification—data from Pew 2020	59
Fig. 4.1	This bar graph shows the percentage of Americans who consider these actions patriotic from Fox News Poll (2014)	66
Fig. 4.2	This bar graph shows the number of words associated with these emotions when Americans consider their feelings of love and hate toward America	72
Fig. 5.1	The percentage clicking to schedule blood donation by experimental treatment	82
Fig. 5.2	The predicted percentage saying they donated blood in 2012 by patriotic beliefs, calculated from Model 3 in Table 5.1	84
Fig. 5.3	The predicted number of groups volunteered for in 2012, calculated from Model 3 in Table 5.4	91
Fig. 6.1	The predicted probabilities of self-reported voting in the 2020 Presidential elections, calculated from Model 3 in Table 6.2	101
Fig. 6.2	The predicted probabilities of validated voting in the 2012 Presidential elections, calculated from Model 3 in Table 6.3	103
Fig. 8.1	This graph shows the point estimate and 95% confidence intervals of the percentage of respondents expressing at least one major problem with the United States. Data from 2012	127
Fig. 8.2	This graph shows the predicted level and 95% confidence intervals of belief in conspiracy ideation. See text for details of the conspiracy ideation psychology scale used—data from 2021	130

Fig. 8.3	This graph shows the predicted level and 95% confidence intervals of belief in both birtherism and trutherism. Data from 2012	133
Fig. 8.4	This graph shows the predicted level and 95% confidence intervals of correctly assessing the economic levels in the preceding 12 months. Data from 2021	135
Fig. 8.5	This graph shows the predicted level and 95% confidence intervals of correctly assessing the economic levels in the preceding 12 months. Data from 2012	136
Fig. 8.6	This graph shows the predicted level and 95% confidence intervals of correctly predicting the economic levels in the next 12 months. Data from 2012	137
Fig. 10.1	This bar graph shows the distribution of local patriotism	169
Fig. 10.2	This scatterplot shows the relationship of local patriotism and national patriotism	171
Fig. 10.3	This box plot shows the mean and 95% confidence intervals of the willingness to donate to help solve the town's biggest problem for the treatment and control groups	177
Fig. 10.4	This box plot shows the mean and 95% confidence intervals of the willingness to donate to help solve the town's biggest problem for the treatment and control groups	178

List of Tables

Table 3.1	Demographics determinants of patriotism	50
Table 3.2	Determinants of patriotism	55
Table 3.3	Determinants of pride and shame in America	60
Table 4.1	Sentiment analysis of writing about feelings of love or hate toward America	71
Table 4.2	Sentiment analysis of writing about feelings of love or hate toward America by race and ethnicity	73
Table 4.3	Sentiment analysis of writing about feelings of love or hate toward America, by ideology	74
Table 5.1	Determinants of donating blood in 2012	85
Table 5.2	Determinants of civic engagement activities in 2020	86
Table 5.3	Determinants of number of types of volunteer activities in 2020	88
Table 5.4	Determinants of number of types of volunteer activities	90
Table 6.1	Determinants of feeling that voter turnout is a civic duty and not a choice in 2012	99
Table 6.2	Determinants of voter turnout in the 2020 presidential election	100
Table 6.3	Determinants of presidential validated voter turnout in 2012	102
Table 6.4	Determinants of presidential validated voter turnout in 2016	104
Table 6.5	Bivariate correlation between patriotism and political activities in 2012	105

Table 6.6	Determinants of number of acts of political participation in 2012	107
Table 6.7	Determinants of participation in protest, march, rally, or demonstration	108
Table 7.1	Determinants of political trust in 2021	116
Table 7.2	Determinants of political trust in 2012	117
Table 7.3	Determinants of political efficacy in 2021	118
Table 7.4	Determinants of political efficacy in 2012	119
Table 7.5	Determinants of satisfaction with democracy in 2021	120
Table 7.6	Determinants of satisfaction with democracy in 2012	120
Table 8.1	Determinants of conspiracy ideation in 2021	129
Table 8.2	Determinants of believing in birtherism and trutherism in 2012	132
Table 8.3	Determinants of correctly knowing the state of the economy in 2021	134
Table 8.4	Determinants of correctly knowing the state of the economy in 2012	134
Table 8.5	Determinants of Correctly Predicting the Economy in 2013	137
Table 9.1	Determinates of an authoritarian personality 2012	148
Table 9.2	Determinates of symbolic racism for white respondents 2012	148
Table 9.3	Thermometer feelings toward Gays and Lesbians 2021	149
Table 9.4	Thermometer Feelings Toward Gays and Lesbians 2012	150
Table 9.5	Thermometer feelings toward muslims 2021	151
Table 9.6	Thermometer feelings toward muslims 2012	151
Table 9.7	Support for immigration 2021	152
Table 9.8	Support for immigration 2012	153
Table 10.1	Determinants of participation in local politics	173
Table 10.2	Determinants of civic participation	174
Table 10.3	Determinants of trust in local government	176
Table A1	Correlation matrix patriotism and 2012 ANES volunteering items	196
Table A2	Attitudes towards gays and lesbians	199
Table A3	Attitudes towards Muslims	199
Table A4	Attitudes towards immigration	200
Table A5	Government trust	200
Table A6	Efficacy	201
Table A7	Democracy satisfaction	201

CHAPTER 1

Introduction

Abstract This chapter introduces the overarching research questions: What is the impact of patriotism on citizens in a democracy, and should patriotism be encouraged? The chapter provides an overview of the theoretical approach, previewing how patriotism can act as a motivating "contractual" force for collective action without producing blind obedience. It also summarizes the empirical methods—original surveys, experiments, and qualitative research—and outlines the main findings, setting the stage for the book's central argument that patriotism generally enhances, rather than undermines, democratic citizenship.

Keywords Patriotism · Democratic Citizenship · Empirical Research · Collective Action · Public Opinion · Political Behavior

What is the impact of patriotism on citizens? Most Americans are patriotic, but important differences exist among politically relevant subgroupings, such as ideology or partisan identification (see Frankovic 2021, Pew Research Center 2014). Despite some political theorists judging patriotism negatively for its impact on citizenship (e.g., Kateb 2006), we do not know enough about its effect on the attitudes and behaviors of citizens. While some work on patriotism focuses on patriotism's potential relationship topics, such as bigotry (e.g., Heinrich 2020), a broad

S. Richey, *Patriotism and Citizenship*,
https://doi.org/10.1007/978-3-031-89885-3_1

overview of how citizenship[1] interacts with patriotism is missing from prior literature. Debates over whether education should promote patriotism revolve around an analysis of whether it is worthy of inclusion in pedagogy (Kodelja 2020). However, since the impact of patriotism on beliefs and behaviors is not fully understood, the cost–benefit analysis of its inclusion in education cannot be accurately derived. We need to know what consequences derive from patriotism to fully understand whether this is a goal that society should promote. This book aims to demonstrate empirically how patriotism, when understood as a reciprocal social contract, positively influences civic engagement, political participation, and trust in democratic institutions, ultimately arguing for its constructive role in strengthening democratic citizenship.

I define patriotism as a love of country, and it has distinctive features that set it apart from related concepts such as national identity, national pride, and nationalism. While national identity refers to a sense of belonging to a specific nation and sharing its culture, traditions, and values, patriotism emphasizes an emotional and devoted relationship with one's country, often expressed through support and loyalty. National pride involves a feeling of satisfaction and esteem for one's nation, typically based on achievements and attributes, but patriotism extends beyond pride to encompass a profound and enduring affection and commitment to the country's well-being.

Unlike nationalism, which can imply a sense of superiority and often an aggressive stance toward other nations, patriotism is more about a deep love and respect for one's country without denigrating others. Nationalism, especially in its modern form, has also become associated with populist movements that emphasize a "nation-first" approach. This rise of populism often centers on a rejection of globalism, an exclusionary stance on immigration, and a focus on protecting national sovereignty and identity against perceived external threats or influences. While populist nationalism can galvanize political engagement, it often does so by fostering divisions both within and between nations.

[1] Citizenship, in the context of this research, refers to the status of being a member of a political community endowed with rights and responsibilities. Crucial to my understanding of this term is that the concept encompasses not only legal entitlements, such as the right to vote and work within a country but also the civic responsibilities of participation in the community's democratic processes and adherence to its laws and ethical norms.

This book explores the intricate relationship between patriotism and various dimensions of citizenship within the United States. Through a comprehensive empirical analysis, which includes the utilization of novel surveys, in-depth interviews, and a wealth of diverse datasets (data described in-depth on page 45), I undertake the task of unraveling the influence of patriotism on some of the most important elements of citizenship, including civic engagement, political participation, and the levels of trust within our society.

The research below presents a unique perspective on patriotism, advocating for its role as a reciprocal social contract. This viewpoint suggests that patriotism can significantly enhance the fabric of our democratic[2] society. By examining the nature of patriotism, I aim to uncover how individuals perceive their duty to contribute to America in exchange for the benefits they receive from it.

This research contributes to our scholarly understanding and holds practical implications for educators, policymakers, and citizens alike. By recognizing the potential of a constructive and inclusive form of patriotism, we can work toward a society where democratic values are upheld, and citizens are motivated to actively participate in shaping the future of their nation. Using data from multiple novel surveys, interviews, experiments, and dozens of other datasets from other sources, I show that patriotism is highly correlated with many normatively beneficial aspects of citizenship and is not associated with uncritical judgment or xenophobia as often suggested. Additionally, I show below that being less patriotic correlates with lower validated voter turnout, civic engagement, increased incorrect predictions about the economy in good times, and lower political trust, political efficacy, and satisfaction with democracy. This research provides a fuller picture of the impact of patriotism on public opinion and political behavior than has been provided previously in political theory or political psychology. It demonstrates the clear benefits of patriotism for liberal democratic societies.

Outside academia, there is great cultural turmoil and angst over patriotism, particularly its role in education (Waxman 2021), which is matched

[2] Democracy is defined in the context of this research as a form of government in which power is held either directly by the people or through elected representatives. It is characterized by principles such as political equality, majority rule, and the protection of fundamental freedoms and minority rights. Democracy emphasizes the importance of public participation in governance, the rule of law, and safeguarding civil liberties.

by a similar debate inside academia (Murphy 2006; Merry 2009). Some argue that patriotism has an important role in fostering a civic education (Boyte 2003), while others are more skeptical of its influence on children's civic abilities (Archard 1999; Reimann 2021). Education and patriotism also have been found to interact in their influence on political behavior (Straughn and Andriot 2011). Callan (1999) discusses the tension in accurately portraying problems with America's past, such as slavery, in history classes, for example, and the risk of education being accused of promoting anti-American views.

Most of these debates in mass media are not empirically grounded and often consist of ideological diatribes (see, e.g., Miller 2023). Almost daily, mass media reports stories of some contentious debate involving patriotism. This includes fierce disagreement over whether it should be taught in schools or evidenced in our cultural traditions. Accusations of those lacking patriotism on one side versus complaints of cultural chauvinism on the other are widespread and unsolvable due to the lack of empirical evidence to help resolve these debates. This book takes a non-ideological empirical approach to examine the possible outcomes that derive from patriotism.

Chiefly lacking is a theoretically grounded empirical analysis of the effect of patriotism on citizenship. I start in Chapter 2 by developing novel theories of how patriotism influences attitudes and behavior based in part on theories of collective action. Using the latest methodologies, novel surveys, qualitative data, and experimental research, the research in this book proceeds from this theoretical framework to provide a thorough understanding of the impact of patriotism on the main topics citizenship that prior scholars have focused on.

Specifically, in Chapter 2, I present my theory of how collective action can be used to understand patriotism's impact on political behavior and public opinion derived from conceptualizing patriotism as contractual. I show in qualitative research in Chapter 4 that patriotism is almost always expressed in terms of a contract. Patriotic citizens say they want to repay America for what its governmental and societal systems have given them. This conceptualization is contractual because the citizen can withhold their love of America if the national government does not do its part to provide citizens with rights, freedoms, security, and sufficient infrastructure to provide a happy life. In exchange for receiving something profoundly important, citizens often want to give back to America. The most important impact that would derive from patriotism on citizenship is how citizens repay America through sacrifice or choose not to because they are unhappy with it. Chapter 2 develops a theoretical model of these intertwined relationships and how they relate to collective action.

A long literature on collective action shows that behavior and actions are motivated primarily through cost–benefit analyses of whether the action will lead to success. As has been known since Downs (1957) and Olson (1965), it is not likely that an individual's action will directly lead to a successful outcome in a mass democracy. There are too many actors, and the problems are too significant for one person's actions to fix the problem or alter the outcome. This canonical insight is as relevant today for understanding behavior as it was when it was first created, and it serves as the foundational starting point for any understanding of when someone will act on a societal problem.

Political scientists and some sociologists have steadily developed the critical insight that there are potential instrumental, solidarity, and psychological benefits from any action (e.g., Riker and Ordeshook 1968; Wilson 1973). Unless these additional solidarities and psychological benefits are incorporated into our understanding of why people act, any action will be irrational in a mass democracy with hundreds of millions of people. Simply put, one person's actions are almost always irrelevant, with no influence on something's success or failure. However, since the population is constantly involved in some form of societal or political action—e.g., voting, boycotts, protests, volunteering—there must be some other benefit derived from these actions. Once the separate benefits are understood, it is possible to see how actions that do not derive an instrumental benefit, such as achieving a policy goal, are still rational for the individual to take due to these other benefits. These benefits can be solidarity derived from belonging to a group or psychological benefits derived from some psychological impulse to be willing to incur the costs of the action.

In Chapter 2, I posit that the critical impact of having patriotism is that it supplies a psychological benefit that will outweigh the cost of action to patriotic people. In Chapter 2, I create a model that shows how being more patriotic will make someone more likely to incur the costs of sacrifice to help the country. This problem in collective action can be expressed in various actions, but the fundamental cost–benefit analysis will remain the same. Whether it is political participation, volunteering, civic engagement, taking the time to learn about current affairs and politics, or even direct efforts at collective action, fundamentally, we need some psychologically derived explanation to explain these behaviors. Patriotism provides that explanation because if you love the country, you will be willing to incur these costs for its improvement.

Further, one potential consequence of patriotism is xenophobia (see Raghunathan 2017). Since xenophobia is mainly derived from other psychological factors, such as authoritarianism, social dominance orientation, and outgroup animus, loving the country is not necessary to explain those behaviors because other, more directly related psychological explanations explain having these feelings. In other words, conceptualizing patriotism as part of a contract between the individual and America suggests that there will not necessarily be a relationship between loving the country and animus for any particular subgroup within the country. The cost–benefit analysis does not offer any explanation of any impact on xenophobia.

Notably, a cost–benefit analysis that applies toward loving America may also apply toward one loving their municipalities. In Chapter 10, I show that loving one's municipality impacts local politics similarly to having national-level patriotism.

I use this theoretical basis to develop a series of hypothesis tests conducted on observational survey data and survey experiments. These tests are examined through quantitative textual analysis of qualitative responses to questions about patriotism. I find robust support for this theory across all methodologies.

Findings on the Impact of Patriotism

Using new survey data augmented with data from the American National Election Studies (ANES), my findings are based on testing a new theory of patriotism: patriotism impact derives from a contractual relationship with the nation. I use qualitative evidence from over 500 responses to examine qualitative data on what patriotism means by asking respondents to write open-ended paragraphs on their feelings toward America. While most respondents mentioned problems they disliked, they also expressed profound gratitude for the freedoms and opportunities in America. Thus, these open-ended qualitative responses show a nuanced view of America that is not blind patriotism or nationalistic. Instead, respondents have a clear-eyed view of this country's inequities and troublesome past but also profound hope for its future. I also use a text-as-data quantitative text analysis approach to investigate these responses, breaking down sentiment analysis into important demographic sub-groups and partisan groups. These results show clearly that Americans conceptualize patriotism and contractual terms as they are repaying America for the freedoms and opportunities its governmental and societal systems have given them.

In the subsequent chapters, flowing directly from this theory, I find that patriotism has a strong positive correlation with political participation and civic engagement and diffuse support for America's system of governance. These positive correlations are robust to multiple specifications, regression modeling techniques, and various control variables known from the prior literature to correlate with these variables. I also find no evidence that patriotism correlates with xenophobia. For example, I find it does not impact feelings of xenophobia as measured by anti-Muslim feelings and opposition to immigration.

In addition to these standard social science academic regression modeling techniques, I also use survey experiments to demonstrate that priming patriotic feelings leads to more willingness to sacrifice. I show that priming patriotic feelings makes participants in a survey experiment more likely to click a link to sign up with the American Red Cross to donate blood. Specifically, a control group was randomly assigned to be told that America has a crisis in donating blood, and they could click an actual link to the American Red Cross website to set up a blood donation in their area. Only 7.9% of participants in the control group who did not prime patriotism clicked the link. However, priming feelings of love toward America in an otherwise similar prompt led to 15.8% clicking the link to donate blood to the American Red Cross. Donating blood is a classic example of something universally needed but is easy to free-ride and not do. Showing that priming patriotism makes people more willing to incur an individual cost to ensure a broadly distributed benefit confirms that patriotism is beneficial to solving collective action problems[3]. This

[3] Collective action problems refer to situations where individuals in a group have a common interest in achieving a goal but face challenges in coordinating and mobilizing efforts due to conflicting personal interests or the temptation to free-ride on the efforts of others. These problems arise because the success of the collective action—such as public goods provision, environmental conservation, or social movements—benefits all members of the group, regardless of individual contribution. However, the cost of participation may deter individual action, leading to underinvestment or failure to act collectively. The essence of these problems lies in reconciling individual incentives with the collective benefit, making it crucial for mechanisms like patriotism, which can enhance cooperation and willingness to contribute to collective goals, overcoming the inherent dilemmas of collective action.

experiment confirms the causal mechanisms described in my theory and is robustly shown through the positive correlations with socially beneficial behaviors and patriotism.

I also introduced a novel conception of patriotism based on a love of one's municipality. I measure this local patriotism and show that it profoundly impacts whether one is involved in political participation at the local level, civic engagement, trust in local government, and willingness to donate money to help the town. Applying the theories developed concerning national-level patriotism to feelings of love toward the municipality validates the fundamental causal mechanisms because it shows that these mechanisms work at different levels of government. A vast literature exists on local politics, but this research shows that a critical omitted variable from this literature is local patriotism. Municipalities have a profound impact on quality of life. This level of government is responsible for many of the most important aspects of human happiness, such as education, public health, policing and criminal justice, enforcing environmental and safety regulations, and transportation. By introducing the novel concept of local patriotism and showing his profound impact on town politics, this book provides insight into improving involvement and cooperation with this crucial level of government.

Prior Understandings of the Impact of Patriotism

Several modern classics in this literature have impacted debates around patriotism in the United States. This book differs from these works because it focuses on what having or lacking patriotism does to the attitudes and behaviors of citizens of advanced democracies such as the United States. While I focus on how patriotism influences citizenship, these works cover different aspects of patriotism in the United States. Most of these works are theoretical analyses of the underlying ideas of patriotism. For example, Curren and Dorn (2018) focus on empirical depictions of the impact of patriotism on students. However, no current book investigates the impact of having or not having patriotism in a data-analytic social-scientific manner.

Generally speaking, one can hardly understate the interest in this topic to the public, scholars, and policymakers. For our understanding of how to live in a multicultural democracy, there is a growing demand for information and research on patriotism. This book addresses these topics and adds to them in meaningful ways. First, it is far more rigorous and in-depth than most popular opinion-based books about patriotism's impact on American political life, explicitly concerning democracy. Even most academic research on democracy relies on observational data, but here, I also use experiments to look inside the "box" of decision-making to accurately see how patriotism can be used as a tool to promote citizenship. Furthermore, while patriotism is somewhat researched, this is the first book to seriously grapple with how patriotism interacts with these various elements of citizenship.

I will next provide a detailed outline of each chapter. I detail the book's main topics and describe the chief outcomes of the research. I also detail the new survey data and experimental research the book engages in to summarize the main results.

Annotated Table of Contents and Detailed Chapter Outline

Chapter Two: A Contractual Theory of Patriotism

This chapter delineates my theory of how patriotism can benefit citizenship by showing that it solves collective action problems through its contractual nature. The loving feelings of patriotism are based on gratitude for what society has given and the subsequent willingness to repay these gifts. Based on this contractual theory of patriotism, this chapter creates models to show how patriotism is a beneficial feature of citizenship due to its ability to provide a psychological benefit that will explain the willingness to incur costs to support a societal good. This chapter also creates theoretical models of how the impact of patriotism on decision-making will be contingent on whether the national government is viewed as acting positively or negatively. This chapter also explains how this book adds to several theoretical debates by providing new evidence on the beneficial impact of patriotism on modern liberal democratic societies.

Chapter Three: Who is Patriotic and Who is Not

Chapter 3 is an in-depth statistical analysis of the levels of patriotism in America, how those levels have changed over time, and which demographic and political subgroupings are more and less patriotic. While I find high levels of patriotism across sub-groupings, this chapter also delves into the non-trivial percentage of the population who express dislike or hatred of America. Across various samples and measures of patriotism, around 3% of Americans express hatred toward America. Perhaps more consequential, across the same varied measures and samples taken in different years, around 8 to 10% say they dislike America. Additionally, around 10 to 15% express no feelings—they neither like nor dislike America. Thus, around 25% of the population is not patriotic and has been almost wholly ignored in prior literature. Also, this chapter explores different ideological and partisan groupings and their relationship to patriotism. To be clear, most Americans are patriotic across every measured demographic subgroup and party identification, but not every ideological grouping. This chapter shows interesting variances exist in the total level of patriotism across ideological groups.

Chapter Four: What Patriotism Means to People

This chapter examines qualitative data on what patriotism means to 500 Americans who were asked to write open-ended paragraphs on their feelings toward America. This sample was matched to nationally representative data on age, gender, and race, providing a more diverse sample than is typical of qualitative research. What emerges is a fascinating picture of the inner conflicts of many Americans. While almost every respondent mentions substantial problems in the country they dislike, these people also express profound gratitude for the freedoms and opportunities this country provides them. Rather than blind patriotism, these open-ended qualitative responses show a nuanced view of America. These Americans are neither uncritically obedient nor uncritically radical. Instead, they have a clear-eyed view of this country's inequities and troublesome past but also profound hope for its future. Almost no prior literature has explored this in-depth into how Americans' view of their relationship with their country. I also use a text-as-data approach using quantitative text analysis to investigate these responses, including breaking down sentiment analysis into important demographic sub-groups and partisan groups.

Chapter Five: Patriotism and Collective Action

This chapter investigates the relationship between patriotism and collective action using two methodologies. First, it examines survey data that shows a clear relationship between patriotism and greater civic engagement. Civic engagement is almost always concerned with improving society and is the classic example of a collective action problem. Additionally, this chapter uses experimental evidence to show that a random half of the survey respondents were primed with a patriotic message or more likely to be willing to go to a page to sign up to donate blood to the American Red Cross. Both methodologies come to the same conclusion: patriotism increases the likelihood of engaging in civic engagement. This is further evidence of the theory that patriotism encourages citizens to pay a cost to help society.

Chapter Six: Patriotism and Voter Turnout and Political Participation

This chapter analyzes newly collected survey data combined with older survey data, showing that no matter how patriotism is measured, it consistently correlates with validated voter turnout. This chapter tests the hypothesis that turnout positively correlates with political participation because it increases the likelihood that someone will be willing to take on the cost of electoral participation. They engage in turnout because they believe it will better the nation they care about. Consistent with the theory explicated in Chapter 2, other forms of partisan participation do not correlate with patriotism. As voter turnout is almost universally held in the literature to be a positive for democracy, it empirically demonstrates one clear avenue in which patriotism benefits citizenship.

Chapter Seven: Patriotism and Diffuse Support

Diffuse support is the combined expression of support for a governmental system. It is often measured through political trust, external political efficacy, and support for democracy in democratic systems. Research in comparative politics has shown diffuse support has decreased in recent decades in advanced postindustrial liberal democracies. I review the literature on this topic in Chapter 7, which also shows that greater diffuse support leads to more stability within the system, greater compliance with public policy, and more willingness to sacrifice for the country's greater good. I also review the empirical research showing that nations with greater diffuse support have easier times with vexing cultural transitions, more resilience toward natural disasters, and more efficiency in passing legislation and policymaking. It is crucial to understand what creates support for democratic systems broadly.

In this chapter, I test whether patriotism correlates with greater diffuse support. Using novel survey data, I find a strong positive correlation between patriotism and political trust, external political efficacy, and support for democracy in democratic systems, even after controlling for other known determinants of diffuse support. This shows patriotism's importance for citizens' willingness to work with the government to improve societal improvements.

Chapter Eight: Patriotism and Political Judgment

A chief worry of people skeptical of the need for patriotism is that it will make citizens unwilling or unable to critique society's problems. They advocate that it is better to have citizens who are not emotionally attached to their nation to remain objective in their critical analysis of the nation to improve their political judgment. However, I theorize that there are situations in which patriotism will benefit political judgment. Political judgment in this chapter is measured in multiple ways: by being able to recognize that there are problems in the United States, correctly predicting future outcomes involving the country, and not believing in conspiracy theories. In line with the theoretical predictions, patriotism is shown not to correlate with whether or not someone can see the problems in the United States, correlates with having more correct assessments of future positive economic conditions, and with less belief in antigovernment conspiracy theories. These results show that a common belief that patriotism delimits sound political judgment is, in fact, empirically shown to be incorrect.

Chapter Nine: Patriotism and Authoritarianism, Racism, Bigotry, and Xenophobia

One of the most vexing issues with patriotism is its potential relationship with authoritarianism, racism, bigotry, and xenophobia. A possible concern is that patriotism will correlate with a dislike for marginalized populations in their country that they deem not to belong. Most past research, however, shows that it is not true that the more one loves America, the more likely one will dislike people seen as deviating from their conceptualization of mainstream Americans. The positive influence of patriotism on citizenship shown in previous chapters would be deeply complicated if patriotism simultaneously correlates with various forms of discrimination and xenophobia. Thus, we must adjudicate the relationship between patriotism and xenophobia. In this chapter, I investigate this relationship by examining longstanding patterns and survey data augmented with novel survey data and questions. I find that patriotism is generally not correlated with authoritarianism, racism, bigotry, and xenophobia.

Chapter Ten: Local Patriotism

Patriotism is generally understood as a national concept. In this chapter, I posit people hold similarly strong feelings toward their municipal area. I show how local patriotism influences local politics based on my theories of patriotism in national politics. Using novel preregistered survey data from an online sample matched to nationally representative data regarding gender, age, and race, I show that people have feelings of love, indifference, or hate toward their municipality. I also find a strong positive correlation between loving one's municipality and participation in local politics, civic participation, and trust in local government. I also conducted two preregistered survey experiments that show that priming feelings of love and hate toward one's town strongly motivates the willingness to sacrifice to solve local collective action problems. Specifically, stimuli evoked these feelings and made participants much more likely to donate the payment they earned from completing the survey to solve a town problem. These results show the crucial importance of local patriotism for understanding local politics.

Chapter Eleven: Conclusion

I conclude by summarizing the arguments and results. Beyond a simple summary, I examine this book's new insights about patriotism. I conclude the book by suggesting new ways that future researchers can analyze patriotism jointly fruitfully. I also examine some policy proposals to make citizens more patriotic.

References

Archard, David. 1999. "Should We Teach Patriotism?" *Studies in Philosophy and Education* 18: 157–173.

Boyte, Harry C. 2003. "Civic Education and the New American Patriotism Post-9/11." *Cambridge Journal of Education* 33 (1): 85–100.
Callan, Eamonn. 1999. *Creating Citizens: Political Education and Liberal Democracy*. Oxford: Oxford University Press.
Curren, Randall, and Charles Dorn. 2018. *Patriotic Education in a Global Age*. Chicago: University of Chicago Press.
Downs, Anthony. 1957. *An Economic Theory of Democracy*. New York: Harper.
Frankovic, Kathy. 2021. "What Does It Mean to Be Patriotic in 2021?" *YouGov*. YouGov, July 1. https://today.yougov.com/topics/politics/articles-reports/2021/07/01/what-does-it-mean-be-patriotic-2021.
Heinrich, Horst-Alfred. 2020. "Causal Relationship or Not? Nationalism, Patriotism, and Anti-immigration Attitudes in Germany." *Sociology of Race and Ethnicity* 6 (1): 76–91.
Kateb, George. 2006. *Patriotism and Other Mistakes*. New Haven: Yale University Press.
Kodelja, Zdenko. 2020. "Education and Patriotism." In *Handbook of Patriotism*, edited by M. Sardoč. Cham: Springer. https://doi.org/10.1007/978-3-319-54484-7_19.
Merry, Michael S. 2009. "Patriotism, History, and the Legitimate Aims of American Education." *Educational Philosophy and Theory* 41 (4): 378–398.
Miller, Andrew Mark. 2023. "Study Contradicts Claims Critical Race Theory Isn't in Schools, Over 90% Students Exposed to It." *Fox News*, March 3. https://www.foxnews.com/us/study-contradicts-claims-critical-race-theory-isnt-schools-90-students-exposed.
Murphy, James B. 2006. "Tug of War." *Education Next* 3 (4). https://www.educationnext.org/tugofwar/.
Olson, Mancur. 1965. *The Logic of Collective Action: Public Goods and the Theory of Groups*. Cambridge: Harvard University Press.
Pew Research Center. 2014. "Section 9: Patriotism, Personal Traits, Lifestyles and Demographics." Pew Research Center, June 26. https://www.pewresearch.org/politics/2014/06/26/section-9-patriotism-personal-traits-lifestyles-and-demographics/
Raghunathan, Suman. 2017. "Too Many Americans Think Patriotism Means Racism and Xenophobia." *The Nation*, September 11. https://www.thenation.com/article/archive/too-many-americans-think-patriotism-means-racism-and-xenophobia/
Reimann, Thor. 2021. "Patriotic Education: Pride or Problem?" *Harvard Political Review*, August 2. https://harvardpolitics.com/patriotic-education/.
Riker, William H., and Peter C. Ordeshook. 1968. "A Theory of the Calculus of Voting." *American Political Science Review* 62 (1): 25–42.

Straughn, Jeremy Brooke, and Angie L. Andriot. 2011. "Education, Civic Patriotism, and Democratic Citizenship: Unpacking the Education Effect on Political Involvement." *Sociological Forum* 26 (3): 556–580.
Waxman, Olivia B. 2021. "Critical Race Theory Is Simply the Latest Bogeyman.' Inside the Fight Over What Kids Learn About America's History." *Time Magazine*, July 16. https://time.com/6075193/critical-race-theory-debate/
Wilson, James Q. 1973. *Political Organizations*. New York: Basic Books.

CHAPTER 2

A Contractual Theory of Patriotism

Abstract This chapter develops the core theoretical framework, positing that patriotism functions as a psychological benefit in citizens' cost–benefit calculations for collective action. When individuals perceive their country as offering freedoms and opportunities, they feel gratitude and a desire to "repay" those benefits through pro-social or civic acts. The chapter introduces formal models illustrating how a sense of mutual obligation—"I owe something to my country"—can spur volunteerism, voting, and other participatory behaviors, and it addresses concerns about whether patriotism can foster social exclusion or unthinking loyalty. The theory underpins the empirical analyses presented in later chapters.

Keywords Contractual Theory · Gratitude · Psychological Benefit · Collective Action · Formal Models · Normative Citizenship

What impact does patriotism have on the attitudes and behavior of citizens in a democracy? This is an essential pedagogical question because civic education often involves patriotic rituals and symbology (Archard 1999). In this chapter, I create theories of potential influences from patriotism to provide a theoretical basis for the hypothesis testing below. I create and model a novel theory of how patriotism interacts with citizenship based on a contractual conception of how citizens will want to

S. Richey, *Patriotism and Citizenship*,
https://doi.org/10.1007/978-3-031-89885-3_2

repay society for what it has given them. I posit that the loving gratitude of patriotism derives from the feeling that one must repay what America has provided them. We know from the psychology literature on gratitude that it has a profound influence on beliefs and behaviors in settings other than politics, implying that it is potentially influential in political beliefs and behaviors (see a review of this literature in Boggiss et al. 2020). Having received profoundly important rights, freedoms, security, and a stable infrastructure, citizens may feel a duty to sacrifice for their country's benefit. The contractual nature of patriotism results from the exchange of what the national government and societal systems provide citizens with and the subsequent sacrifice citizens feel obligated to provide in return.

I posit, then, that the sacrifice derived from the contractual nature of patriotism will resolve collective action problems and profoundly affect political behavior. Delamater, Katz, and Kelman (1969) provide early survey evidence that being involved with a nation is explainable due to three social-psychologic benefits: "symbolic, an orientation to the nation's symbols and attendant emotional satisfactions; or normative, an orientation toward norms and the associated rewards and sanctions; or functional, a concern with the material and other benefits derivable from membership in the national system" (Delamater et al. 1969). Each one of these benefits sparks involvement with the nation. The citizens gain a reward from society and are then motivated to work for its involvement. Thus, a chief impact of patriotism may be to motivate citizens to cooperate in collective action problems in return for benefits that the society provides them.

Collective action refers to activities undertaken by a group of individuals to achieve common objectives, particularly when individual efforts are insufficient. In the context of patriotism, collective action is understood as the mobilization of citizens driven by a shared love for their country to participate in acts that benefit the public good. This can range from voting and community service to broader political and societal support and engagement. The linkage between patriotism and collective action is premised below on the idea that patriotic sentiment can encourage individuals to transcend personal interests for the collective welfare of the nation. This emotional bond to the country serves as a powerful motivator for engaging in activities that may require personal sacrifice but are deemed necessary for the country's betterment.

Beyond behavioral influences, I theorize that patriotism should also affect beliefs about the nation, which (as I show below) primarily influences political trust and related concepts. Additionally, I show that assessments of the country's successes or failures will be influenced by patriotism, and these assessments should have profound political impacts. Related to this contractual nature is that there is nothing associated with wanting to repay America for what has been given that would make someone more discriminatory or xenophobic. In all circumstances theorized and examined below, patriotism has a positive normative impact on citizenship.

My theoretical perspective also allows for more nuance than most prior literature on this topic in understanding the impact of patriotism because it incorporates the potential impact for those who dislike or hate the country. Prior research on patriotism has mostly ignored the unpatriotic. Although most pundits and scholars assume Americans to be patriotic, I show in Chapter 3 that about 5 to 10% of Americans have little love for the United States and are angry about its actions. The prior literature on American politics has not focused much on the public opinion and political behavior of those Americans who are angry and have little love for their nation. These home-grown anti-Americanists are unhappy with the larger society, which may significantly impact their political beliefs and actions. I seek to create a theory that will allow empirical testing of the impacts of being patriotic and unpatriotic on public opinion and political behavior.

Prior Theories of Patriotism

It is surprising how often patriotism's impact is ignored in academic literature because current political debates often revolve around accusations of blind, unthinking patriotism or knee-jerk anti-Americanism. One key exception is Smith (2021), who articulates the challenges facing the notion of patriotism in contemporary America, highlighting its transformation from a unifying principle to a source of division, exacerbated by extreme politicization from all sides. Where patriotism once symbolized a collective American identity, Smith (2021) shows how it has now been co-opted into a tool for division; on one side, it aligns with nationalism and a divisive "us versus them" mentality, and on the other, it's criticized as a barrier to recognizing diverse ethnic, religious, or racial identities, posing a challenge to the ideals of global cosmopolitanism.

Smith (2021) unpacks patriotism from these polarized interpretations, proposing a version of patriotism that is inclusive enough to accommodate both a dedication to one's country and the acknowledgment of global and multicultural allegiances. Smith argues that true patriotism involves both intellectual and emotional commitment, advocating for a version of patriotism that unites individuals around the foundational values of equality. This perspective presents patriotism not as a divisive force, but as an essential and dignifying quality vital for the cohesion and moral integrity of democratic societies. This is crucial for my empirical analysis of the potential ways that patriotism impacts everyday politics and civic engagement.

Much empirical work on patriotism studies, however, its impact on the distinction between patriotism and nationalism without testing the impact on other aspects of political behavior and public opinion, such as political participation, civic engagement, and diffuse support that I research below (See De Figueiredo and Elkins 2003; Karasawa 2002; Kosterman and Feshbach 1989). While early research on patriotism often conflated it with nationalism (see, e.g., Tamir 1992; Sullivan et al. 1992), modern research uses a more nuanced approach, defining patriotism as a positive appreciation for the nation and willingness to sacrifice for its greater good. In contrast, nationalism is described as a feeling that one's nation is superior to others. Blind patriotism is essentially another phrase for nationalism used in psychology. The literature presents nationalism (or blind patriotism) as a harmful component of citizenship (Schatz et al. 1999).

Several political theorists, however, view patriotism as pathological. Indeed, MacIntyre famously described it as "a permanent source of moral danger" (MacIntyre 1995, 226). These arguments have a significant, though often overlooked or unsaid, cognitive component. Kateb (2006) and others have attacked the concept of loving one's country by stating that it causes citizens to lose the ability to analyze their nation's actions rationally. The entirety of MacIntyre's famous quote reveals a fundamental flaw in this line of thinking. He writes that patriotism is "a permanent source of moral danger because of the way it places our ties to our nation beyond rational criticism" (MacIntyre 1995, 226). Patriotism and quality decision-making are supposed to be highly negatively correlated. My research below shows that they are not necessarily so, and unpacking these concepts reveals a worthwhile extension of our theoretical understanding of patriotism.

One exception in political theory is described by Viroli (1995), who conducted a significant analysis of these issues that separate patriotism from nationalism. Notably, he outlines a theoretical model, which shows that people have used patriotism for centuries to achieve goals and that these people commonly separate it from nationalism. He examines the difference in xenophobic beliefs in national supremacy that nationalists have and patriots do not. His theory suggests that love of country does not necessarily mean the denigration of an out-group or a claim of supremacy among the in-group. According to this research, the history of civic republicanism shows that many have used the language of patriotism to achieve great national goals without using revanchism. Thus, the common fear of many that hatred is needed to motivate behavior may be unfounded. People trying to motivate collective action can use the language of love of country without reverting to attacking an enemy or stressing their supremacy. This theory is a breakthrough because it provides an eloquent analysis and evidence as to why patriotism is not necessarily xenophobic or supremacist (see also Muller 2007). And, crucially, while nationalism correlates with bigotry and xenophobia, patriotism does not (De Figueiredo and Elkins 2003).

Some scholars argue that patriotism encompasses multiple categories, most prominently represented by constructive and constitutional patriotism. An important distinction comes from Schatz, Staub, and Lavine (1999), who argue that patriotism has two dimensions, with an oft-ignored dimension of constructive patriotism. Constructive patriotism is shown by individuals who see societal problems and work toward solutions because they love their country, often requiring sacrifice for the greater good (Schatz et al. 1999). Constructive patriots may sometimes be angry and ashamed of America's actions, but they still love their country. These constructive patriots generally have traits that are healthy for democracy, and these scholars argue that they must be distinguished from those citizens who are never ashamed of or angry at the United States. I find below that almost everyone has some problem with the United States, and so I focus love of America in this research.

Another conception of patriotism is constitutional patriotism. Constitutional patriotism features a deep attachment and allegiance to the nation's *raison d'etre* and essential documents, but it does not devolve into a type of blood and soil nationalism (Muller 2007). Instead, its critical point is that anyone can be a full member of a nation if they have an allegiance to its foundational national aspirations, essential documents, and civic culture. In this way, constitutional patriotism welcomes immigrants and historically marginalized subgroups as patriotic members of society.

While prior research has focused on nationalism and blind patriotism a lot and a little on constructive patriotism, it has essentially ignored the unpatriotic. Moreover, research on anti-Americanism usually focuses on non-Americans, such as Europeans who are against America (e.g., Roger 2005, but also see Hollander 1995). The empirical literature up to this point has investigated other types of patriotism in a few articles, but it has not expressly examined non-patriots. These would be citizens who do not like their country and differ substantially from the constructive patriots described in Schatz, Staub, and Lavine (1999). These anti-Americanists potentially have profoundly different beliefs about the national government and general societal systems and their responsibility to sacrifice for it. Thus, prior research has not thoroughly investigated patriotism because it has not focused on the minority who are not patriotic.

In addressing the nuanced spectrum of patriotism, it's pivotal to differentiate between "constructive" and "blind" patriotism. Constructive patriotism embodies a critical love for one's country, encouraging individuals to recognize its shortcomings and strive for societal improvement. This form of patriotism fosters a balanced critique and allegiance, driving democratic engagement through informed and thoughtful participation. Conversely, blind patriotism is marked by an unquestioning loyalty that overlooks flaws and discourages critique, potentially leading to a passive acceptance of governmental decisions without scrutiny.

Furthermore, delineating national identity from patriotism clarifies their distinct roles within civic engagement. National identity refers to a sense of belonging to a country, often based on shared history, culture, or language, without necessarily involving evaluative judgments about the country's moral or political standing. Patriotism, however, integrates an affective commitment to the country, imbued with values and judgments about its worth and moral standing. By distinguishing these concepts, we can better understand the layers of influence on citizens' engagement and the complex interplay between personal identity, patriotic sentiment, and democratic participation. This clarification enriches the theoretical framework, offering a clearer lens through which to view the impact of patriotism on democracy and citizenship.

Based on the general lack of theorizing about the impact of patriotism on other forms of beliefs and behavior than discrimination and xenophobia, I have created theories below that will allow me to empirically establish the impact of being patriotic or unpatriotic on the most important aspects of citizenship. I now examine how patriotism can benefit modern democratic societies.

A Contractual Theory of Patriotism

Returning to the book's central question, the impact of patriotism on political beliefs and behavior is not well understood, and many questions arise about its influence on citizens. I posit that patriotism provides enough affection[1] that we will toil to correct our nation's problems. My idea is that patriotism inspires us not to defect in our daily collective action problems. Without affection, what drives the motivation to be involved in fixing the country's problems by undertaking the requirements to understand the pressing issues? We know that rational ignorance does not benefit society but does benefit individual shirkers (Nie et al. 1976). Some scholars—often called civic nationalists—stress that it is crucial to find inspiring national myths to motivate the rationally ignorant not to freeload (see Abizadeh 2004). I similarly argue that patriotism motivates sacrifice through a contractual process and create theories and empirical tests below to show how this operates in American society.

Many politicians, for example, invoke patriotism to instill these values. For example, in his inaugural address, Barack Obama stated, "We must choose our better history," inspiring us to work diligently to improve America (Obama 2009). Here, he was using patriotism as a motivating device. Nevertheless, it is crucial to note that by saying "better history," Obama clarified that America has a worse history. Obama's style of patriotism does not negate the ability to be ashamed of America's mistakes. However, there is nothing mythical about stating that America has better

[1] Within the context of patriotism is carefully defined to distinguish it from related concepts such as attachment and devotion. "Affection" in this manuscript refers specifically to the emotional bond and positive feelings citizens have towards their country, which motivates engagement and sacrifice for the collective good. This is distinct from "attachment," which implies a deeper, perhaps more enduring psychological bond, and "devotion," which suggests a level of commitment or loyalty that might not necessarily involve positive emotions.

(Dillow, Goodboy, and Bolkan 2014).

and worse histories; it is instead a clearheaded analytical appraisal of its past. After making this rational cleavage between better and worse, one can become emotionally attached to the better history. Rationality and emotional bonds are, therefore, not mutually exclusive. Thus, the style of patriotism Obama utilizes to motivate shared sacrifice has the advantage of facilitating the emotional bonds that civic nationalists say are needed to solve significant problems while still allowing the critical analysis required for government by the people. Based on these ideas, I now state and formalize my contractual theory of patriotism in the next section.

A Contractual Theory of Patriotism

My contractual theory of patriotism is based on the idea that love of America is given in return for what the national government and societal systems have given the person. This is contractual because if the national government and societal systems does not fulfill its end of the bargain, the person can withhold patriotic sentiment. National government can give or withhold rights, freedoms, and basic levels of safety, infrastructure, and support. If a person receives these supremely important things, they may be inclined to be grateful for it. In return for these precious gifts, the person will be more inclined to sacrifice for the collective good of the nation. Since the national government and societal systems have supported them, they will support America by doing their part.

My idea of explaining patriotism's impact on beliefs and behaviors through a contractual lens echoes John Locke's Second Treatise of Government, focusing on a reciprocal exchange between individuals and their society (see Locke 1980). This tacit consent, mentioned in Locke's conception of a social contract, underpins the mutual responsibilities and benefits between a nation and its citizens. The idea that love of country arises from what society offers aligns with Locke's notion that political legitimacy is based on the consent of the governed, contingent on the protection of rights and liberties. While every citizen may not consciously enter into this "contract," the societal benefits and the expectation of contributing to the common good implicitly draw upon Locke's principles of governance and civic responsibility.

The contractual theory of patriotism I propose shares conceptual space with Locke's social contract, emphasizing a reciprocal relationship between the individual and the state. This theory posits that patriotic sentiment is contingent upon the state's provision of rights, freedoms, and security to its citizens. Such a contract implies that patriotism is not a blanket allegiance but a reflective commitment, grounded in the state's fulfillment of its obligations. This perspective allows for a nuanced understanding of patriotism, beyond mere emotional attachment, suggesting that it is both a moral and rational response to the benefits received from society. While not every citizen may consciously enter into this agreement, the theory suggests that societal benefits engender a sense of duty and gratitude, motivating contributions to the common good. This approach aims to recast patriotism as a constructive force, fostering civic engagement and loyalty that is informed and conditional.

It is pivotal to elucidate how this contractual framework enriches the conventional conceptions of patriotism. The contractual theory posits that patriotism evolves from a reciprocal relationship between the individual and the state rather than being an unconditional emotional allegiance. This relationship is contingent upon the state's provision of fundamental rights, safety, and welfare to its citizens. In essence, the emotional attachment and willingness to make sacrifices for the country, such as participating in national defense, stem from abstract affection and tangible recognition of the benefits and protections received. Thus, the idea of a "contract" is integrated into the fabric of patriotism by grounding emotional attachment in the tangible exchange between the individual and the society. This perspective does not negate the traditional view but adds a layer of rationality and conditionality, suggesting that the state's fulfillment of its obligations to its citizens fosters genuine commitment to the country.

Notice that this theoretical perspective presupposes that there is nothing natural or inalienable about rights and freedoms. Empirically, that is without question true, as a majority of countries do not give substantial rights and freedoms (see Freedom House 2023). However, a long natural rights tradition is referenced in America's founding documents (Maier 1998). Chapter 4 details qualitative and quantitative evidence, however, that most Americans perceive these rights and freedoms as something "given" to them by America, not endowed by their creator. Many explicitly reference that other countries often do not give their citizens rights and freedoms. Thus, it is likely that since they conceptualize America giving them something as important as rights and freedoms—in addition to safety, etc.—they will be inclined to give back to America through sacrifice.

Based on these ideas, there are two potential impacts that we can theoretically derive from patriotism. First, patriotism should help resolve collective action problems. Second, patriotism will alter views of the country, depending on whether the national government's and societal systems' actions are worthy of support or not. The converse of both predicted outcomes should hold for those who lack patriotism; they should be less likely to help resolve collective action problems and more negative in assessing the country's actions.

In the next sections, I delineate models of these theoretical perspectives and conclude by making empirically testable predictions based on these theories.

A Model of the Contractual Theory of Patriotism

Before I can create theoretical models of patriotism's impact, I must first create a basic model of what influences patriotism, as it will be the key term in the models below. Equation (2.1) shows my contractual theory of what influences the likelihood of expressing patriotic sentiment. It creates two sets of predictors and includes an error term. The first set of predictors accounts for my theory on the contractual nature of patriotism. The basic idea is that patriotism is given in return for what society has given. In exchange for being given rights, freedoms, and general conditions of safety and infrastructure, someone will express gratitude and love for the country. In addition, the model includes a term for socialization. Decades of exposure to socialization in mass media, holidays, and public schooling will tend to make people more patriotic. Finally, the norms of the social network that one exists in will influence how likely the person is to express patriotism freely or not. Social pressure will act as a force to increase or decrease expressions of patriotism. Finally, the model may not include all possible influences on patriotism, and any individual may not understand the other model terms correctly. The error term picks up any residual influences from misspecification or misperception for these cases.

$$\mathrm{E}(dp) = [(r + f + c) * (s) * (n)] * e \tag{2.1}$$

In Eq. (2.1), $\mathrm{E}(d_p)$ is the level of expressed patriotism. The r term represents the rights given. The f term represents the freedoms given. The c term represents the social and material conditions that one will be thankful or unthankful for. The s term represents the socialization of patriotic and unpatriotic beliefs. The *n* term represents how the expression of patriotism is altered to match the norms of the social networks that the person is embedded into. The model suggests that *ceteris paribus*, more rights, freedoms, and better conditions will increase the likelihood of expressed levels of patriotism. Now that patriotism has been modeled, we can create models of how it will affect beliefs and behaviors.

Model of Collective Action and Patriotism

I use models of collective action as a basis for my theory of how patriotism influences collective action. Research on collective action problems, such as freeriding, typically uses modeling to understand the micro-foundations of when someone will likely incur the costs of participating in collective action (see Oliver 1993 for a review.) For example, Finkel, Muller, and Opp (1989) model the conditions when collective action problems can overcome freeriding. Equation (2.2) shows their basic model, which I will develop to create a model of the relationship between collective action and patriotism.

$$E(A) = \left[(u + d) * c_g\right] * V \tag{2.2}$$

Finkel, Muller, and Opp's (1989) model in Eq. (2.2) depicts *E(A)* as the expected utility of performing a political action. *V* is the value an individual derives from achieving the goal that is the direct outcome of the action. The chance that the group will be successful is denoted by c_g. The minimum contribution set is defined as whether every group member is necessary to achieve its goal. Every member being needed puts profound pressure on each member to participate in achieving the goal, a circumstance expressed in the Equation by *u*. Finally, the belief that one should do their duty to help the group achieve its goals is expressed by *d*.

And it is this *d* term that is crucial for the explication of my model. The original conceptualization of *the d* term—*d* standing for duty—in early rational choice models was formulated by Riker and Ordeshook (1968). They examine the act of voting, but their model's logic can be applied to any political activity incurring costs. Riker and Ordeshook (1968) suggest that positive feelings of duty to vote—the *d* term—could be based on at least five reasons: (1) Satisfaction with compliance with the ethic of voting; (2) Satisfaction with support for the democratic system; (3) Satisfaction with partisan preference; (4) Satisfaction with deciding or going to the polls; (5) Satisfaction with affirming one's efficacy in the political system (Riker and Ordeshook 1968, 28). Together, these psychological benefits derived from the satisfaction of voting provide enough benefit in the cost–benefit analysis that many people engage in this collective action.

Downs (1957) did not include this *d* term and showed that without it, no rational actor should ever vote because it is nearly impossible for their vote to decide an election with hundreds of thousands or millions of people. Riker and Ordeshook (1968) provided the theoretical basis to explain why people take on the onerous task of political participation when they cannot influence the election. Of course, these factors are stochastically distributed across the population and influence citizens across a large range of possible levels of participation. Differential levels in the political socialization of these factors explain differences in decisions to participate in collective action.

Since my argument essentially boils down to patriotism's omission from Riker and Ordeshook's (1968) list of positive influences on feelings of duty, it is important to review each listed satisfaction and show that these are unrelated to or not a subset of patriotism. Satisfaction 1 and 2 are closest to patriotism but are unique factors, not explicitly and exactly patriotism. Although these may be related to or correlated with it, they are not specifically patriotism. For example, Satisfaction 1 is a psychological principle in which a person feels better about themself by fulfilling an action they have been socialized to believe is important. This satisfaction concerns the specific psychological fulfillment provided by voting, but it is not a direct measure of patriotism. Satisfaction 2 concerns support for democracy but not specifically loving one's country.

The final three potential reasons are also unrelated to patriotism. Satisfaction 3 concerns supporting a party or candidate one is enamored of, which is clearly not patriotism. Satisfaction 4 concerns a need for cognition[2] and the simple enjoyment of going out to vote. Some people may enjoy the intellectual pursuit of understanding politics or being involved in something. Neither option involves patriotism. Satisfaction 5 concerns the satisfaction of the idea that one can influence a political system. This is related to political efficacy, but it is more about the psychological enjoyment of providing input into the political system.

[2] See Cacioppo and Petty (1982).

While this list illustrates many ways people can derive a sense of duty that would motivate them to incur costs through collective action, it is not exhaustive. Crucially, Riker and Ordeshook (1968) admit that there are probably a whole host of other factors that may elicit feelings of duty; as they say, "doubtless there are other satisfactions" (Riker and Ordeshook 1968, 28). It is crucial, therefore, to add more fully to our understanding of why citizens incur costs that are not likely explained by a direct cost–benefit analysis regarding whether their participation is necessary and sufficient to achieve societal goals and promote the public good. The chief point is that patriotism elicits a sense of duty omitted from the current understanding of collective action.

Equation 2.3 demonstrates my fully explicated model by including the new term to denote patriotism.

$$E(A) = \left[\left(u + d_p + d_s\right) * c_g\right] * V \tag{2.3}$$

Equation 2.3 takes this basic explanation of why someone would be involved in collective action and separates the *d*-term into two components. I posit that patriotism is one of the chief reasons one feels a duty to commit to solving collective action problems. To show this in the model, I separate all other forms of satisfactions that one might feel a duty to with the term d_s—with the *s* standing for the satisfactions that Riker and Ordeshook (1968) mentioned and all other potential ones—from another term, which represents one's love of America and is denoted by the term d_p. The term d_p for any individual is derived from the processes explained in the prior section on the contractual theory of patriotism and explicated in Eq. 2.1.

Ceteris paribus, any increase in the patriotism term will increase the likelihood of civic engagement that benefits America.[3] Any duty to support a specific candidate or change the social position of any societal subgroup will motivate participation but will not be under the d_p term but actuated in the model by the d_s term. The patriotism term in the

[3] Civic engagement refers to individual and collective actions designed to identify and address issues of public concern. It encompasses a wide range of activities, including voting, volunteering, participating in group activities focused on public policy, engaging in community service, and actions to influence government. Civic engagement aims to improve the quality of democracy and community life by promoting the involvement of citizens in the decision-making processes and the implementation of solutions to social and political issues.

model makes someone more likely to engage in collective action to help America as a whole, thereby resolving free rider problems. It is plausible if someone has enough love for America that they are willing to engage in the action simply because they love it.

In this theoretical model, patriotism's influence is not absolute. It is restricted by whether people have other forms of satisfaction for doing the action (d_s), the likelihood that the action will be successful (c_g), and the value that they ascribe to the action (V). Additionally, this action is more likely if they believe everyone must perform it to achieve the goal ($\underline{u}$). Based on my formally stated theory, I state a series of empirical predictions derived from the logic of my theory below.

Model of Decision-Making and Patriotism

In addition to collective action, I developed a theory on how patriotism can affect cognition in decision-making about attitudes toward America. Neyman and Pearson (1933) model the initial theoretical discovery in decision science with Eq. (2.4). Equation (2.4) shows an iterative process that models a binary choice (P). New evidence (y) in support of either hypothesis (P_1, P_2) has a probability that it is believed and accepted (p). The reasons p can be lower than 1 include but are not limited to a lack of comprehending the evidence, lack of noticing the evidence, lack of being convinced by the evidence, and so on. Evidence accumulates in support of either hypothesis. If $\frac{P_{1n}}{P_{2n}}$ is greater than 1, hypothesis (P_1) is supported, and if it is less than 1, hypothesis (P_2) is supported.

$$\frac{P_{1n}}{P_{2n}} = \frac{p_1(y_1)p_1(y_2)\cdots p_1(y_n)}{p_2(y_1)p_2(y_2)\cdots p_2(y_n)} \tag{2.4}$$

Modern decision science had a significant breakthrough with the Ratcliff (1978) Drift-Diffusion model, denoted in Equation 2.5. The Drift-Diffusion model expands on the Neyman and Pearson (1933) model. The change in understanding is noted with *dx* in Equation 2.5. *Adt* represents that change in the understanding of evidence since the last piece of evidence was considered. CdW represents random noise associated with any error in a decision-making process involving humans. Here, $A > 0$ if H_1 is correct, and $A < 0$ if H_2 is correct.

$$dx = Adt + cdW, \cdots x(0) = 0 \tag{2.5}$$

Equation (2.6) takes the Drift-Diffusion model in Equation (2.6), adds two terms, and changes the two hypotheses to explain my theoretical model of patriotism influencing decision-making fully. Patriotism is defined as a term that goes from - ∞ for those who entirely hate America, purely indifferent at 0, and fully patriotic at ∞ for any individual. Again, the term p for any individual is derived from the processes explained in the prior section on the contractual theory of patriotism and explicated in Equation 2.1. All other factors influencing decision-making are in ***Z***.

$$dx = (Adt + cdW) + p * Z, x(0) = 0 \tag{2.6}$$

Here, $A > 0$ if H_1 is greater pro-American beliefs, and $A < 0$ if H_2 is greater anti-American beliefs. These beliefs may or may not be correct, depending on the validity of America's actions. Note that at extreme levels on either side, p will overwhelm most evidence or explanatory factors. Also, while purely evidence-based decision-making would set p at 0, having p at 0 is only necessary but insufficient for a purely evidence-based decision because $\boldsymbol{Z}$ and $\boldsymbol{cdW}$ also interfere with evidentiary reasoning.

Based on this theory, whether patriotism equates to better decision-making depends entirely on the nation's actions. If the national government and general societal systems are doing good, then patriotism will lead the person to support the nation correctly. However, this support is not derived from a cognitive analysis of the validity of the national government and general societal system's actions. Instead, patriots are mechanistically determined to support all actions of the nation. Therefore, more patriotism delimits assessment when the national government and general societal systems are acting badly.

Conversely, lacking patriotism or hating the country will make the person less likely to correctly assess the national government and general societal system's actions if they are doing good but will promote a correct decision if they are acting negatively. Furthermore, of course, this term is often sublimated by the other terms in the model for those with less intense belief in patriotism. Thus, patriotism is one factor out of many that will influence the quality of the assessment of the nation's actions. Based on this, we can expect that patriotism promotes better assessments when the country is doing well. Conversely, patriotism will deleteriously influence assessments when the country is doing poorly.

Empirical Predictions Derived from the Theories of Patriotism

The theory expressed in Eq. 2.3 posits that patriotism promotes citizens to cooperate when faced with collective action problems (see, e.g., Tamir 1992). I test below patriotism's impact on several topics related to the fundamental ideas of collective action problems. These topics are studied because they are theoretically relevant to patriotism and essential topics that have generated much prior research. Here, we should see that these measures of various forms of sacrifice to the larger society of the United States positively correlate with patriotism. The data and methods I use to test these hypotheses are described in subsequent chapters.

Voter Turnout and Political Participation

First, I predict that patriotic people will vote more often because they are more willing to incur the costs of voting due to their love of America. We have long known that civic duty is the primary driver of voter turnout, which Riker and Ordeshook (1968) call the "d" in their famous Equation. "D" stands for duty, and those who are less patriotic should feel less of a societal norm to fulfill their civic duty. The same logic will not extend to all forms of political participation, though, because each specific activity may not be perceived as benefiting the country as a whole but merely a subset within the nation.

Patriotism is about the love of the nation, and actions such as voting, which are linked to America's democratic system, can generally correlate positively with patriotism. On the other hand, actions that are beneficial to one particular subgroup but not necessarily to the entirety of the nation or that challenge the foundational myths upon which America has been justified will not be correlated with patriotism. Patriotism concerns the love of the nation as a whole, not a particular subgroup, and certainly not a critique of the nation's validity.

- Prediction 1: Patriotism will correlate with more validated voter turnout.
- Prediction 2: Patriotism will not correlate with political participation designed to support an ideological or sociodemographic group exclusively

- Prediction 3: Patriotism will not correlate with protest and similar forms of political participation.

Civic Participation

Similarly, the social capital literature details the great importance of volunteering to society (Putnam 2000). I measure this by volunteering in the community and donating blood. I expect both forms of sacrifice to be positively correlated with patriotism.

- Prediction 4: Patriotism will correlate with more volunteering.
- Prediction 5: Patriotism will correlate with being more likely to donate blood.

Political Judgement

Theorists such as MacIntyre (1995) view patriots as blind in their ability to criticize their country's problems rationally, and there are thus unjustifiably favorable predictions from patriots. It may also be that those who hate America are also unthinkingly hating it, and if so, they will be too negative in their assessment of America. The assumption often is that being negative is critical, but that is only true if there is a legitimate thing to be pessimistic about. In favorable situations, negativity will correlate with incorrect judgment.

I first test the impact of patriotism on political judgment using predictions of the United States. The ANES asks questions about future economic performance. Using the economy as a test, I predict that the less patriotic will be more likely to be incorrectly pessimistic about the future of the American economy in the year ahead. Since the survey was taken in 2012, the year ahead for these respondents' predictions was the US economy in 2013. By every objective measure, the US economy improved from November 2012 to November 2013. In this period, unemployment went down (from 7.4 to 6.7%) (Organization for Economic Co-operation and Development 2018), real GDP went up $740 per capita (US Bureau of Economic Analysis 2018), inflation went down from 1.96 to 1.75% (US Bureau of Labor Statistics 2018a), wages went up 2.2%, and so on (US Bureau of Labor Statistics 2018b). Poor judgment will be shown if the unpatriotic are more likely to mispredict a bad economy.

- Prediction 6: Patriotism will correlate with correct predictions about the United States economy.

I also expect the less patriotic to be suspectable of believing in conspiracy theories due to motivated reasoning. Since their prior beliefs are that there is something negative about America, they may be more likely to believe erroneous opposing theories about it.

- Prediction 7: Patriotism will correlate with less support for anti-government conspiracy theories.

Diffuse Support

Diffuse support is necessary in a liberal democratic society that requires general recognition and legitimacy from its people (Easton 1975). Moreover, diffuse support helps society weather crises (Aldrich 2012). All societies have crises, and empirical evidence shows that the most resilient are those where citizens have a general belief that the system is trustworthy, that it generally cares for people like them, and that the people have a say in what happens (Dalton 2004). These can be expressed as political trust, external political efficacy, and satisfaction with democracy (in an established democracy like the United States). Patriotism will make one more likely to believe that the general system is trustworthy and responsive. This diffuse support will be beneficial in times of crisis when society needs legitimacy.

I test this by first examining the relationship with political trust. I know the benefits of political trust have been shown in many settings, as societies with more institutional trust are more efficient and better working (Hetherington 2004; Putnam 1993, 2000). In addition, political trust may be influenced by patriotic values, as having negative feelings about the United States may lead some to believe that the government is less trustworthy. For this reason, I test the hypothesis that patriotism correlates with more trust in America's government.

- Prediction 8: Patriotism will correlate with more trust in government.

Also, I test whether patriotism will encourage us to believe that our actions matter in political society. For example, patriotic people may be more likely to believe that the system will be responsive to their efforts. I operationalized this by measuring political efficacy, which has been found to correlate with beneficial properties (Karp and Banducci 2008). Showing patriotism correlates with greater political efficacy will be a necessary extension in this line of research.

- Prediction 9: Patriotism will correlate with more political efficacy.

A primary concern now is that democracy is losing support across the globe. Debates on it are often imbued with explicit and implicit accusations of lack of patriotism for supporters of democracy. I predict that those less patriotic will be more likely to be dissatisfied with democracy because it is synonymous with the American system of government.

- Prediction 10: Patriotism will correlate with more satisfaction with democracy.

Xenophobia

One of the most common mass critiques of patriotism, often seen in op-ed pages but not the academic literature on this point, is that it correlates with belligerence toward out-groups (see, e.g., Marshall 2020). The sometimes-made corollary implication is that those lacking patriotism will be less likely to be against out groups. Thus, to test this untested corollary of the assumption of patriotism's relationship with xenophobia, I examine patriotism's relationship with psychological predispositions and attitudes toward salient out-groups: authoritarian personality, symbolic racism, attitudes toward Muslims, gays and lesbians, and immigrants. If patriotism is not associated with an animus for these out-groups, it will confirm the theoretical work on the confluence of patriotism with xenophobia (Cohen and Nussbaum 1996).

- Prediction 11: Patriotism will not correlate with the authoritarian personality.
- Prediction 12: Patriotism will not correlate with symbolic racism.
- Prediction 13: Patriotism will not correlate with negative attitudes toward Muslims.
- Prediction 14: Patriotism will not correlate with negative attitudes toward gays and lesbians.
- Prediction 15: Patriotism will not correlate with opposition toward immigration.

Empirical Predictions Derived from the Collective Action Theory of Local Patriotism

Additionally, this theory may help understand local politics. The extensive literature on how national-level patriotism affects national-level politics serves as a helpful starting point to understand how local patriotism may affect local politics. The literature on patriotism almost universally assumes that this concept concerns the love of the nation-state. Moreover, the literature has consistently found that national patriotism correlates with participation in national-level politics, such as voter turnout. This finding leads to the expectation that local patriotism will correlate with local political participation. As such, we will test all these predictions again at the local level in Chapter 10 with a novel measure of local patriotism and specific questions about local politics.

Conclusion

Patriotism is a common political phenomenon at the individual level, influencing several vital aspects of public opinion and political behavior. Specifically, collective action and its relation to patriotism is worth investigating. To do so, I create a contractual theory of patriotism based on the idea that patriotism concerns love and gratitude for what a national government and general societal systems have given someone, in addition to other factors. Based on this idea, I posit that patriotic beliefs influence the willingness to incur the costs of collective action, profoundly impacting political behavior and public opinion. Additionally, I showed that theoretically, we could expect patriotism to positively impact rational decision-making when the country is conducting itself and, conversely, delimit rationality when it is doing wrong.

The political theorists who argue that patriotism is a moral hazard ignore the civic problems of not having patriotism. Rather than rejecting patriotism, as many political theorists advocate (see Kateb 2006 or MacIntyre 1995), maybe society should try to build patriotism. Although not significant, the unpatriotic may correlate with many normatively undesirable properties and should also be the focus of more research. A more precise understanding of the impact of lacking patriotism will improve our understanding of patriotism's role in modern politics.

I theorized that patriotism affects many vital issues, and its nuances deserve more attention from researchers. In the chapters below, I operationalize collective action through commonly studied political and civic participation measures, feelings of diffuse support, political judgment, and xenophobia.

References

Abizadeh, Arash. 2004. "Historical Truth, National Myths and Liberal Democracy: On the Coherence of Liberal Nationalism." *Journal of Political Philosophy* 12 (3): 291–313.

Aldrich, John H. 2012. *Why Parties?: A Second Look*. Chicago: University of Chicago Press.

Archard, David. 1999. "Should We Teach Patriotism?" *Studies in Philosophy and Education* 18 (2): 157–173.

Boggiss, Anna L., Nathan S. Consedine, Jennifer M. Brenton-Peters, Paul L. Hofman, and Anna S. Serlachius. 2020. "A Systematic Review of Gratitude Interventions: Effects on Physical Health and Health Behaviors." *Journal of Psychosomatic Research* 135: 110–165.

Cacioppo, John T., and Richard E. Petty. 1982. "The Need for Cognition." *Journal of Personality and Social Psychology* 42 (1): 116–131.

Callan, Eamonn. 1999. *Creating Citizens: Political Education and Liberal Democracy*. Oxford: Oxford University Press.

Cohen, Joshua, and Martha C. Nussbaum. 1996. "For Love of Country: Debating the Limits of Patriotism." In *For Love of Country: Debating the Limits of Patriotism*, ed. Joshua Cohen, 3–17. Boston: Beacon Press.

Curren, Randall, and Charles Dorn. 2018. *Patriotic Education in a Global Age*. Chicago: University of Chicago Press.

Dalton, Russell J. 2004. *Democratic Challenges, Democratic Choices: The Erosion of Political Support in Advanced Industrial Democracies*. Oxford: Oxford University Press.

De Figueiredo, Rui J. P., and Zachary Elkins. 2003. "Are Patriots Bigots? An Inquiry into the Vices of In-Group Pride." *American Journal of Political Science* 47 (1): 171–188.

Delamater, John, Daniel Katz, and Herbert C. Kelman. 1969. "On the Nature of National Involvement: A Preliminary Study." *Journal of Conflict Resolution* 13 (3): 320–357.

Dillow, Megan R., Alan K. Goodboy, and San Bolkan. 2014. "Attachment and the Expression of Affection in Romantic Relationships: The Mediating Role of Romantic Love." *Communication Reports* 27 (2): 102–115.

Downs, Anthony. 1957. "An Economic Theory of Political Action in a Democracy." *Journal of Political Economy* 65 (2): 135–150.

Easton, David. 1975. "A Re-Assessment of the Concept of Political Support." *British Journal of Political Science* 5 (4): 435–457.

Finkel, Steven E., Edward N. Muller, and Karl-Dieter. Opp. 1989. "Personal Influence, Collective Rationality, and Mass Political Action." *American Political Science Review* 83 (3): 885–903.

Freedom House. 2023. *Freedom in the World*. Technical Report. Accessed at https://freedomhouse.org/report/freedom-world/2023/marking-50-years

Hetherington, Marc J. 2004. *Why Trust Matters: Declining Political Trust and the Demise of American Liberalism*. Princeton: Princeton University Press.

Hollander, Paul. 1995. *Anti-Americanism: Critiques at Home and Abroad, 1965–1990*. New York: Oxford University Press.

Karasawa, Minoru. 2002. "Patriotism, Nationalism, and Internationalism Among Japanese Citizens: An Etic–Emic Approach." *Political Psychology* 23 (4): 645–666.

Karp, Jeffrey A., and Susan A. Banducci. 2008. "Political Efficacy and Participation in Twenty-Seven Democracies: How Electoral Systems Shape Political Behaviour." *British Journal of Political Science* 38 (2): 311–334.

Kateb, George. 2006. *Patriotism and Other Mistakes*. New Haven: Yale University Press.

Kosterman, Rick, and Seymour Feshbach. 1989. "Toward a Measure of Patriotic and Nationalistic Attitudes." *Political Psychology* 10 (2): 257–274.

Locke, John. 1980. *Second Treatise of Government*. Edited by C. B. Macpherson. Cambridge, MA: Hackett Publishing.

MacIntyre, Alasdair. 1995. "Is Patriotism a Virtue?" In *Theorizing Citizenship*, ed. Ronald Beiner, 209–228. Albany: SUNY Press.

Maier, Pauline. 1998. *American Scripture: Making the Declaration of Independence*. New York: Alfred A. Knopf.

Marshall, Yannick Giovanni. 2020. "Patriotism is Racist." *Al Jazeera*, February 6. https://www.aljazeera.com/opinions/2020/2/6/patriotism-is-racist.

Muller, Jerry Z. 2007. "Us and Them: The Enduring Power of Ethnic Nationalism." *Foreign Affairs* 86 (2): 18–35.

Neyman, Jerzy, and Egon S. Pearson. 1933. "On the Problem of the Most Efficient Tests of Statistical Hypotheses." *Philosophical Transactions of the Royal Society of London. Series a, Containing Papers of a Mathematical or Physical Character* 231: 289–337.

Nie, Norman H., Sidney Verba, and John R. Petrocik. 1976. *The Changing American Voter*. Cambridge: Harvard University Press.

Obama, Barack. 2009. *A More Perfect Union [Speech]*. Philadelphia, PA: National Constitution Center. https://obamawhitehouse.archives.gov/the-press-office/remarks-senator-barack-obama-race-delivered-constitution-center-philadelphia. Accessed 30 May 2025.

Oliver, Pamela E. 1993. "Formal Models of Collective Action." *Annual Review of Sociology* 1 (1): 271–300.

Olson, Mancur. 1965. *The Logic of Collective Action: Public Goods and the Theory of Groups*. Cambridge: Harvard University Press.

Organization for Economic Co-operation and Development (OECD). 2018. *Education at a Glance 2018: OECD Indicators*. Paris: OECD Publishing.

Putnam, Robert D. 1993. *Making Democracy Work: Civic Traditions in Modern Italy*. Princeton: Princeton University Press.

Putnam, Robert D. 2000. *Bowling Alone: The Collapse and Revival of American Community*. New York: Simon & Schuster.

Ratcliff, Roger. 1978. "A Theory of Memory Retrieval." *Psychological Review* 83 (2): 59–108.

Riker, William H., and Peter C. Ordeshook. 1968. "A Theory of the Calculus of Voting." *American Political Science Review* 62 (1): 25–42.

Roger, Phillip. 2005. *Americanism: New Perspectives on the History of an Ideal*. Chapel Hill: University of North Carolina Press.

Schatz, Robert T., Ervin Staub, and Howard Lavine. 1999. "On the Varieties of National Attachment: Blind versus Constructive Patriotism." *Political Psychology* 20 (1): 151–174.

Smith, Steven B. 2021. *Reclaiming Patriotism in an Age of Extremes*. New Haven: Yale University Press.

Sullivan, John L., George E. Marcus, Stanley Feldman, and James E. Piereson. 1992. *Political Tolerance and American Democracy*. Chicago: University of Chicago Press.

Tamir, Yael. 1992. *Liberal Nationalism*. Princeton: Princeton University Press.

US Bureau of Economic Analysis. 2018. "National Income and Product Accounts." Washington, DC: U.S. Department of Commerce. https://www.bea.gov/

US Bureau of Labor Statistics. 2018a. "Labor Force Statistics from the Current Population Survey." Washington, DC: U.S. Department of Labor. https://www.bls.gov/cps/

US Bureau of Labor Statistics. 2018b. "Employment Projections." Washington, DC: U.S. Department of Labor. https://www.bls.gov/emp/
Viroli, Maurizio. 1995. *For Love of Country: An Essay on Patriotism and Nationalism*. Oxford: Oxford University Press.
Wilson, James Q. 1973. *Political Organization*. New York: Basic Books.

CHAPTER 3

Who Is Patriotic And Who Is Not

Abstract Using historical and contemporary survey data, Chapter Three investigates variations in patriotic sentiment across demographic groups, ideological subgroups, and party affiliations in the United States. Findings show that most Americans report high levels of patriotism, but a consistent minority (around 25%) exhibits dislike, hate, or indifference toward the country. The chapter highlights how expressions of patriotism—or its absence—vary by age, race, ideology, and partisanship. These data confirm that patriotism is not uniformly distributed and that some segments of the population reject or withhold patriotic feelings entirely, raising important questions for democratic cohesion.

Keywords Patriotism Levels · Demographics · Ideology · Partisanship · National Identity · Survey Data

Before diving into patriotism's impact on American beliefs and behaviors, we need to know who is patriotic and who is not. Understanding the implications of patriotism in American politics will be difficult without understanding those who have patriotism, those who are indifferent, and those who lack patriotism. To do so, this chapter provides an in-depth statistical analysis of the levels of patriotism in America, how those levels have changed over time, and which demographic subgroupings are more

S. Richey, *Patriotism and Citizenship*,
https://doi.org/10.1007/978-3-031-89885-3_3

and less patriotic. Also, this chapter explores different ideological and partisan groupings and their relationship to patriotism. I find that most Americans are patriotic across every measured demographic subgroup, party identification, and ideological grouping, but interesting variances exist in the total level of patriotism across these groups.

For example, while I find high levels of patriotism across sub-groupings, this chapter also delves into the non-trivial percentage of the population who express dislike or hatred of America. Across various samples and measures of patriotism, around 3% of Americans express hatred toward America (discussed below).These data are from an online survey from 2021 matched to nationally representative data for age, gender, and race. It is weighted for representativeness for Hispanic ethnicity, political ideology, and party identification. There were 600 respondents.[1] Perhaps more consequential, across the same varied measures and samples taken in different years, around 8% to 10% say they dislike America. Additionally, around 10% to 15% express no feelings—they neither like nor dislike America. In total, around 25% of the population is not patriotic and has been almost wholly ignored in prior literature. Due to these variations in beliefs about America, it is important to examine who is patriotic and who is not. The following section examines general levels of patriotism in a novel cross-sectional survey, other cross-sectional surveys taken over time, and cross-national surveys.

General Levels of Patriotism

It cannot be overstated how clearly survey data show Americans are patriotic. For example, Fig. 3.1 shows results from a novel national representative survey. conducted in the fall of 2021, around three out of four

[1] In Spring 2021, a study was conducted with a sample of 600 individuals recruited from an online platform to examine various socio-demographic dynamics. This sample was meticulously compared against nationally representative data to ensure its adequacy in representing the broader population across key demographic variables: age, race, and gender. The primary aim was to ascertain whether the online sample mirrored the diversity and distribution found in the general population, thereby validating the reliability and generalizability of the findings. By aligning the sample's demographic composition with that of the national benchmarks, researchers sought to minimize biases that often plague online surveys, ensuring that the insights derived would be reflective of societal patterns at large. This methodological rigor is crucial, especially in studies targeting nuanced understandings of social behaviors or attitudes, where demographic representation plays a significant role in the validity of the conclusions drawn.

Americans either like or love their country. This finding is less patriotic than is typical of other surveys and is suggestive of the difficult time the country was in at the height of the delta variant of the coronavirus pandemic, economic turmoil, and recoiling from the events of the January 6th attack on the U.S. Capitol and the George Floyd murder. Even in tumultuous times, most Americans like or love their country. Additionally, I show below that patriotism extends across almost every possible subgrouping or way of dividing society.

When we examine the breakdown of the data more specifically to degrees of hate or love for America, we see that most Americans have positive feelings about it. Figure 3.2 shows patriotism data from the 2012 ANES broken down by whether they hate, dislike, neither dislike nor like, like, or love America. There is a clear skew in the data toward positive feelings in the direction of America, with 2/3rds saying they love it. In

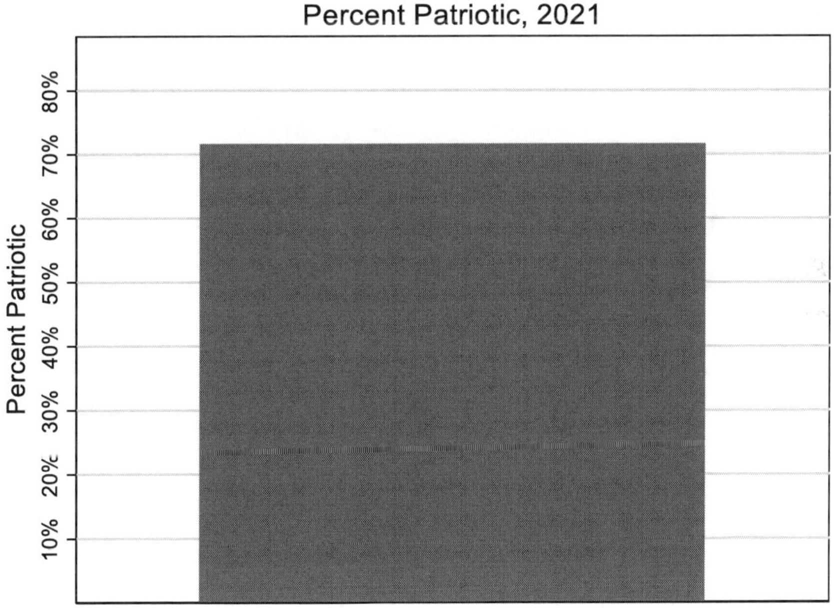

Fig. 3.1 Patriotism data from a 2021 online survey showing the percentage that said they like or love America

addition, 23% say they like America, and around 10% have either no feelings or negative feelings toward it. This shows that very high levels of patriotism exist in society and helps us explain why we will not see too many differences by demographic or political characteristics since there are not so many people who dislike America.

One thing to note from these two data sets, separated by 9 years, is that patriotism seems to decline. Of course, the problem with comparing overtime rates of patriotism is that the data used in Figs. 3.1 and 3.2 are different samples taken with different modalities, survey methodologies, questionnaires with differing question orders, and question wordings. Any difference could be due to differences in the samples, how they were taken and how, and the surveys were implemented. To better examine change over time, we need to use survey data with the same methodologies, using the exact question wordings preferably by the same survey company. While we can never know that the exact numbers found by any

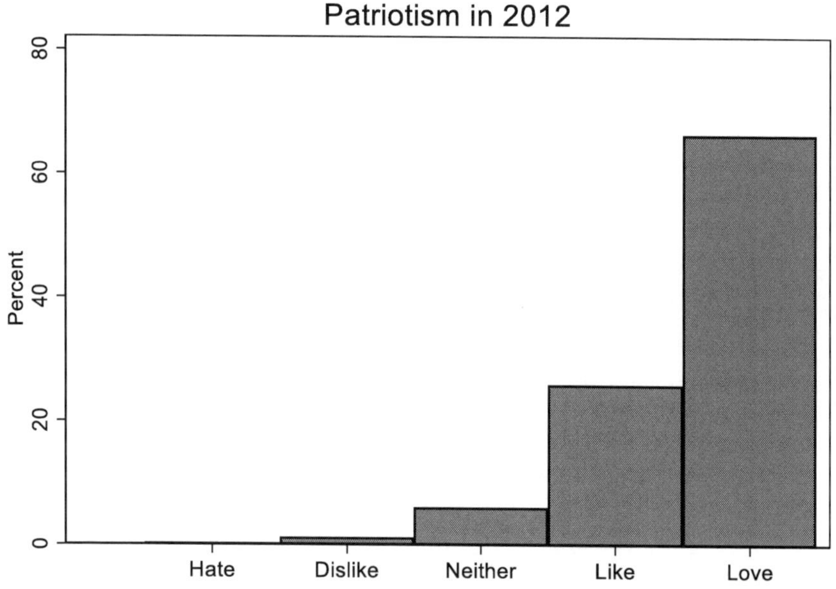

Fig. 3.2 A histogram of patriotism data from the 2012 ANES, shown as the percent who say they hate, dislike, neither dislike nor hate, like, or love America

company's methodologies will be accurate, the trend over time should reveal how patriotism has changed in America.

Unfortunately, direct measurements of patriotism—defined as love of country—that are worded the same and fielded by the same company over time are unavailable. While love and pride are distinct concepts, we can also examine pride in America as a somewhat related concept due to less availability of data on love of country. Meitinger (2018) found that using pride in the country as a measure of patriotism has low validity, especially in the cross-country context, so these data should be analyzed cautiously. While it is clear that pride is not the same as the love of country, pride in America should be correlated with it, and it may work as an acceptable proxy variable for patriotism to a certain extent.

Figure 3.3 shows the percentage of Americans who are extremely proud to be Americans from the Gallup Poll Social Survey (Gallup Organization 2022). These data have the advantage of being asked using the same methodologies by the same company over 20 years. Figure 3.3 shows that while there has been some decline recently in those extremely proud to be American, most U.S. citizens are extremely proud of being American. The decline, however, is statistically significant, which suggests that this decline is a factor to consider going forward.

Another way to consider America's patriotism is to compare it to similar nations to see how different our conceptualization of patriotism is. Interestingly, Pew (2020) conducted nationally representative surveys in France, Germany, the United Kingdom, and the United States that asked a question about pride and shame in one's nation. As discussed in Chapter 2, one conceptualization of patriotism is whether one is a constructive or blind patriot (see Schatz et al. 1999). By asking respondents whether they are mostly ashamed, both proud and ashamed, or mostly proud, these surveys give us an approximation of constructive and blind patriotism and those who are unpatriotic. We can use these data to compare these four nations' citizens' opinions about their nation.

Figure 3.4 shows the mean of those who feel mostly proud, both proud and ashamed, and mostly ashamed of their country. Surprisingly, Americans express similar pride in their nation as these three liberal European nations. Americans are actually about as patriotic as residents of these other nations. This suggests that nations with strong traditions of democracy, free markets, civil liberties, and high levels of human development engender a high degree of patriotism in their citizenry. In fact, the United States and the United Kingdom have almost identical distributions across

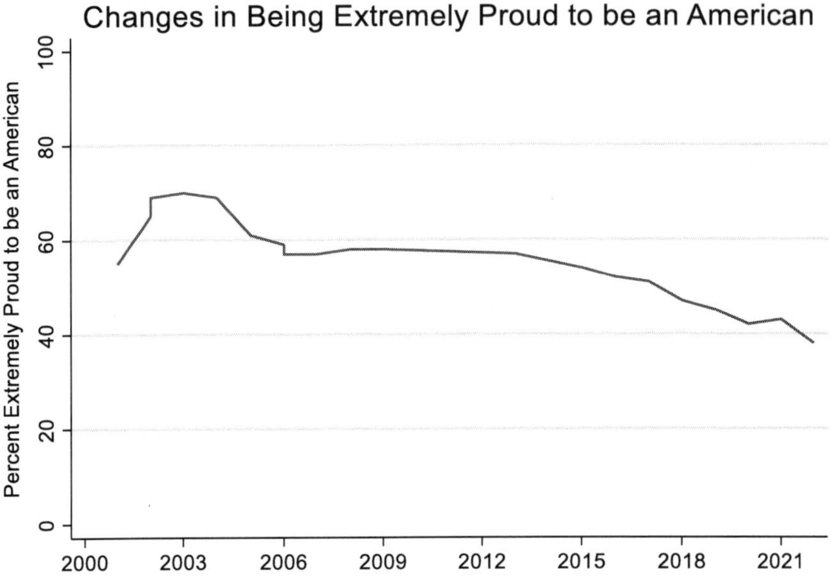

Fig. 3.3 This graph shows the percentage who are extremely proud to be an American. Data from the Gallup Poll Social Survey

these three conceptualizations of national shame and pride. Related to the discussion below about the unpatriotic, note that all four nations have a small group that is mostly ashamed of their country, suggesting the importance of this ignored group.

In sum, the aggregate level of patriotism in America is very high, shown in multiple forms of measurement captured in nationally representative surveys over time and across nations. I now discuss more in-depth the unpatriotic.

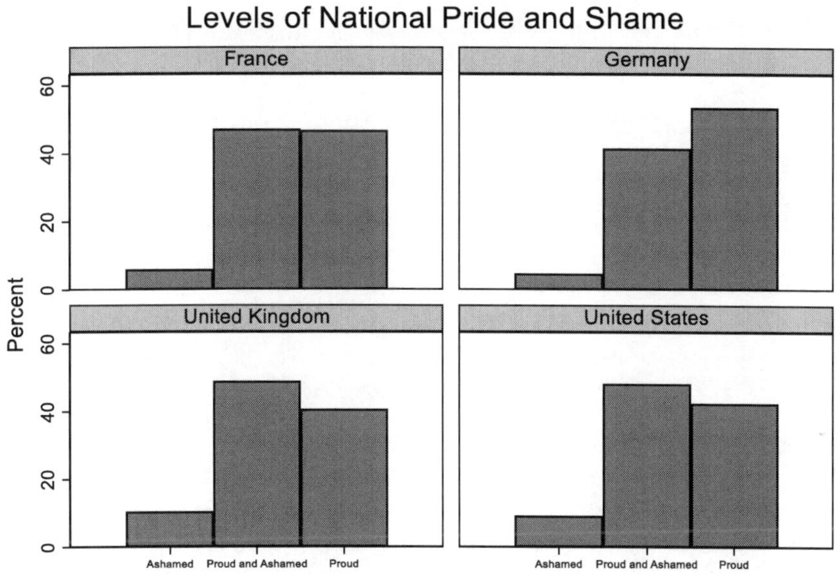

Fig. 3.4 This bar graph shows the mean of those who feel mostly proud, both proud and ashamed, and mostly ashamed of their country. Data from nationally representative samples in France, Germany, the United Kingdom, and the United States from Pew (2020)

The Unpatriotic are a Real, But Small Group in America

Survey data repeatedly show that around 5 to 10% of Americans dislike or hate America. This may seem small, but many important subgroups[2] commonly studied by social science—such as Asian Americans, LGBT Americans, and Jewish Americans—are a smaller percentage of the U.S. population. It is highly plausible that political outcomes derive from disliking or hating your country. Thus, it is crucial to study these Americans who dislike or hate their own country and analyze the impact of these beliefs on their attitudes and behaviors.

[2] To be clear, I define subgroups as: Demographic subgroups are specific segments of a population defined by distinct characteristics, such as age, gender, race, ethnicity, income level, or education.

This surprisingly high level of anti-Americanism among Americans is not just a function of question wording or response type. For example, a 2021 poll gave a ten-point scale of answer options on how great America is and still found that around 11% rated America less than 5, implying not great, and 3% gave it a 1 out of 10, signifying that America was not great in any way (IPSOS 2021). It is also not limited to question wording issues due to respondents not comprehending what patriotism means, as similar distributions occur with surveys that define patriotism. For example, a 2018 nationally representative survey defined it before it asked the question, "Patriotism is defined as devoted love, support, and defense of one's country, or as having "national loyalty." How patriotic toward America do you consider yourself to be?" (Social Science Research Solutions 2018). 58% chose very patriotic, 28% said somewhat patriotic, 5% said not very patriotic, and 8% said that they were not at all patriotic. Dozens of other surveys show similar results.

The repetition of this finding across many surveys with differing questions, modalities, and samples strongly suggests that between 5 and 10% of Americans do not like America. For example, a 2021 nationally representative poll asked, "In the last five years, would you say you have become more or less likely to think of yourself... as patriotic? More likely, less likely, neither more nor less likely, never thought of myself this way" (PRRI 2021). In agreement with all the other data, 10% answered that they never thought of themselves as patriotic. A 2022 Gallup poll using gold-standard survey methodology found that 4% of Americans had no pride at all in being American (Gallup Organization 2022). What is striking about this result is that these respondents were also given another option of having "only a little pride in being American," which many social scientists would predict Americans will select due to social disability bias. This makes it clear that these respondents did not just have little pride in being American but genuinely had none. Dozens of surveys have found similar results: a small but real group of people who lack patriotism at similar levels say that they dislike or hate their country. This group is entirely ignored in the academic literature on this topic.

This distribution also helps explain why patriotic education is so controversial. Since about one in ten people are not patriotic, and a large plurality are very patriotic, it makes sense that this topic would engender fierce debate. For example, a nationally representative 2022 poll asked parents if they believe that their child's school teaches patriotism in a way that is consistent with their values (NPR 2022). Only 42% said yes, while

15% said no, and interestingly, 8% said that their school does not teach about this. Another nationally representative 2022 poll asked, "Public schools are also sometimes expected to instill values important to our society. Please tell me if you think instilling patriotism is essential for public schools, important but not essential, not that important, or something public schools should not do" (Selzer 2022). Around 38% said it was essential to instill patriotism through public schools, 37% said it was important but not essential, 13% said it was not important, and tellingly 8% said it is something that schools should not do. If 8% do not want it done and 38% think it is essential to do, we can expect a lot of conflict on this topic in schools.

Finally, it is important to distinguish the group that has neither positive nor negative feelings toward America from those who dislike or hate it, which is around 10% in samples that allow a response of neither/nor (see, e.g., Fig. 3.2 above). Zahra (2010) examined the phenomenon of national indifference, which may apply to this rather large group of around 10%. These people seem indifferent to the nation, neither positive nor negative toward it. Thus, while America is highly patriotic, there are interesting and important subgroups of Americans who have divergent opinions. In the section below, I explore how demographic factors correlate with the distribution of patriotism.

Patriotism and Demographics

Now, turning to examining demographic factors and their correlations with patriotism, Table 3.1 shows an ordered logistic regression model for demographic determinants of patriotism from novel survey data taken in 2021 matched to nationally representative data for age, gender, and race and weighted for representativeness for party identification, ideology, and Hispanic ethnicity.[3] The only demographic characteristic that correlates with patriotism is age. This means that being female, having higher education or income, or being black or Hispanic are not discernibly different from others in these categories in terms of levels of expressed patriotism. Note that since it is highly unlikely that patriotism alters the self-categorization into these identity groups on surveys, typical concerns with regression models involving bi-causality are not likely applicable.

[3] These results are similar without using weights.

This is a striking result because many of the most intense debates in American society at their core revolve around accusations of either nationalistic blind patriotism or anti-Americanism that are ascribed to demographic groups. Yet the data clearly shows that most groups, except for young and old, are not distinct in patriotism.

Figure 3.5 shows a boxplot of patriotism data from the same 2021 data, shown as the mean with 95% confidence intervals of those who say they hate, dislike, neither dislike nor hate, like, or love America, separated by age groups. On a 5-point scale, those who are 65 and older are about 1.5 points higher in expressed levels of patriotism than those who are 18 to 19. Interpreting these differences, we see that those who are older have a fairly linear growth pattern in increasing patriotism, and by around age 45, the mean is to like America. The mean is between neither liking nor disliking and liking America for those younger than 45. The difference between the lowest and highest categories in age is about 1.4 standard deviations in patriotism.

Whenever age is considered in social science, a common question is whether this is specific to this year's youth or a long-term pattern where people grow more patriotic as they age. In other words, it could be that young people throughout modern history are less patriotic than older

Table 3.1 Demographics determinants of patriotism

Variable	*Coef*	*S.E*
Age	0.357***	0.064
Female	–0.180	0.218
Education	–0.035	0.120
Income	0.072	0.043
Black	–0.402	0.368
Hispanic	0.338	0.292
Cutpoint 1	–2.872***	0.799
Cutpoint 2	–0.621	0.647
Cutpoint 3	1.137	0.716
Cutpoint 4	3.270***	0.696
N	551	
chi2	52.330***	

Note Cells represent unstandardized coefficients and standard errors for an ordered logistic regression model for determinants of patriotism. Data from 2021, weighted
+p<.10, *p<.05, **p<.01, ***p<.001

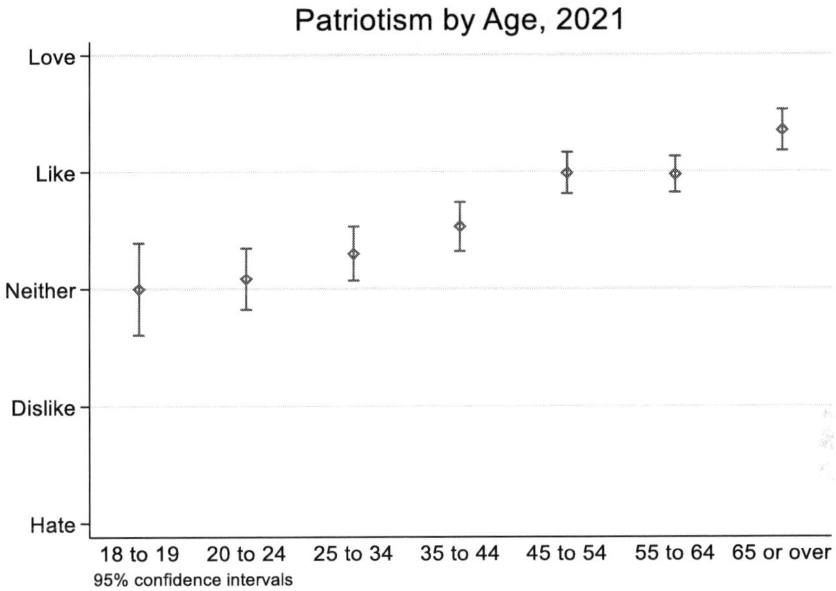

Fig. 3.5 A boxplot of patriotism data from 2021, shown as the mean with 95% confidence intervals of those who say they hate, dislike, neither dislike nor hate, like, or love America, separated by age groups

people. Conversely, it could be that in 2021, young people are disproportionately less patriotic, which would not necessarily be an effect of aging but rather something that's happening to this generation of young people. To investigate this, I examine an earlier measurement of patriotism in the 2012 ANES sample and show that, in fact, young people seem to have always been less patriotic than their elders, and it is not something specific to the political circumstances of now.

This null finding for the other demographic groups replicates with other data. Although some datasets do show a statistically significant difference between being black and white in levels of patriotism, for example, these differences are hardly ever substantively significant. For example, a similar ordered logistic regression model to Table 3.1 conducted with 2012 ANES data does show a statistically significant difference between black and white respondents and levels of patriotism. However, when examining the expressed levels of patriotism, we see that they are very similar in substantive significance if not statistical significance. Figure 3.6 is a histogram that shows the percentage of people expressing different feelings toward America, differentiated by race and ethnicity. There is almost no discernible difference in the distribution of patriotic beliefs across being black, white, or Hispanic, even though the regression model shows that the coefficient for black is statistically significant and lower.

The phenomenon of national disidentification highlights that individuals from immigrant backgrounds often do not resonate with the identity of their receiving countries, displaying attitudes that can range from disengagement to outright antagonism (see Maliepaard and Verkuyten 2018). Huntington (2004) suggests similar process might be happening in the United States with immigration. That's why it is important to examine the potentiality that the children of immigrants may have national disidentification expressed through lower levels of patriotism. To investigate this

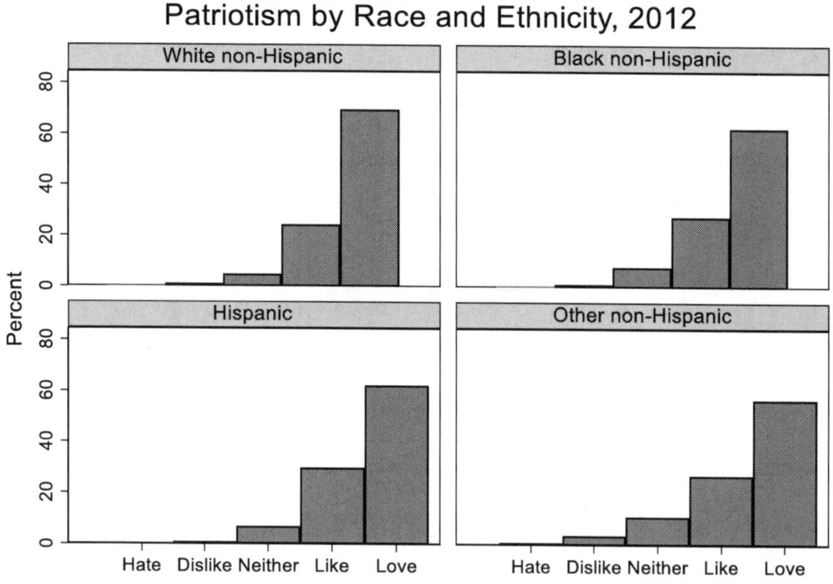

Fig. 3.6 This histogram shows the percentage expressing different feelings toward America, differentiated by race and ethnicity. Data from ANES 2012

possibility, Fig. 3.7 shows 2012 ANES data for second-generation Americans and other Americans who expressed Patriotism categorized again into responses of "Love," "Like," "Neither," "Dislike," and "Hate." It differentiates between those with both parents born in the United States, one parent born in the United States, and neither parent born in the United States. The graph includes 95% confidence intervals, indicating a statistical measure of the range within which the true value of the responses is expected to fall. Figure 3.7 shows that feelings of patriotism among second-generation Americans are substantially similar to non-second-generation Americans, although there is a statistically significant difference. The mean for those with both parents born in the United States is 4.59 on a 1–5 scale, those with one parent born in the United States have a mean of 4.51, and neither parent born in the United States are at 4.48. This visual representation shows that the patriotism levels among different groups of second-generation Americans are similar.

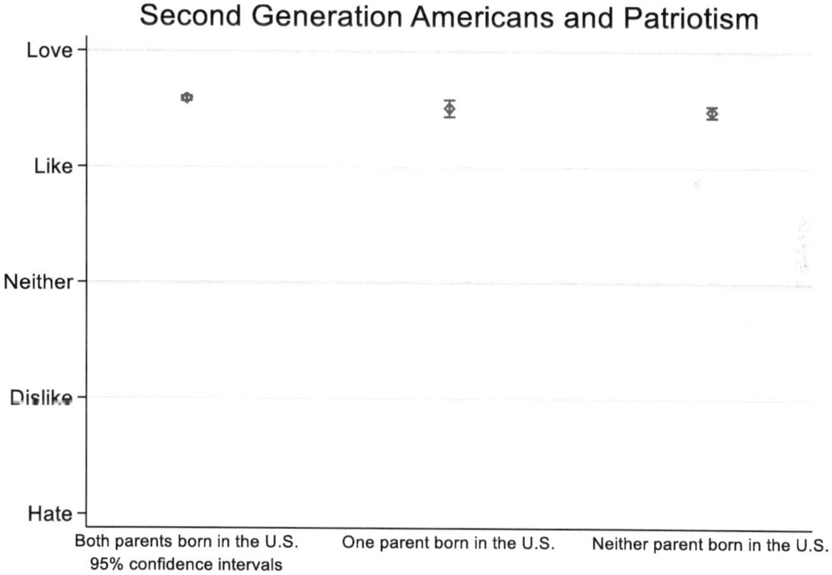

Fig. 3.7 This graph shows the percentage and 95% confidence intervals expressing different feelings toward America, differentiated by parental nativity—data from ANES 2012

A similar finding occurs when distinguishing between constructive, blind patriotism, or being unpatriotic. Figure 3.8 is a histogram that shows the mean with 95% confidence intervals of Americans who feel mostly proud, both proud and ashamed, and mostly ashamed of America, differentiated by gender. As we can see, the distribution of men and women in being constructive, blind, and unpatriotic is essentially the same. Also note that Table 3.2 below shows a fully explicated regression model where gender has no explanatory power once political ideology and partisanship are accounted for. Table 3.2 also shows again that older Americans tend to be mostly proud of their country. Thus, one demographic difference in patriotism in the United States that is substantively significant is the difference between old and young.

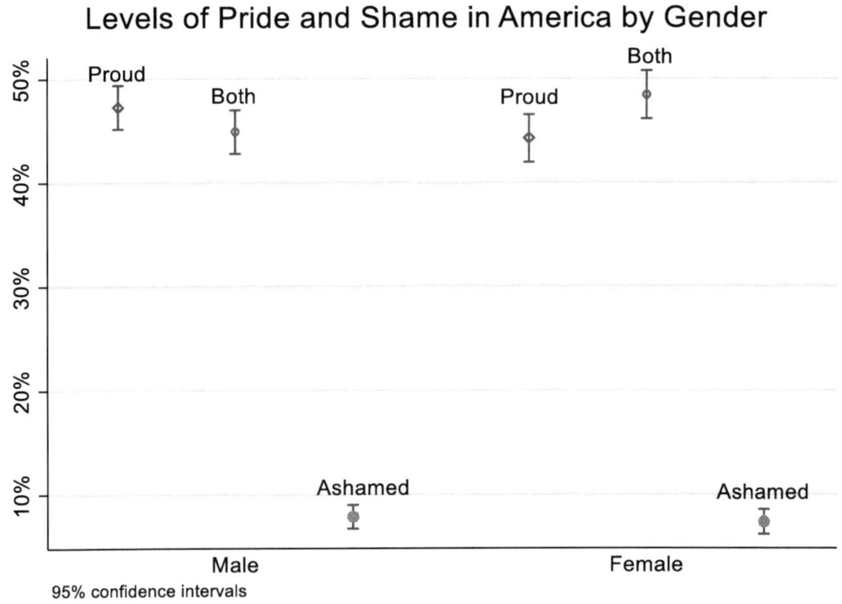

Fig. 3.8 This histogram shows the mean with 95% confidence intervals of Americans who feel mostly proud, both proud and ashamed, and mostly ashamed of America, differentiated by gender. Data from Pew 2020

Table 3.2 Determinants of patriotism

Variable	*Coef*	*S.E*
Republican	0.520	0.393
Ideology	−0.242*	0.108
Age	0.319***	0.065
Female	−0.111	0.221
Education	0.017	0.122
Income	0.032	0.046
Black	−0.330	0.368
Hispanic	0.313	0.326
Cutpoint 1	−3.919***	1.018
Cutpoint 2	−1.635	0.901
Cutpoint 3	0.219	0.942
Cutpoint 4	2.506**	0.925
N	551	
chi2	74.500***	

Note Cells represent unstandardized coefficients and standard errors for an ordered logistic regression model for determinants of patriotism. Data from 2021, weighted
+p<.10, *p<.05, **p<.01, ***p<.001

Patriotism and Ideology and Partisan Identification

Compared to the relatively muted results for demographic variables, we see clear evidence of the profound effect of ideology on patriotism. This matches Hanson and O'Dwyer's (2019) findings from a q-methodology study of American national identity, which mainly found a left–right dimension in conceptualizing patriotism and nationalism (also see Satherley, Yogeeswaran, Osborne, and Sibley (2018) for an example of this from New Zealand). Table 3.2 shows the same regression model shown in Table 3.1 with the same data but with party identification and ideology added as independent variables. Ideology has a strongly negative effect, whereas those who are more liberal are less likely to be patriotic. Republicans are not more likely to be patriotic than other partisan identifications. Also note that in this model specification, the only demographic variable that is significant is age. Having a liberal ideology has a strong negative impact on patriotism.

It is important to check if this relationship is linear or, by each step, increases the likelihood of being less patriotic. Figure 3.9 shows the mean of Americans who feel patriotic, differentiated by ideology. It shows that it is only those who are very liberal where there is a large decrease in patriotism. Up to and including those who are somewhat liberal, the vast majority of citizens are patriotic. In the very liberal group, however, patriotism drops to around 41%. And while that is still a significant portion of the group that is patriotic, it is one of the very few categories in which we see the majority are not patriotic.

A similar result is obtained when we differentiate patriotism by whether the person is constructive, blind, or unpatriotic. Using Pew (2021) data, Fig. 3.10 shows the mean with 95% confidence intervals of Americans who feel mostly proud, both proud and ashamed, and mostly ashamed of America, differentiated by ideology. The only ideological category where the level of being mostly ashamed is larger than the level of being mostly proud is for those who are very liberal. Almost twice the number of very liberal Americans are mostly ashamed rather than mostly proud of America. Even in this category of very liberal, the mostly ashamed group

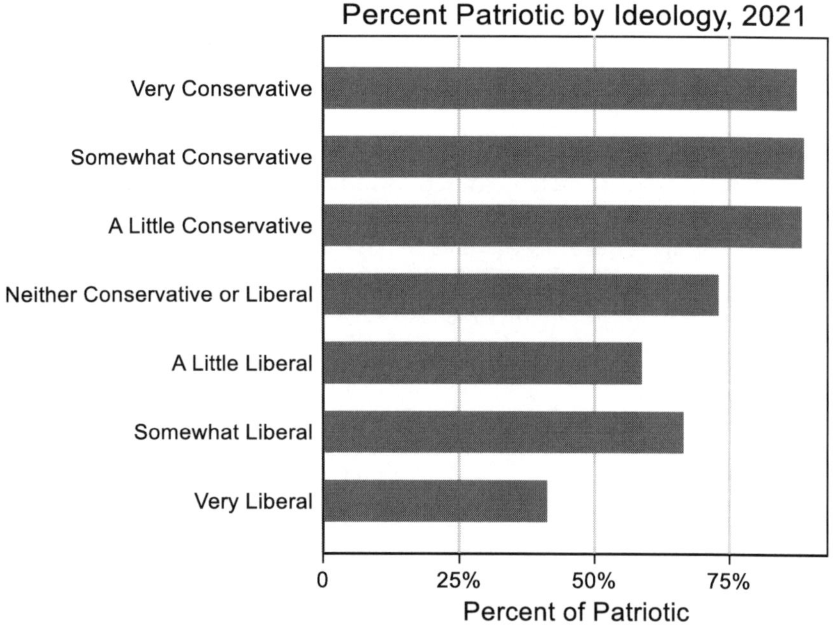

Fig. 3.9 This bar graph shows the mean of Americans who feel patriotic, differentiated by ideology

is only 34%, signifying that around 2/3 of very liberal people are proud of America.

Figure 3.11 also shows a distinction by partisan identification where Republicans are much more likely to be mostly proud, Democratic respondents are much more likely to be both proud and ashamed, and independents are some mix of the two. Interestingly, although ideology showed a large percentage of very liberal people are mostly ashamed of America, Democratic respondents are proud of America. The key distinction is that these Democratic respondents match constructive patriotism because they are also ashamed of some of the country's actions. Also important is that despite Republicans being less likely to be mostly ashamed, there is still around 5% of Republicans who are mostly ashamed of America. Across all three partisan identification groups, there are between 5 and 10% of people who are mostly ashamed of America. In sum, the main finding gained by examining partisan identification is that

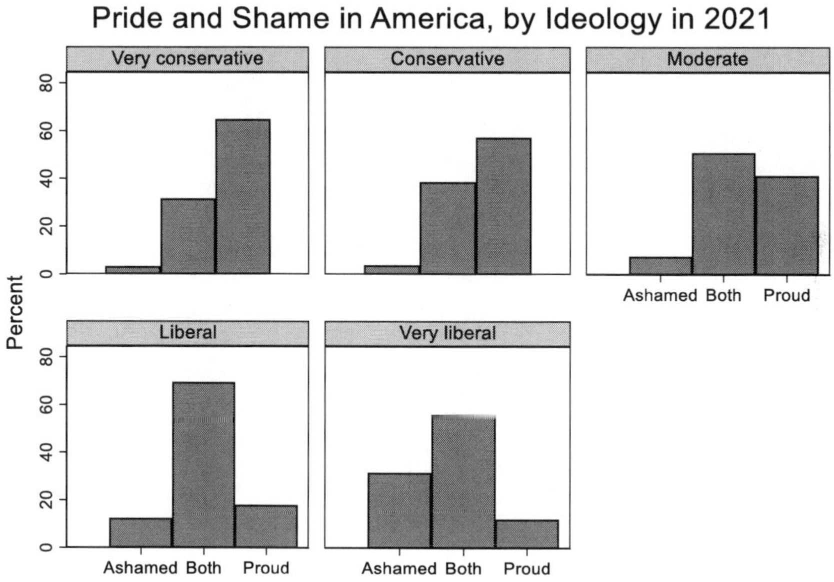

Fig. 3.10 This histogram shows the mean with 95% confidence intervals of Americans who feel mostly proud, both proud and ashamed, and mostly ashamed of America, differentiated by ideology. Data from Pew 2020

Republicans have more blind patriotism whereas Democratic respondents have more constructive patriotism, which matches prior literature on this topic (Schatz et al. 1999).

Table 3.3 shows a multinomial probit regression model for determinants of pride and shame in America. Respondents saying that they were both proud and ashamed is the base category. Importantly, the only predictor of being both proud and ashamed of America is that those who are liberal are more likely to be mostly ashamed of America. Interestingly, all the other demographic and political variables in this model are not statistically significant showing that ideology is their primary driver of feelings of being mostly ashamed of America. When examining those who are mostly proud as compared to those who are both proud and ashamed of America, the model shows that having a liberal ideology decreases the likelihood of being mostly proud as does being a Democratic partisan or an independent. In terms of demographic variables, Hispanics and the elderly are more likely to be mostly proud of America as compared to being both proud and ashamed of America. Additionally, females are less likely than males to be mostly proud of America. This regression model shows similar results as to the others, the main driver of these beliefs of patriotism is ideology, and across most demographic groups, there is not much variation except that the elderly are more patriotic, including blind patriotism, than the younger generation.

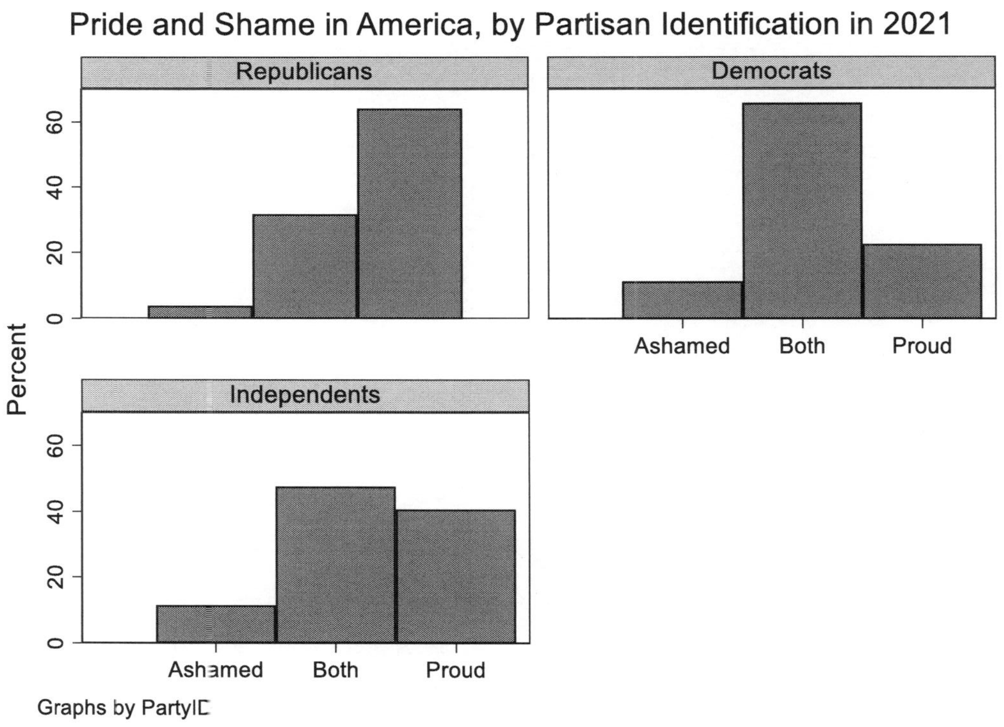

Fig. 3.11 This histogram shows the mean with 95% confidence intervals of Americans who feel mostly proud, both proud and ashamed, and mostly ashamed of America, differentiated by partisan identification—data from Pew 2020

Table 3.3
Determinants of pride and shame in America

Variable	*1*	*S.E.2*
Proud		
Ideology	–0.256***	0.076
Democrat	–1.089***	0.207
Independent	–0.581***	0.174
Black	–0.173	0.238
Hispanic	0.574**	0.219
Income	0.001	0.032
Education	–0.025	0.040
Age	0.012**	0.004
Female	–0.359**	0.137
Intercept	1.006*	0.400
Ashamed		
Ideology	0.384***	0.099
Democrat	–0.548	0.302
Independent	–0.028	0.268
Black	0.170	0.273
Hispanic	–0.026	0.295
Income	–0.045	0.043
Education	0.000	0.056
Age	–0.008	0.005
Female	0.178	0.185
Intercept	–1.974***	0.575

Note Cells represent unstandardized coefficients and standard errors for the multinomial probit regression model for determinants of pride and shame in America. Respondents saying that they were both proud and ashamed is the base category
+ $p < 0.10$, *$p < 0.05$, **$p < 0.01$, ***$p < 0.001$

Conclusion

Through various measures and samples, this chapter shows that Americans are highly patriotic. This extends across almost every subgroup, and with very few exceptions, Americans are patriotic. The primary ideological grouping that is, on average, unpatriotic is those who are very liberal on a seven-point ideology scale. Even in this group, around 45% are patriotic. In every other racial, gender, age, income, education, and partisan identification subgrouping, most Americans in these categories are patriotic. The data also show clearly that around 5% to 10% of Americans are unpatriotic, and some measures show a similar percentage expressing dislike or hatred of America.

There are differences in how patriotism can influence beliefs and behaviors based on politically salient subgroups. We do not know enough about how this variance affects political outcomes for these different groups. The following chapters explore how patriotism correlates with critical political outcomes, which are deemed valuable in democratic societies by scholarly literature.

Before we analyze the relationship between patriotism and political phenomena, it is crucial to understand at a deeper level what patriotism means to Americans. The next chapter takes a qualitative approach to analyze how Americans conceptualize their relationship with their country. Using a novel set of 500 open-ended answers where respondents were instructed to write a paragraph on what patriotism means to them, we see a nuanced view that articulates what is best described as constructive patriotism. These Americans love their country but are deeply worried about its problems. Far from blind patriotism, these Americans expressed profound shame over America's historical problems and current failures. Simultaneously, they are deeply thankful for the freedoms and opportunities this country has given them and highly optimistic about America's future.

References

Gallup Organization. 2022. *Gallup Poll, Question 1*, 31119654.00015. Gallup Organization, Cornell University, Ithaca, NY: Roper Center for Public Opinion Research, Dataset.

Hanson, Kristen, and Emma O'Dwyer. 2019. "Patriotism and Nationalism, Left and Right: A Q-methodology Study of American National Identity." *Political Psychology* 40 (4): 777–795.

Huntington, Samuel P. 2004. *Who Are We? The Challenges to America's National Identity*. New York: Simon & Schuster Inc.

Ipsos. 2021. *Ipsos Understanding Society: Wave 10 June 2021, Question 1*, 31118534.00000. Ipsos, Cornell University, Ithaca, NY: Roper Center for Public Opinion Research, Dataset.

Maliepaard, Mieke, and Maykel Verkuyten. 2018. "National Disidentification and Minority Identity: A Study among Muslims in Western Europe." *Self and Identity* 17 (1): 75–91.

Meitinger, Katharina. 2018. "What Does the General National Pride Item Measure? Insights from Web Probing." *International Journal of Comparative Sociology* 59 (5–6): 428–450.

NPR. 2022. *NPR/Ipsos Poll, Question 34*, 31119555.00033. Ipsos, Cornell University, Ithaca, NY: Roper Center for Public Opinion Research, Dataset.

Pew. 2020. *Pew Research Center Global Attitudes & Trends Fall 2020 Questionnaire*. Dataset.

Pew Research Center. 2021. *Public Trust in Government: 1958–2021*. Washington, DC: Pew Research Center. https://www.pewresearch.org/politics/2021/05/17/public-trust-in-government-1958-2021/. Accessed 30 May 2025.

PRRI. 2021. *PRRI American Values Survey, Question 71*, 31118794.00070. Ipsos, Cornell University, Ithaca, NY: Roper Center for Public Opinion Research, Dataset.

Satherley, Nicole, Kumar Yogeeswaran, Danny Osborne, and Chris G. Sibley. 2018. "If They Say "Yes", We Say "No": Partisan Cues Increase Polarization Over National Symbols." *Psychological Science* 29 (12): 1996–2009.

Schatz, Robert T., Ervin Staub, and Howard Lavine. 1999. "On the Varieties of National Attachment: Blind Versus Constructive Patriotism." *Political Psychology* 20 (1): 151–174.

Selzer, J. Ann. 2022. "The Erosion of Civic Trust and the Role of Public Opinion." *Journal of Democracy* 33 (1): 45–59.

Social Science Research Solutions. 2018. *SSR Omnibus Survey, Question 4*, 31116569.00003, Social Science Research Solutions (SSRS). Cornell University, Ithaca, NY: Roper Center for Public Opinion Research, Dataset.

Zahra, T. 2010. "Imagined Noncommunities: National Indifference as a Category of Analysis." *Slavic Review* 69 (1): 93–119.

CHAPTER 4

What Patriotism Means to Americans

Abstract This chapter examines qualitative data from 500 Americans who wrote open-ended paragraphs describing their feelings toward the United States. The results reveal a nuanced patriotism: respondents commonly criticize America's failures while expressing gratitude for its freedoms and opportunities. Text-as-data analyses confirm that most Americans hold a "clear-eyed" love for their country, neither blind nor uncritical. This chapter thus complicates simplistic portrayals of patriotism by showing how it often involves an ongoing negotiation of pride, hope, and concern for societal problems.

Keywords Qualitative Research · Text-as-Data · Mixed Sentiments · Open-Ended Responses · Critical Patriotism · Public Opinion

Scholars have offered multiple definitions of patriotism, which can be interpreted in multiple ways. So, knowing what it means to Americans is crucial before investigating how patriotism influences citizens. This chapter analyzes survey data and qualitative responses on what patriotism means and how citizens view their relationship with America to analyze the potential definitions of patriotism deeply, described in-depth below. I use publicly available survey data from large survey companies, augmented by a new online sample matched to nationally representative

S. Richey, *Patriotism and Citizenship*,
https://doi.org/10.1007/978-3-031-89885-3_4

data for age, gender, and race—data described below. In this novel survey, respondents were instructed to write about how they feel love and hate toward America. Most respondents wrote over a paragraph, providing unusually rich data to analyze this crucial question.

This mixed method approach has advantages because the nationally representative survey data provides extensive coverage of society. Comparatively, the qualitative data allows a much more nuanced and in-depth understanding of conceptualizing these ideas. I will analyze the paragraphs written about patriotism using quantitative text analysis, which has the advantage of being objective and reproducible to transcend the typical flaws inherent in qualitative research. Combined, the survey data qualitative research and the quantitative text analysis provide an in-depth picture of how Americans view patriotism.

The research below shows that Americans' vision of patriotism is highly nuanced. They are often extremely grateful for the freedoms and opportunities America provides and the sacrifices made by those who serve it. Conversely, they also see its many problems. Based on the theoretical understandings that previous scholars on patriotism have presented, most Americans would be described as constructive patriots because they recognize and are deeply thankful for all America gives them, but they also see its issues.

In the next section, I examine available survey data that asks Americans to conceptualize how they show patriotism and describe what is patriotic.

What Patriotism Means to Americans

One way to know how Americans conceptualize patriotism is by asking them in a nationally representative survey. For example, List 1 shows such a survey from 2018 asking for an open-ended response: "In just a few words, how do you show your American patriotism?" (Social Science Research Solutions 2018). The respondents were allowed to list only one activity. Still, political participation, civic engagement, and respect and support for elected officials and the government were all top of mind for many in this sample.

List 1: How Americans Show Patriotism

23% Flying/saluting/honoring/displaying/respecting the flag (in general).

15%	Respecting/supporting the troops/veterans/military.
13%	Being a good American/good citizen; honoring/respecting my country; being a good person.
11%	Voting.
8%	Respecting/following the constitution/laws.
7%	Participating in civic engagement/community involvement.
5%	Served/serving in the armed forces.
5%	Participating in the national anthem/Pledge of Allegiance/moment of silence/patriotic songs.
5%	Working/paying taxes.
4%	Celebrating/attending parades/patriotic events (4th of July, Memorial Day, etc.)
4%	Buying American-made products.
3%	Respecting/supporting elected officials/leadership/government.
2%	Wearing patriotic clothing.
*	Other.
19%	Don't know/no answer.

List 1 shows the percentage of responses from a 2018 nationally representative survey that asked, "In just a few words, how do you show your American patriotism?".

List 1 is incredibly interesting for what follows in the next chapters because it shows that the correlations below match what a different sample of Americans think of when they consider how to show patriotism. Many of the same actions used as dependent variables below align with how these Americans think to show their patriotism, implying that greater patriotism leads to a greater number of the expressed actions. This implies that these open-ended responses match the predictions based on the theory. The data in List 1 gives greater validity to the correlation between patriotism and political participation, civic engagement, and diffuse support shown below.

One limit of the data in List 1 is that it allows respondents to choose only one way to show patriotism. It is highly plausible that someone who verbalized the most chosen outcome of flying the flag may simultaneously view respecting veterans as patriotic, for example. Figure 4.1 shows data from a nationally representative survey that gave a selection of closed-ended options from which the respondent could select all that apply. The disadvantage of these data is that, unlike the open-ended questions in List 1, the respondents were limited to choosing only the offered selections. As in List 1, voting features prominently in how Americans conceptualize what it is to be patriotic in Fig. 4.1. Additionally, many respondents selected the forms of civic engagement offered on this closed-ended list. The similarity between the two samples is striking and validates the hypotheses evaluated empirically below.

Interestingly, in the open-ended responses, no respondents said owning a gun was a way to show patriotism, but when explicitly offered this as a potential option, 50% did so in Fig. 4.1 Also, note that between both samples, no citizens said or selected anything involving the dominance of other nations or subgroups within our society. This outcome could be derived from social desirability bias; however, the possibility exists that these feelings are not related to patriotism in the minds of most Americans. I will empirically test this in the chapter examining xenophobia and patriotism below.

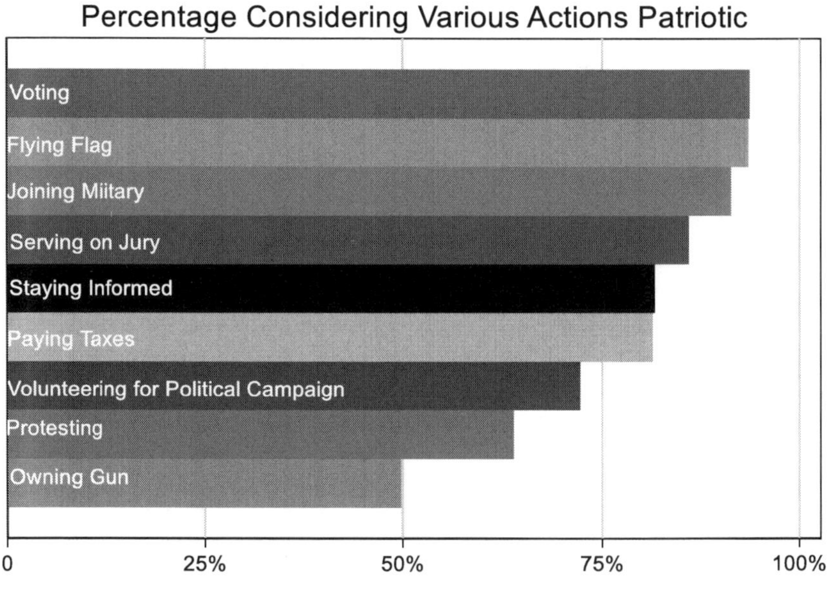

Fig. 4.1 This bar graph shows the percentage of Americans who consider these actions patriotic from Fox News Poll (2014)

While these surveys are fascinating, in the next section, I examine a novel qualitative data set of 500 Americans describing their love and hate for America. This is a much richer and more nuanced set of data to analyze. First, I will explain how this question was responded to by selecting representative quotes, which is common in qualitative research. I will then analyze the same data set using quantitative text analysis.

Qualitative Text Analysis

In the fall of 2021, I had an online sample of 500 Americans matched to nationally representative data for age, gender, race, and ethnicity write an open-ended paragraph or more about their feelings of love and hate toward America. Their thoughtful responses showed great nuance of feeling toward America. Reading their responses made it clear that there was tremendous optimism about and appreciation for the freedom and opportunities that America provided and, simultaneously, great frustration with the social divisions, political turmoil, and inequalities in both historical and present-day America. In this section, I show exemplary quotes demonstrating the general feelings of the three main groups toward America. A majority are overtly positive in their expressed feelings toward America, a smaller but sizeable group has mixed feelings, and a small group dislikes or hates America.

Most respondents wrote about their love of America even though the writing prompt asked about love and hate. Particularly important to them was the opportunity and freedom available in America. For example, a slightly liberal, young Black man wrote, "I love America because everyone has relatively equal freedom to choose their path in life and equal opportunity compared to the vast majority of other countries around the world."[1] Similarly, a conservative, elderly Hispanic man wrote, "I love my country, it gave my family an opportunity to be free and indeed, my father, a Cuban immigrant, fought in WW 2 to defend that freedom." Hundreds of other respondents expressed similar feelings, showing that their patriotism derived from well-considered opinions about what the country had offered them.

[1] Many of these quotes have grammatical errors. I left these writing mistakes in the quotes intentionally, due to a desire to convey the exact nuance of the respondent's writing.

Throughout these responses, patriotism was conceived of in contractual terms. America had given them something (freedom, opportunity), and they had given something back (love). Many specifically mentioned freedom of religion. As a somewhat conservative, elderly, White woman wrote, "I love that I have the freedom to practice and believe any religion that I want." Her expression of love derived from her appreciation of her religious freedoms, which is essential because the theoretical model in Chapter 2 depends on deriving a psychological benefit of giving back to America. The theoretical model articulated in Chapter 2 shows that political participation, civic engagement, and other forms of collective action derive from patriotism when people wish to give back to the country that has given them something. These qualitative textual responses show that this logic was clearly in the minds of these respondents. Examine the grammatical structure of this response from a somewhat conservative, middle-aged, White woman: "I love America because of all the freedoms we enjoy here." Her love was given because she had received something vital: freedom.

Another group expressed a mix of both hatred and love for America or aspects therein. Many in this group expressed admiration for the nation's ideals but did not believe the country always lived up to them. For example, a very liberal, young, multiracial male said, "I love what America has the potential to stand for when it comes to allowing its citizens and potential ones when it comes to freedom and the promise of a better life for those who want it. But America has proven that it is willing to uphold ideas that go against that like banning abortion and criminalizing drugs." Similarly, a slightly conservative, middle-aged Asian woman explained, "I feel neither love nor hate for America, but somewhere in between. I like the relative freedom we have, such as almost total freedom of speech and other choices…we do have a lot of civil liberties relative to a lot of other countries, which we often take for granted. On the other hand, local, state, and federal governments have gotten way out of hand concerning infringing on those liberties. There is no longer any privacy…citizens are under constant surveillance. Don't even get me started on civil forfeiture…what a complete travesty that is. There are cameras everywhere and a lot of the police are simply a street-gang in uniform. Political corruption has become so normalized we have become numb to it and accept it without a thought." In sum, this group expressed hope that America could live up to its ideals but is concerned about current realities.

As with the quantitative question on love or hate of America analyzed in Chapter 3, a small minority of people clearly articulated hatred toward this country. Most often, the people who expressed hatred toward America were angry about racial oppression, social inequality, and economic distribution issues. For example, a very liberal, young, White male declared, "It has deliberately become a nation built upon exploitation and lack of consideration for people of color and those of lower socioeconomic status. Its government is corrupt with little to [no] ability to lessen its corruption over time." Similarly, a slightly liberal, middle-aged, White woman complained, "I absolutely hate this country. You don't get paid to go on maternity leave when you have a child. Some people don't even get to keep their jobs because they don't qualify for FMLA. It's disgusting that people don't have insurance. Everything is so messed up. I've never been insured. I haven't had my teeth looked at in 20 years. Basically, I have to hope I don't die." These in-depth writings show that the 5 to 10% of Americans who consistently select dislike or hatred of America on survey questions shown in Chapter 3 have clearly thought out and well-articulated reasons for their feelings. Thus, the findings in Chapter 3 are not based on some artifact of survey wording or other methodological issues. Rather, they are based on a genuine dislike for or hatred of America. This significant finding has been overlooked in the literature on patriotism.

These selected quotes are examples based on my reading of this sample's texts. However, my selection could be based on arbitrary factors and not accurately represent those writings. For a more objective summary of these writings' meanings, I turn to quantitative text analysis in the next section.

Quantitative Text Analysis

In this section, I examine these passages using quantitative text analysis, which has grown in usage due to the creation of readily available software allowing for easy yet sophisticated text analysis (see a detailed explanation in Grimmer et al. 2022). The software uses a text-as-data approach to quantify certain words' usage and assign them sentimental or emotional values. It lets researchers know which words are used most often and provides summarized quantitative metrics of the text's general meaning. Political Science particularly has been a leader in using quantitative text analysis to understand public opinion. For example, Ferrario and Stantcheva conducted a quantitative text analysis on open-ended survey questions about policy concerns. In particular, I use a specific type of quantitative text analysis called sentiment analysis to examine what patriotism means to these Americans.

Sentiment Analysis

Although similar in goals to traditional content analysis, quantitative text analysis is advantageous because it is objective and reproducible. It also allows access to deeper text trends inaccessible to human readers through the software's ability to simultaneously analyze large text quantities in a way the human mind cannot. The obvious disadvantage is that this is a comprehensive analysis of general text trends and is not precise about specific word meanings that context can alter. I use this approach to augment the more traditional qualitative text used in the last section. Quantitative text analysis provides these passages an objective analysis to help us understand how these Americans view their country, supplementing the prior section's more subjective selection.

Sentiment analysis as a tool to understand public opinion on politics has been growing. Every English word is coded as positive, negative, or neutral. Very small words are removed, as are punctuation, numbers, and other nonrelevant characters. The software tabulates the number of positive, negative, and neutral words and gives a quantitative summary of the sentiment of the text. Van Atteveldt, van der Velden, and Boukes (2021) show that the method is far from perfect for analyzing textual sentiment and is best used as a simple metric to augment human reading. I follow the best practices recommended by Chan et al. (2021) in that I check for the influence of content length and use a suitable sentiment dictionary, but I do not assume the dictionary's validity or reliability, nor do I use multiple dictionaries to test the same statistical hypothesis.

Table 4.1 shows a sentiment analysis of writing about feelings of love and hate toward America from a 2021 online survey matched to nationally representative data for age, gender, and race. It shows that the median word is positive at 0.65. This implies that these respondents are generally optimistic when writing about their feelings of love and hate toward America. Note that there is a sizable percentage of negative words, as the first quartile is –0.4. Thus, quantitatively, these respondents are generally

Table 4.1 Sentiment analysis of writing about feelings of love or hate toward America

Min	*1st Qu*	*Median*	*Mean*	*3rd Qu*	*Max*
-7.1000	-0.4000	0.6500	0.7262	1.7500	12.2000

positive toward America, but they also express concerns and some negative feelings. This quantitative assessment matches the nuanced feelings reported in the previous sections.

Table 4.1 shows a sentiment analysis of writing about feelings of love and hate toward America from a 2021 online survey matching nationally representative data in the United States for age, gender, and race.

Of course, there is more to feelings than simple positiveness and negativeness. To explore other emotions expressed in the text, I utilize the NRC Emotion Lexicon, described as an association of English words with the following eight basic emotions: anger, fear, anticipation, trust, surprise, sadness, joy, and disgust (see Mohammad 2020). Just as the previous sentiment analysis tagged every word in the English language as positive, negative, or neutral, this lexicon associates each English word with these eight common emotions. Naturally, some words are not associated with any emotion. Running this textual analysis gives you the total number of words in a body of text that can be tagged with one of these emotions.

Figure 4.2 shows a bar graph of the number of words associated with these emotions when Americans consider their feelings of love and hate toward America. Particularly, the most common emotion expressed is trust. This finding will be replicated later when I examine the relationship of patriotism to political trust with survey data. On the other hand, the least common emotion is surprise, which makes sense as most people are probably not surprised when considering their feelings about something as commonplace as America. The second most common emotion is joy, which makes sense because patriotism is often discussed as a love of one's country, and love for one's country should be similar to joy. The subsequent most common emotions, fear and anger, are negative, which again conveys the nuance of these writings toward America. The emotional attachment to America provokes positive feelings, such as joy and trust, and negative feelings, such as fear and anger. Accordingly, this

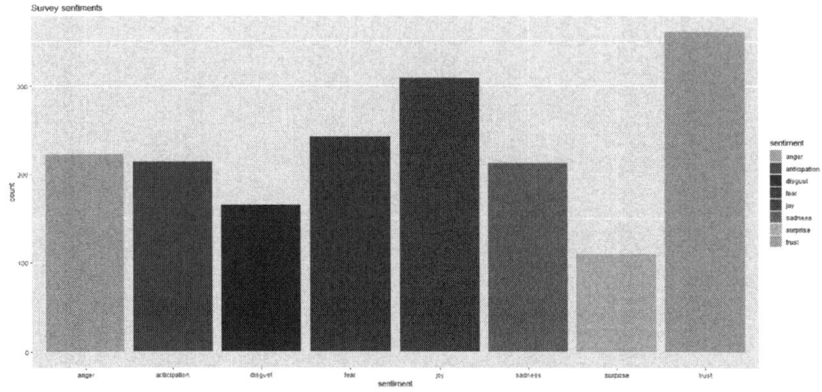

Fig. 4.2 This bar graph shows the number of words associated with these emotions when Americans consider their feelings of love and hate toward America

emotional understanding of patriotism derived through this quantitative textual analysis suggests that most Americans have favorable emotions toward their country, but this is not blind patriotism. Similar to the combination of positive and negative sentiments in the text, positive and negative emotions are associated with America.

The quantitative textual analysis of what Americans generally think and feel about America is fascinating and provides deep insight into what Americans believe, but it is important to break these feelings down into significant sociological subgroups. Mass aggregate feelings and emotional attachments about America could belie important differences between subgroups. In the next section, I examine different American subgroups' feelings using the same methodologies.

Sentiment Analysis by Subgroups

Beyond the general attitude of patriotism, it is interesting to select politically relevant subgroups and see how their language differs. We can take the same approach as the prior section to analyze the positiveness and negativeness of the words used when discussing subgroups' love and hatred of America. Table 4.2 shows the same sentiment analysis but differentiated by race and ethnicity. Groupings of white, black, Hispanic, and

Asian respondents are analyzed because these groups have enough respondents in the sample. As in Chapter 3, where we examined closed-ended survey questions, we see no statistically significant differences in the sentiment of these groups. American Political Science constantly studies race relations and attitudes between races. However, quantitative and qualitative analysis, including the sentiment analysis of written text, finds no distinctions across these groups regarding patriotism. As in the prior section, the mean and median are positive, implying that across these four racial and ethnic groups, respondents use more positive words when describing their feelings of love and hate toward America.

Table 4.2 shows a sentiment analysis of writing about feelings of love and hate toward America from a 2021 online survey matched to nationally representative data in the United States for age, gender, and race by race and ethnicity.

The main group that showed a distinctive pattern in attitudes toward America in Chapter 3 comprised the very liberal. Thus, using the same sentiment analysis to analyze ideology is important, Table 4.3 shows a sentiment analysis of the writing by those who were very conservative, neither liberal nor conservative, or very liberal. The very conservative respondents and neither liberal nor conservative respondents had the same median sentiment score of 0.75. The only group I found lacking an overall positive sentiment toward America was the very liberal group whose median score was 0 and mean score was slightly negative. I examined other factors like age, gender, income, and education, and sentiment analysis showed no statistically significant differences. This again highlights the same finding shown in Chapter 3: Very liberal respondents are the only group with a negative attitude toward America.

Table 4.3 shows a sentiment analysis of writing about feelings of love and hate toward America from a 2021 online survey match to nationally

Table 4.2 Sentiment analysis of writing about feelings of love or hate toward America by race and ethnicity

Race or Ethnicity	*Min*	*1st Qu*	*Median*	*Mean*	*3rd Qu*	*Max*
White	–7.1000	–0.4000	0.6250	0.7336	1.800	12.2000
Black	–6.6500	–0.4750	0.5000	0.4596	1.3625	5.5500
Hispanic	–2.8000	–0.0125	0.5750	0.8327	1.5750	4.9000
Asian	–6.8000	–0.0750	0.7500	0.9717	2.2375	7.3500

Table 4.3 Sentiment analysis of writing about feelings of love or hate toward America, by ideology

Race or Ethnicity	*Min*	*1st Qu*	*Median*	*Mean*	*3rd Qu*	*Max*	*Sig. diff Median*
Very Conservative	−4.5500	0.0000	0.7500	0.5324	1.7500	3.6500	
Neither	−3.2500	−0.0500	0.7500	0.9742	1.7500	8.3500	0.999
Very Liberal	−7.1000	−0.9000	0.0000	−0.0066	1.1250	7.3500	0.000

representative data in the United States for age, gender, and race, by race and ethnicity.

Conclusion

This chapter shows that much of the worry about Americans blindly and uncritically accepting patriotism confuses the term with nationalism. The patriotism expressed by most of the survey responses and the qualitative research conducted in the fall of 2021 shows great nuance in its appreciation of America's problems and successes. The survey results show that Americans' views of patriotic expressions and actions align with the theoretical predictions that this concerns solving collective action problems. Specifically, they mentioned political participation, community engagement, respect for officials, etc., strongly suggesting a link between these activities and patriotism in the respondents' minds. It further suggests that having greater patriotism will generate more of these activities.

Patriotism is shown in the qualitative responses as the outcome of a contractual relationship with one's country. The deep gratitude that patriotic people feel derives from their country's gifts, such as freedom and opportunity. Since they believe America has given them freedom and opportunity, they respond by giving back gratitude, love, and commitment. Because they were given freedom and an opportunity by America, they responded by loving it. The descriptions of patriotism as blinding or unthinking ignore that this contractual component derives from citizens contemplating what America has given them. It seems likely that the scholars and pundits who paint patriots as unthinking simply disagree with them over the levels of opportunity and freedom available in America.

However, that is not a disagreement over patriotism; it is a disagreement over the empirical reality of America's levels of freedom and opportunity.

This is a crucial distinction because it is not really a debate about cognition. These scholars who view patriots as unthinking ignore that a thinking person can express gratitude and love if given something of value. At its core, this is an ideological disagreement over what America provides rather than an analysis of the validity of patriotism. Political theorists who criticize and critique patriotism should address whether or not it is valid to feel gratitude and love in exchange for being provided something that someone views as extremely valuable. For patriotism to be irrational, unthinking, and so forth, it would have to be irrational and unthinking to engage in this kind of contractual exchange of love. No theorist to date has dealt with this, and almost all political theories on patriotism presuppose that America is an unequal, oppressive society. Whether stated overly or not, they conclude that a contractual exchange cannot be rational because America has not provided its end of the bargain. However, that is an ideological disagreement these scholars have with patriotic Americans over what constitutes a sufficient level of opportunity and freedom and has nothing to do with the inherent rationality of patriotism.

In the next chapter, I begin to examine the impact of patriotism, by analyzing its relationship with collective action.

References

Chan, C.-H., J. Bajjalieh, L. Auvil, H. Wessler, S. Althaus, K. Welbers, W. van Atteveldt, et al. 2021. "Four Best Practices for Measuring News Sentiment Using 'off-the-Shelf' Dictionaries: A Large-Scale p-Hacking Experiment." *Computational Communication Research* 3 (1): 1–27.

Grimmer, Justin, Margaret E. Roberts, and Brandon M. Stewart. 2022. *Text as Data: A New Framework for Machine Learning and the Social Sciences*. Princeton University Press.

Fox News. 2014. *Fox News Poll: Obama/U.S. Military/Iraq: June 2014, Question 43*, USASFOX.070214.R21. Shaw & Co. Research/Anderson Robbins Research, Cornell University, Ithaca, NY: Roper Center for Public Opinion Research, 2014, Dataset.

Mohammad, Saif M. 2020. *Sentiment Analysis: Automatically Detecting Valence, Emotions, and Other Effectual States from Text*. arXiv:2005.11882v2 https://doi.org/10.48550/arXiv.2005.11882

Social Science Research Solutions. 2018. *SSR Omnibus Survey, Question 4*, 31116569.00003. Social Science Research Solutions (SSRS), Cornell University, Ithaca, NY: Roper Center for Public Opinion Research, Dataset.

Wouter van Atteveldt, Mariken A. C. G. van der Velden, and Mark Boukes 2021. "The Validity of Sentiment Analysis: Comparing Manual Annotation, Crowd-Coding, Dictionary Approaches, and Machine Learning Algorithms, Communication Methods, and Measures." *Communication Methods and Measures* 15 (2): 121–140.

CHAPTER 5

Patriotism and Collective Action

Abstract This chapter tests the link between patriotism and collective action. Survey-based evidence shows that individuals reporting higher patriotism are more likely to engage in civic activities (e.g., volunteering). A survey experiment primes participants with patriotic sentiments and measures their likelihood of taking tangible action (e.g., signing up to donate blood). The findings indicate that patriotic attachment can indeed inspire greater willingness to pay personal costs that benefit society, supporting the central contractual theory of patriotism as a motivator for helping one's country.

Keywords Collective Action · Survey Experiment · Civic Engagement · Sacrifice · Public Goods · Pro-Social Behavior

This chapter investigates the relationship between patriotism and collective action. It focuses on civic engagement as a measurable proxy for collective action, and a specific form of sacrifice for the group is focused on: blood donation. Across many measures of civic engagement and through the measurement of donating blood, we see that patriotism strongly correlates with collective action. Crucially, I also conducted a survey experiment, which allows me to make causal statements about the relationship between patriotism and civic engagement. The strong

S. Richey, *Patriotism and Citizenship*,
https://doi.org/10.1007/978-3-031-89885-3_5

combination of results from nationally representative survey data and experimental evidence where the causation can be directly measured provide strong evidence of those with more love of their nation or more likely to sacrifice for it.

A chief finding of this book is the underappreciated role of patriotism in promoting someone willing to undertake the costs of volunteering. As the main theories described in Chapter 2 revolve around ideas over willingness to sacrifice being motivated by love of country, establishing this empirically with both observational and experimental data grounds the theory in a strong evidentiary basis. Based on the robustness of these findings, we can be confident that those with greater patriotism will be more likely to volunteer in their communities. The experimental evidence below shows that communities should activate patriotic feelings to promote sacrifice for the group. Together, these findings are strong evidence that if civic education promotes patriotism, there will be direct benefits derived from it by having a more engaged citizenry in their local communities.

Collective Action and Civic Engagement

The relationship between collective action and civic engagement is clear; one can think of civic engagement as a subset of collective action. While collective action is often associated with interest group activity, more general broad-based volunteering with charitable organizations or civic groups also is a form of collective action. For example, Oliver (1984) defines collective action as "activities which produce collective or public goods" (Oliver 1984, 602). Under this definition, any service group that provides public goods would be an endeavor that involves collective action. Oliver (1984) further states that "(t)he concept of collective action provides a framework for understanding the common dilemmas in a wide variety of situations, and many scholars have treated participation in community organizations as a form of collective action" (Oliver 1984, 602). Having the willingness to sacrifice for others should be related to patriotism. While nothing in this theory would suggest that partisan or ideological-based interest groups would be motivated by patriotism, it may motivate civic engagement. Thus, while it is true that collective action can involve traditional conceptions of interest groups, it does not have to and can also come from involvement in more traditional forms of civic engagement.

In most situations, collective action, civic engagement, civic participation, and civil society are directly combined. Pfaff and Valdez (2010) describe this complex intertwined relationship as "(c)ollective action lies at the heart of any vibrant civil society because civic engagement requires individuals to work together as part of a group" (Pfaff and Valdez 2010, 498). Basically, civil society requires civic participation to achieve goals, and civic participation derives from civic engagement, a form of collective action. Being willing to sacrifice for the group motivates someone to get involved in groups to solve problems in their community. The more someone is involved in these groups, the greater the level of civic engagement this person has.

In addition to civic participation in groups, more straightforward forms of collection action involve simple sacrifice that does not necessarily involve group participation. Below I measure this by blood donation as a form of collective action, but there are many other ways, such as abiding by the law, paying taxes, cooperating with environmental and other initiatives, not littering, and so on. These actions do not require groups but sacrifice or, at least, not cheating others, which is also collective action. Civic engagement is best thought of as an articulated form of collective action that I show in the next section greatly benefits society.

Benefits of Civic Engagement

A large literature shows the great benefit of a willingness to volunteer (Putnam 2000). Civic engagement profoundly impacts communities (Putnam et al. 1993; Skocpol 2003). Research shows that communities with actively engaged citizens have communities with better education outcomes (Jeynes 2012), are more resilient to disasters (Aldrich and Meyer 2015), are healthier at both the individual and group levels (Kawachi and Berkman 2014), and have less crime (Ling et al. 2019). Pancer (2014) summarizes a vast amount of research as finding that "(s)tates and countries with high levels of civic participation experience better health and mental health, with lower rates of disease, mental health problems, and suicide. They also have lower crime rates. Research evidence indicates that they are also more prosperous economically, have healthier and better-educated children, and are better governed." (Pancer 2014, 8). Simply put, all things being equal, more civic engagement produces a better society at both the individual and group levels.

While Theiss-Morse and Hibbing (2005) show that civic engagement may not make perfect democratic citizens, it is still shown to improve the communities through direct action to solve problems vastly (Levine 2013). Not only does it benefit the community, but active involvement in voluntary endeavors also has a profound impact on the happiness of the individual volunteer (see Borgonovi 2008). Hero (2003) shows civic engagement could empower local racists to exclude outsiders. However, this did not necessarily apply to the civic engagement examined below because nothing in these measurements of civic engagement would augment an exclusionary social movement. Civic engagement is typically about voluntary activities and charitable organizations with no direct role in de facto racial segregation. The negative outcomes that Hero (2003) shows are dated to a particular social and economic time when white resistance to integration utilized the tools provided by collective action to achieve their racist goals. However, this was conducted in a particular historical context after segregation in housing was deemed illegal in the 1960s, which is not descriptive of involvement in activities like the PTA or youth sports today.

In sum, a large amount of literature shows that there are benefits from civic engagement and collective action, and if patriotism can promote these activities, it will benefit society. I now examine experimental research to explore the causal relationship between patriotism and collective action.

Experimental Results

I start with experimental evidence because causation with experiments is clear. The only difference between the treatment and control groups is assumed to be the random assignment of participants to different stimuli. The similarity of the treatment and control group can be observed by examining the balance between these groups on political and socioeconomic variables which are measured pretreatment. Since the only apparent difference between these groups is exposure to a stimulus promoting patriotic thinking, we can be confident that patriotism elicits any behavior change. Randomization produced balance across a broad pretest set of variable.

Additionally, the problem of generalizability is often an issue with experiments that use convenience samples. This survey experiment has respondents matched to nationally representative data for age, gender, and race and is broadly geographically dispersed across the United States.

Therefore, compared to most experimental studies in psychology that use college students, for example, this is a far more generalizable sample. It is important to note that the survey experiment also contains a high level of realism because most scheduling of blood donation is done through the Red Cross website linked to the experiment.

The experimental design is based on the emotion induction methodology in psychology (see Lench et al. 2011). This methodology creates stronger emotions in a treatment group than in a control group (Siedlecka and Denson 2019). Experimental psychology research shows that after participants think about emotional attachments, their subsequent actions will be more likely to be influenced by them (see Baumeister et al. 2007 for a critical review). The difference between the treatment and control group in the current study derives only from the randomly assigned inducement of the emotional attachment to their town. Having the treatment group think about their feelings toward America prioritized that emotional attachment in deciding whether to donate blood, while the control group was not necessarily thinking about these feelings. Importantly, if participants do not have feelings of emotional attachment, then stimuli to prompt such feelings will not influence their behavior. Based on its long history in psychology, vetted by dozens of psychometric experiments (see a meta-analysis in Westermann et al. 1996), this design and method are appropriate for this research question and theory.

The experimental procedures had 384 respondents answer pretest questions, and then a random half of the participants were assigned to read a treatment stimulus that promoted patriotism, while another random half was assigned to read a question that omitted the patriotic elicitation. The treatment was worded as, "There is a historically low blood supply now. **Thinking about your love of America,** would you like to schedule a time and place to donate blood? If so, please click Yes, Donate Blood below. If not, please click No, Do Not Donate Blood."

In contrast, the control was worded as, "There is a historically low blood supply now. Would you like to schedule a time and place to donate blood? If so, please click Yes, Donate Blood below. If not, please click No, Do Not Donate Blood." Based on the emotion induction methodology, getting the respondent to think about their love of America should promote patriotism in considering whether or not to donate blood. The only difference in this experiment between the treatment and control is the inducement of patriotic emotional thinking. If this relatively simple inducement can promote more blood donation, it shows a quick and easy methodology for governments to gain compliance over their citizenry. It will signify that simply evoking patriotic symbology can achieve acquiescence to societal goals that require joint sacrifice, such as blood donation. This experiment provides a clear test of whether patriotism is closely related to collective action.

Experimental results in Fig. 5.1 show that exposure to patriotic stimuli doubles the likelihood of being willing to donate blood by clicking on a Red Cross link to schedule blood donation. Randomly assigning someone to think about their love of America increased by 8 percentage points their likelihood of being willing to donate blood. The percentage of those agreeing to donate blood in the control condition was 7.94%, and 15.91% in the treatment condition, a statistically significant difference with a *p*-value of 0.0182. The pairwise correlation between exposure to the patriotic stimulus and willingness to donate blood is 0.1236. This equates to around 1/8th of a standard deviation increase in the willingness to donate blood.

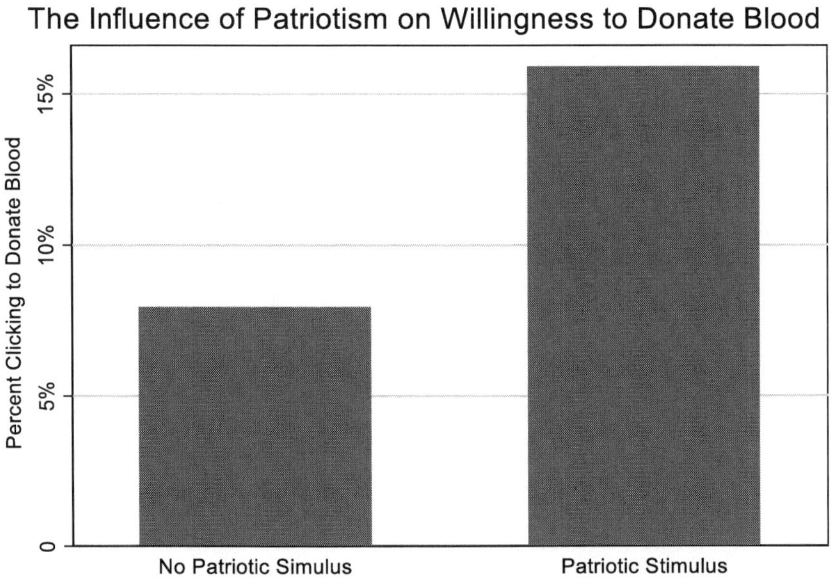

Fig. 5.1 The percentage clicking to schedule blood donation by experimental treatment

This shows that patriotism is a powerful channel by which society can motivate collective action. A simple six-word prompt that got the participant to think about patriotism doubled their likelihood of clicking a link to schedule a blood donation. By merely asking the respondent to think about their love of America, twice as many were willing to sacrifice for this country by donating blood. This has profound implications for understanding how and when individuals undertake the sacrifices necessary for collective action. In the next section I showed these results are replicated by correlational survey analysis.

Survey Results

The experiment clearly shows that eliciting patriotic thinking promotes more likelihood of one form of collective action, and it is important to expand this research to other times samples and types of collective action and civic engagement. Continuing directly with the topic of the previous experiment, the 2012 ANES survey asked questions on blood donation and patriotism. The Donated Blood variable is coded (1) if the respondent said they donated blood in the last 12 months and (0) if not. Figure 5.2 shows that the patriotic also donated blood more often in 2012. The regression results show higher blood donation in 2012 for the patriotic while controlling for the other determinants. Other significant predictors in Model 3 are income and education correlates with a greater likelihood of donation, while being aged, female or black correlates with less likelihood. This serves as another test of a collective action problem that requires individual sacrifice for the benefit of the group and confirms patriotism's positive impact.

Figure 5.2 shows the predicted percentage of people who donated blood in 2012 by patriotic beliefs, calculated from Model 3 in Table 5.1. The effect of moving from loving to hating America is about 8 percentage points less likely to donate blood, about one-half of a standard deviation change. Interestingly, these are around the same percentages shown in the experimental evidence from 2020, which provides a great deal of assurance as to the validity of the experimental results. Again, this shows that the patriotic are more willing to sacrifice for the group's benefit and confirms the effect of the experiment in another sample, time and survey mode.

Beyond blood donation, many important types of civic engagement greatly help communities solve collective action problems. In the 2020

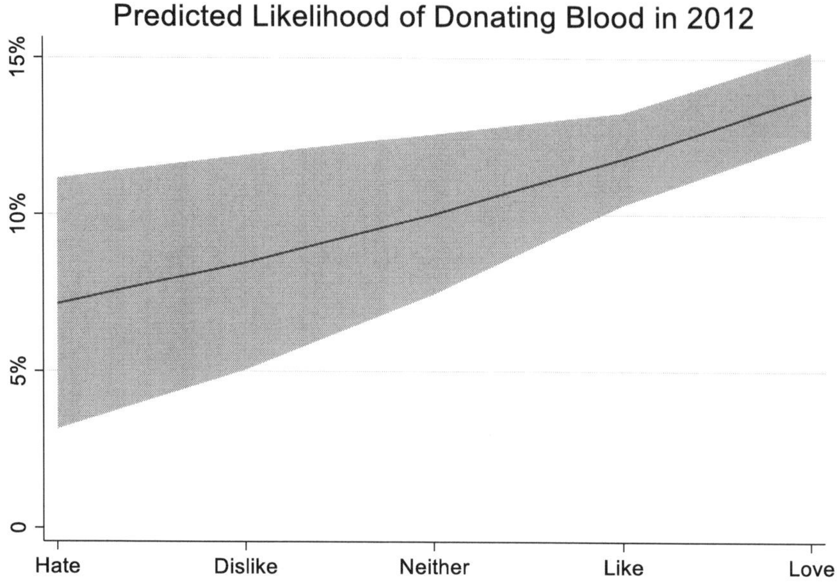

Fig. 5.2 The predicted percentage saying they donated blood in 2012 by patriotic beliefs, calculated from Model 3 in Table 5.1

survey data,[1] respondents were asked about involvement in the following list of common civic engagement activities: church or religious group, PTA, neighborhood organization/HOA, youth sports, Boy Scouts/ Girls Scouts or similar youth groups, Rotary/Masons/Elks or Moose Lodge/ Lions/Kiwanis/or similar group, Chamber of Commerce or local business group, and cleaning up litter project or similar beautification group. Respondents were given three choices of levels of activity in these groups: Haven't Done This (coded 0), Have Done it a Little (1), and Have Done it a Lot (2).

Table 5.2 shows that even after controlling for socioeconomic demographics and the levels of interpersonal trust and interest in politics,

[1] One thing to note is that this survey was taken during the COVID-19 pandemic when much of society was shut down. However, the question asked about this over the prior long-term period before the pandemic will not be influenced by the short-term lockdowns and restrictions over the pandemic. In other words, this question asked about long-term involvement in these groups, predating the pandemic.

Table 5.1 Determinants of donating blood in 2012

Variable	*1*	*S.E*	*2*	*S.E*	*3*	*S.E*
Patriotism	0.184*	0.078	0.139 +	0.079	0.187*	0.085
Media Attention			0.016	0.013	0.033*	0.014
Life Satisfaction			0.034	0.054	−0.014	0.057
Generalized Trust			0.222***	0.059	0.098	0.063
Age					−0.065***	0.018
Female					−0.279**	0.105
Income					0.019**	0.007
Education					0.140**	0.051
Black					−0.563**	0.185
Hispanic					−0.223	0.164
Intercept	−2.762***	0.364	−3.535***	0.422	−3.407***	0.455
N	3539		3530		3397	
chi2	5.920*		24.776***		80.742***	

Note Cells represent unstandardized coefficients and standard errors for logistic regression models for determinants of whether the respondent donated blood in the last twelve months. Data from 2012 ANES, weighted.
+ $p < 0.10$, * $p < 0.05$, ** $p < 0.01$, *** $p < 0.001$

patriotism strongly correlates with joining a religious organization, being involved in the PTA, involvement in a neighborhood or homeowners association, and involvement in youth sports. Table 5.2 continues this list on the next page while controlling for the same control variables and again shows that patriotism has a strong significant positive correlation with Boy Scouts/ Girls Scouts or similar youth groups, Rotary/Masons/ Elks or Moose Lodge/Lions/Kiwanis/or similar group, Chamber of Commerce or local business group, and cleaning up litter project or similar beautification group. Tables 3.2 and 3.3 show the profound importance of patriotism to civic participation.

Indeed, patriotism is the only variable with a significant correlation with involvement in all these groups, implying that patriotism is one of the most important variables for understanding why people get involved in their community. Of course, any correlation or research could have omitted variable bias. However, these strong, consistent results across many different types of activities while controlling for several important control variables demonstrate the importance of patriotism and civic engagement and are augmented by the experimental results above where causation is clear.

Table 5.2 Determinants of civic engagement activities in 2020

Variable	*Religious org*	*S.E*	*PTA*	*S.E*	*HOA*	*S.E*	*Youth sports*	*S.E*
Patriotism	0.526***	0.109	0.827***	0.201	0.331*	0.135	0.672***	0.151
Interpersonal trust	0.054	0.129	–0.048	0.199	0.166	0.171	–0.196	0.162
Interest	–0.03	0.137	0.152	0.222	0.392*	0.188	0.13	0.179
Female	0.124	0.198	0.38	0.315	0.232	0.26	–0.029	0.254
Age	–0.001	0.069	–0.283*	0.114	–0.128	0.091	–0.304***	0.091
Income	–0.004	0.037	0.163**	0.059	0.085	0.047	0.116*	0.047
Education	0.224*	0.102	0.309	0.164	0.523***	0.138	0.21	0.133
Black	0.860**	0.276	0.960*	0.427	0.175	0.389	0.484	0.351
Hispanic	–0.108	0.421	–0.424	0.783	–0.936	0.769	–0.061	0.533
cut1	5.318***	1.123	9.294***	2.041	6.964***	1.616	5.969***	1.468
cut2	6.362***	1.135	11.282***	2.086	8.782***	1.645	7.108***	1.485
N	468		463		467		466	
chi2	45.056***		51.722***		50.554***		47.049***	

Variable	*Youth group*	*S.E*	*Fraternal*	*S.E*	*CoC*	*S.E*	*Litter*	*S.E*
Patriotism	0.791***	0.225	0.715**	0.221	0.644**	0.204	0.202 +	0.112
Interpersonal trust	#######	0.22	0.049	0.219	0.198	0.221	–0.061	0.14
Interest	#######	0.232	0.175	0.245	0.243	0.237	0.136	0.153
Female	#######	0.351	–0.42	0.348	–0.13	0.333	–0.25	0.219
Age	–0.336**	0.127	–0.162	0.12	–0.193	0.116	–0.098	0.075
Income	#######	0.064	0.111	0.063	–0.02	0.06	–0.038	0.04

Variable	*Youth group*	*S.E*	*Fraternal*	*S.E*	*CoC*	*S.E*	*Litter*	*S.E*
Education	#######	0.181	0.308	0.182	0.464**	0.176	0.157	0.114
Black	#######	0.536	–0.51	0.643	0.294	0.491	–0.046	0.335
Hispanic	#######	1.062	–0.141	0.786	–0.285	0.792	0.229	0.447
cut1	6.603**	2.236	8.389***	2.186	8.643***	2.08	2.583*	1.171
cut2	7.852***	2.258	9.893***	2.216	10.079***	2.104	4.738***	1.196
N	468		468		467		468	
chi2	27.289**		34.553***		26.096**		8.352	

Note Cells represent unstandardized coefficients and standard errors for ordered logistic regression models for determinants of whether the respondent engaged in these forms of civic engagement. Data from 2020.

+ $p < 0.10$, * $p < 0.05$, ** $p < 0.01$, *** $p < 0.001$

Another common approach in the literature on civic participation is to summarize the total number of types of volunteer activities the respondent has done to measure the breadth of their commitment to the town (see, e.g., Xenos and Moy 2007; 710). Table 5.3 shows a negative binomial regression model where the dependent variable summarizes the variables measured in Table 5.2. There is a strong positive correlation between patriotism and the number of types of volunteer activities in all three model specifications. The results in Table 5.3 confirm that patriotism not only correlates with these individual acts but generally motivates the respondent to be more involved in their community across a broad summary measure of possible activities. In combination with the more activity-specific results from Table 5.3, this is strong evidence that patriotism correlates with greater civic engagement.

The 2012 ANES also has rich data on volunteering by expanding the traditional single item into a long list of possible ways to volunteer. It asks whether or not the respondent is an active volunteer for a service club, religious group, veterans' group, senior club, women's

Table 5.3 Determinants of number of types of volunteer activities in 2020

Variable	*1*	*S.E*	*2*	*S.E*	*3*	*S.E*
Patriotism	0.273***	0.055	0.254***	0.056	0.257***	0.058
Generalized trust			0.042	0.074	–0.002	0.076
Interest			0.169	0.087	0.165	0.087
Hispanic					–0.033	0.270
Black					0.338	0.186
Education					0.200**	0.066
Income					0.031	0.024
Age					–0.067	0.042
Female					–0.009	0.125
Intercept	–1.171**	0.388	–1.725***	0.468	–2.215***	0.666
lnalpha	0.291**	0.109	0.270*	0.110	0.160	0.115
N	458.000		458.000		458.000	
chi2	22.975***		27.559***		50.760***	

Note Cells represent unstandardized coefficients and standard errors for a negative binomial regression model for determinants of a number of types of volunteer activities the respondent has done in the last twelve months. Data from a 2020 online sample matched to nationally representative data for age, race, and gender.

+ $p < 0.10$, * $p < 0.05$, ** $p < 0.01$, *** $p < 0.001$

group, issue-oriented group, non-partisan civic organization, school club or association, hobby/sport team/youth group, neighborhood association/community group, racial/ethnic group, PTA, a charity, or a community group. Appendix Table A1 shows the pairwise correlation between patriotism and each of these groups. For simplicity, I will summarize these results here. Patriotism has a statistically significant positive bivariate correlation which each of the following groups: service club, religious group, veterans' group, senior club, women's group, issue-oriented group, hobby/sports team/youth group, racial/ethnic group, a charity, or a community group. In the other groups, there was no statistically significant correlation, and there was no group with a statistically significant negative correlation. Although the groups are different, the same basic result is obtained with this sample, patriotism has a general positive correlation across many forms of civic participation.

I also sum the responses of this list of 14 possible ways to volunteer to create a variable for Volunteering, which ranges from 0 to 14. Table 5.4 shows that the patriotic also volunteer for a greater number of types of groups. The results show that the less patriotic have fewer groups they volunteered for while controlling for the other determinants of volunteering. The collective action idea is best expressed as a willingness to sacrifice for others to achieve collective goods. These results show that patriotism leads to more willingness to make the sacrifice of volunteering time and effort. Other significant predictors in this model are well-known in the literature, such as media attention, age, education, and being female or black have a greater correlation with more numbers of types of groups. Interestingly, those with more life satisfaction in this sample were more likely to volunteer in 2012 with more types of groups, and those with greater interpersonal trust were also more likely.

Figure 5.3 shows the predicted number of groups volunteered in 2012, calculated from Model 3 in Table 5.4. Figure 5.3 shows that the effect of moving from hating to loving America is about 1 more group they volunteered for on average in 2012, about one-fourth of a standard deviation change.

In sum, multiple correlational survey analyses showed that patriotism correlates with greater civic engagement, in agreement with the experimental evidence.

Table 5.4 Determinants of number of types of volunteer activities

Variable	*Coef.*	*S.E*	*Coef.*	*S.E*	*Coef.*	*S.E*
Patriotism	0.230***	0.034	0.158***	0.034	0.119***	0.035
Media Attention			0.042***	0.006	0.035***	0.006
Life Satisfaction			0.132***	0.024	0.086***	0.024
Generalized Trust			0.186***	0.026	0.112***	0.027
Age					0.035***	0.008
Female					0.185***	0.044
Income					0.003	0.003
Education					0.272***	0.022
Black					0.169**	0.065
Hispanic					–0.055	0.070
Intercept	–0.770***	0.159	–1.915***	0.183	–2.611***	0.192
lnalpha	0.026	0.052	–0.094	0.055	–0.290***	0.061
N	3427		3418		3291	
chi2	45.014***		197.590***		407.016***	

Note Cells represent unstandardized coefficients and standard errors for a negative binomial regression model for determinants of a number of types of volunteer activities the respondent has done in the last twelve months. Data from 2012 ANES, weighted.
+ $p < 0.10$, * $p < 0.05$, ** $p < 0.01$, *** $p < 0.001$

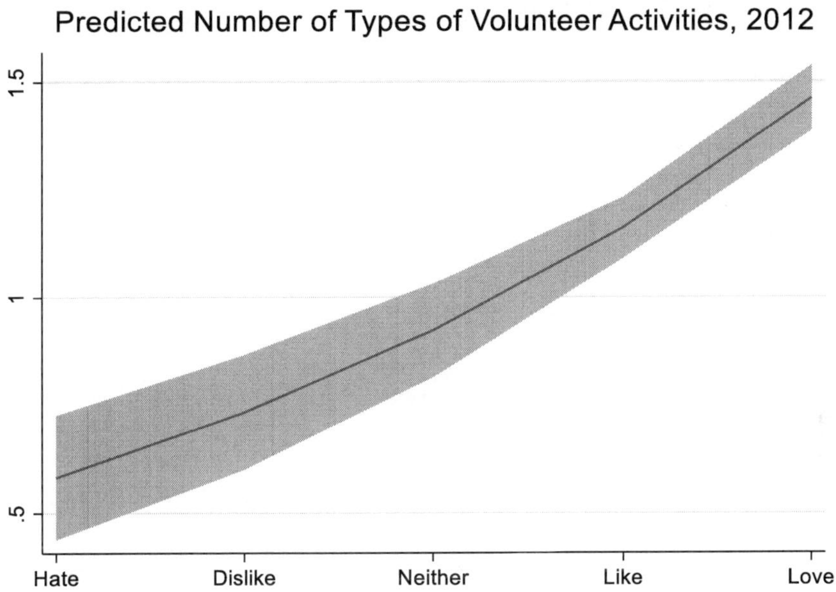

Fig. 5.3 The predicted number of groups volunteered for in 2012, calculated from Model 3 in Table 5.4

Conclusion

This chapter provides strong and clear empirical evidence that patriotism helps resolve collective action problems by motivating civic engagement. The robust findings in nationally representative survey experiments and nationally representative survey correlational analysis show the powerful impact of patriotism on motivating sacrifice for collective goods. Across multiple measures, data, and dates, those higher in patriotism are more likely to sacrifice their time and energy by volunteering to help their community. Higher levels of civic engagement are almost universally considered positive in academic literature. Due to the causal relationship and diverse findings of the positive relationship between patriotism and civic engagement, we can say that this is one area that patriotism benefits society.

In the next chapter, I turn to political participation and, specifically, the act of voting to see whether the same basic mechanisms manifest in these areas. The predictions outlined in Chapter 2 suggest that the same willingness to engage in collective action that derives from patriotism will motivate people to turn out to vote. Much literature has detailed the reason why people bother to vote in an election with hundreds of millions of voters is because civic duty implores them to facilitate the democratic process by spending their time and effort to vote. Since patriotism has shown to be a powerful motivator in getting people to engage in costly activities for the benefit of others, it should lead people to vote more often, and I will test this in the subsequent chapter.

References

Aldrich, Daniel P., and Michelle A. Meyer. 2015. "Social Capital and Community Resilience." *American Behavioral Scientist* 59 (2): 254–269.

Baumeister, Roy F., Kathleen D. Vohs, C. Nathan DeWall, and Liqing Zhang. 2007. "How Emotion Shapes Behavior: Feedback, Anticipation, and Reflection, Rather Than Direct Causation." *Personality and Social Psychology Review* 11 (2): 167–203.

Borgonovi, Franchesca. 2008. "Doing Well By Doing Good. The Relationship Between Formal Volunteering and Self-Reported Health and Happiness." *Social Science and Medicine* 66 (11): 2321–2334.

Hero, Rodney E. 2003. "Social Capital and Racial Inequality in America." *Perspectives on Politics* 1 (1): 113–122.

Jeynes, William. 2012. "A Meta-Analysis of the Efficacy of Different Types of Parental Involvement Programs for Urban Students." *Urban Education* 47 (4): 706–742.

Kawachi, Ichiro, and Lisa F. Berkman, 2014. "Social Capital, Social Cohesion, and Health." In *Social Epidemiology*, edited by Lisa F. Berkman, Ichiro Kawachi, and M. Maria Glymour, 2 edn. New York; online edn, Oxford Academic, 1 March 2015.

Lench, Heather S., Sarah Flores, and Shane Bench. 2011. "Discrete Emotions Predict Changes In Cognition, Judgment, Experience, Behavior, And Physiology: A Meta-Analysis Of Experimental Emotion Elicitations." *Psychological Bulletin* 137 (5): 834–855.

Levine, Peter. 2013. *We Are the Ones We Have Been Waiting For: The Promise of Civic Renewal in America.* New York: Oxford University Press.

Ling, Richard, Scott W. Campbell, Michael Chan, and Johannes M. Bauer. 2019. "The Mobile Communication and Social Cohesion Perspective." *New Media & Society* 21 (7): 1467–1483.

Oliver, Pamela. 1984. "If You Don't Do It, Nobody Else Will: Active and Token Contributors to Local Collective Action." *American Sociological Review* 4 (5): 601–610.

Pfaff, Steve, and Sarah Valdez. 2010. "Collective Action ." In *International Encyclopedia of Civil Society*, edited by H.K. Anheier and S. Toepler. Springer: New York, NY.

Pancer, S. Mark. 2014. *The Psychology of Citizenship and Civic Engagement*, 2015; online edn., Oxford Academic, December 18, https://doi.org/10.1093/acprof:oso/9780199752126.001.0001. Accessed 12 March 2023.

Putnam, Robert D, Robert Leonardi, and Raffaella Y. Nanetti. 1993. *Making Democracy Work. Civic Traditions in Modern Italy*. Princeton, NJ: Princeton University Press.

Putnam, Robert D. 2000. *Bowling Alone. The Collapse and Revival of American Community*. New York: Simon and Schuster.

Skocpol, Theda. 2003. *Diminished Democracy: From Membership to Management in American Civic Life*. Norman: University of Oklahoma Press.

Siedlecka, Ewa, and Thomas F. Denson. 2019. "Experimental Methods for Inducing Basic Emotions: A Qualitative Review." *Emotion Review* 11 (1): 87–97.

Theiss-Morse, Elizabeth, and John R. Hibbing. 2005. "Citizenship and Civic Engagement." *Annual Review of Political Science* 8 (1): 227–249.

Westermann, Rüdiger, Katrin Spies, Gabriele Stahl, and Franz W. Hesse. 1996. "Relative Effectiveness and Validity of Mood Induction Procedures: A Meta-Analysis." *European Journal of Social Psychology* 26 (4): 557–580.

Xenos, Michael, and Patricia Moy. 2007. "Direct and Differential Effects of the Internet on Political and Civic Engagement." *Journal of Communication* 57 (4): 704–718.

CHAPTER 6

Patriotism and Voter Turnout and Political Participation

Abstract Building on the collective action framework, this chapter explores how patriotism influences political engagement, especially voter turnout. Drawing on both new survey data and historical survey datasets, the evidence suggests that patriotic sentiment is a powerful predictor of voting, even when controlling for multiple confounding variables. Although patriotism correlates with higher civic involvement, it does not necessarily predict partisan activism; rather, it fosters engagement that is seen as broadly beneficial to the nation. The chapter concludes that patriotism can serve as a significant catalyst for electoral participation in a democracy.

Keywords Voter Turnout · Political Participation · Civic Involvement · Collective Action · Empirical Analysis · Democracy

This chapter examines whether patriotism correlates with voter turnout. I determine whether this relationship holds across electoral environments, with different candidates, levels of competitiveness, debated policy issues, and other differences, and analyze newly collected survey data combined with older survey data. As voter turnout is universally held in the literature to be a positive for democracy, it provides one clear avenue in which

S. Richey, *Patriotism and Citizenship*,
https://doi.org/10.1007/978-3-031-89885-3_6

patriotism benefits citizenship. This chapter tests the hypothesis that patriotism positively correlates with turnout because it increases the likelihood that someone will be willing to take on the cost of voting. The idea is that someone will turn out to vote because they believe it is their duty to support the nation that they care about.

From an early age, political socialization processes advocate that it is one's duty in a democratic society to vote. Various societal organizations extoll citizens that it is their duty to vote (LeRoux 2007). Patriotic symbology, such as flags and historical figures, are often used to convey that the nation depends on voters enduring the costs of voting so that democracy functions smoothly (White 2008). Campbell shows how schools often feature civic education courses that overtly state that voting is essential for America (but see Weinschenk and Dawes [2022] for evidence on this not working to boost turnout directly). And it works to socialize Americans into believing in the importance of voting for citizens, as a 2022 Pew poll found that 90% of Americans viewed voting in elections as either somewhat or very important to be a good citizen, more than any other activity (Silver 2022). This messaging will have a stochastic influence based on the level of patriotism. Those not inclined to love America will likely ignore or even resist these messaging strategies. However, those who love it will most likely be receptive and feel that it is their duty to vote because of the freedoms and opportunities that America has given them.

According to the theoretical logic outlined in Chapter 2, in the contractual relationship between citizens and America, those who feel more grateful for what the national government and general societal systems have provided will be more likely to engage in costly activities. The well-known literature on voter turnout suggests that costs are a crucial determinant of whether someone votes. Research shows that when voting is made more accessible, voter turnout increases, which implies that costs affect voter decision-making (e.g., Richey 2008). Various reforms that enabled voters to vote more easily—thereby reducing the cost of voting—have led to greater voter turnout (Gronke et al. 2008). Since costs are clearly considered in the calculus of whether to turn out, making someone more willing to endure these costs should alter the calculus and promote greater voter turnout.

On the other hand, no similar political socialization advocates for the benefit of America generally from other forms of political participation, such as donating money to candidates or protesting. Supporting partisan causes through various political participation activities will be influenced by a desire to help the candidate or cause, but there is no reason to think this is related to general patriotism. Over 85% of K-12 students are in public schools, and most children in the remaining 15% are in tax-exempt schools, such as Catholic schools. In both situations, these nonprofit schools cannot advocate for partisan causes. As such civic education in these areas does not promote partisan activity as a civic duty. Therefore, the connection in the minds of citizens between advocating for a candidate through activities such as displaying yard signs or a bumper sticker—often considered forms of political participation by scholars—and patriotism is probably lacking.

Furthermore, more confrontational activities—such as boycotts, protests, demonstrations, and marches—are not promoted in schooling. If these activities were promoted as a civic duty, then perhaps a more robust vision of patriotism would correlate with these forms of participation. However, the current reality in America is that voting is the only form of political participation that society works hard to associate with civic duty.

One might argue in response that helping a cause the person deems beneficial is a form of broadly helping the nation. Nevertheless, it is just as likely that those who are angry at America—and therefore have less patriotism—may be motivated to participate in protest politics, boycotts marches, write letters, attend meetings, and so forth because they are mad at the current situation in America. Depending on the situation and type of political participation, it may very well be that those who are less patriotic and are angry at society will be more likely to participate. The theory explicated in Chapter 2 does not predict that these other forms of political participation will be more likely with patriotism. There is no reason to think that supporting candidates, political parties, or various protest movements will be statistically more likely with those who are patriotic in relation to those who are less patriotic.

In the next section, I examine how voter turnout has been associated in the minds of patriotic people as a civic duty.

Voter Turnout as a Civic Duty

There are two plausible ways to consider voter turnout and its relationship to one's social responsibilities. The first views it as an individual's choice as to whether or not to turn out to vote. This libertarian approach to voter turnout conceptualizes the decision as a matter of personal liberty. The responsibility to society is not considered more important than the individual's ability to choose their actions. Conceptualizing voter turnout as a choice implies that those not voting have made a legitimate decision based on their considerations of the value of voting (Lever 2010). For these individuals who do not conceptualize voting as a duty to society but rather as an individual choice, voting is no different from any other behavior that society should not impose upon in a liberal democracy.

Conversely, a more communitarian approach to considering voter turnout considers it a duty to society. This approach is more related to the contractual theory I advocate as the main impetus for patriotism's impact on citizenship. This argument is that voter turnout is a chore one must undertake because society has given them so much. Similar to the concept of tacit consent, whether overtly stated or not, the people who view voter turnout as a duty conceptualize it as a contractual exchange because these potential voters have received much from America. In response to what they have been given, they should vote. It is the one action that democracy requires. Of course, it is easy to argue that voting may also benefit the person. Further, voting for the vast majority of people is not so onerous that it is an unreasonable ask from society. Some countries have chosen to make voting compulsory because of these conceptualizations of voting as a duty that citizens must perform in exchange for the vast freedoms, opportunities, and security that modern liberal democracies provide them (Chapman 2019).

To investigate this potentiality, I create in Table 6.1 an ordered logistic regression model of a survey question that asks on a one to seven scale whether someone views the act of voting as a personal choice or a civic duty. The data is from the 2012 ANES that was described previously. Specifically, the survey question is worded as, "Different people feel differently about voting. For some, voting is a duty, they feel they should vote in every election no matter how they feel about the candidates and parties. For others voting is a choice - they feel free to vote or not to vote, depending on how they feel about the candidates and parties. For you personally, is voting mainly a duty, mainly a choice, or neither a duty nor a choice?" This question provides unusually rich data that allows testing whether more patriotic people are more likely to view voter turnout as a duty in line with the contractual theory of patriotism.

Table 6.1 shows that patriotism clearly correlates with conceptualizing voter turnout as a civic duty. This robust relationship shows that patriots

Table 6.1 Determinants of feeling that voter turnout is a civic duty and not a choice in 2012

Variable	*1*	*S.E*	*2*	*S.E*	*3*	*S.E*
Patriotism	0.271***	0.041	0.252***	0.043	0.133**	0.050
Ideological			0.288***	0.035	0.259***	0.038
Party ID			0.022	0.016	0.040*	0.018
Black					0.415***	0.122
Hispanic					0.340***	0.097
Female					–0.008	0.068
Age					0.079***	0.011
Education					0.179***	0.033
Income					0.015***	0.004
Cutpoint 1	–0.035	0.180	0.224	0.193	1.044***	0.233
Cutpoint 2	0.708***	0.179	0.976***	0.192	1.824***	0.233
Cutpoint 3	0.867***	0.179	1.138***	0.192	1.982***	0.233
Cutpoint 4	1.363***	0.180	1.644***	0.193	2.499***	0.233
Cutpoint 5	1.500***	0.181	1.785***	0.193	2.653***	0.234
Cutpoint 6	2.052***	0.183	2.352***	0.196	3.268***	0.237
N	5541		5525		4989	
chi2	44.837***		117.084***		221.786***	

Note Cells represent unstandardized coefficients and standard errors for an ordered logistic regression model for determinants of feelings that voter turnout in the 2012 Presidential elections was a civic duty and not a choice. Data from 2012 ANES, weighted
+$p < .10$, *$p < .05$, **$p < .01$, ***$p < .001$

are more likely to view voter turnout as a duty they must perform. This holds in models controlling for political characteristics such as ideologicalness and party identification and a more robust model that controls demographics. Importantly, Model 3 in Table 6.1 still shows a significant positive relationship between patriotism and a feeling of civic duty to vote while controlling for age. This is important because America emphasized civic education more in prior generations, and the elderly would have had greater exposure to these ideas. These robust results show that patriotism still has this effect even when controlling for age. This shows the underlying psychological mechanisms that connect political socialization from patriotism to voter turnout and confirms the basic presuppositions of my theoretical model. In the following sections, I examine the basic relationship between patriotism and voter turnout.

Results for Voter Turnout

Now I conduct the chief test of Prediction 1 that patriotism correlates with voter turnout. Using the novel survey data from the fall of 2021, Table 6.2 shows a logistic regression model of self-reported voter turnout in the 2020 presidential election. Patriotism has a clear and consistent positive correlation with voter turnout across three model specifications. Model 1 is a bivariate model that shows a statistically significant correlation between patriotism and voter turnout. Models 2 and 3 show that even when politically relevant control variables are included in the model, patriotism still correlates positively with voter turnout. Model 2 shows that being more ideological, having a Democratic Party identification, and having political interest correlate with voting in the 2020 presidential election, as expected from the prior literature on this topic. Finally, most of the priorly accepted determinants of voter turnout from social and economic status correlate with voter turnout in Model 3, showing that these data conform to our established understanding of why people vote.

The coefficients from logistic regression models are difficult to interpret directly. Figure 6.1 shows a plot of the effect of patriotism on voter

Table 6.2 Determinants of voter turnout in the 2020 presidential election

Variable	*1*	*S.E*	*2*	*S.E*	*3*	*S.E*
Patriotism	0.564***	0.149	0.624***	0.169	0.440*	0.182
Ideological			0.509**	0.168	0.438*	0.177
Party ID			1.100**	0.345	1.170**	0.378
Interest			0.593**	0.193	0.457*	0.201
Black					−1.329***	0.363
Hispanic					−0.674	0.537
Female					−0.217	0.334
Age					0.294*	0.118
Education					0.432*	0.209
Income					0.101	0.060
Intercept	−3.375***	1.010	−6.318***	1.232	−5.991**	1.824
N	552		552		551	
chi2	14.350***		57.507***		67.893***	

Note Cells represent unstandardized coefficients and standard errors for a logistic regression model for determinants of Voter turnout in the 2020 Presidential election. Data from 2021, weighted. + $p < 0.10$, $^{*}p < 0.05$, $^{**}p < 0.01$, $^{***}p<.001$

turnout while controlling for all the control variables in Model 3 from Table 6.2. Basically, Fig. 6.1 is a graphical representation of the patriotism variable in Model 3 from Table 6.2. Even while controlling for these other well-known factors that produce voter turnout, patriotism significantly impacts the predicted probability that someone would self-report voting in the 2020 presidential election. All things being held constant, Fig. 6.1 shows that the predicted probability of someone who hates America reporting in this survey to have voted in the 2020 presidential election was around 42%. On the other hand, those who love America have a predicted probability of reporting to vote of around 76%. This is a large differential and clearly shows the profound political consequences of patriotism.

One major issue with the data reported in Table 6.2 is that it measures self-reports of voting. Turnout is notoriously noisy data due to the social desirability bias that comes from the norm of voting. Simply put, people often lie and say they voted when they did not. To overcome these

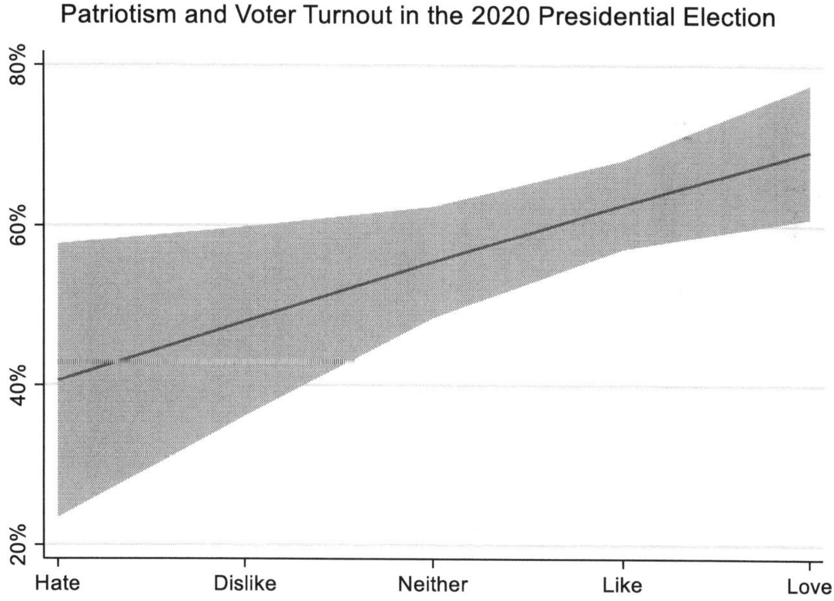

Fig. 6.1 The predicted probabilities of self-reported voting in the 2020 Presidential elections, calculated from Model 3 in Table 6.2

potential biases in the data, Table 6.3 shows a similar logistic regression model with similar covariates included in the three model specifications but with validated voter turnout. The 2012 ANES survey was validated using public records of whether or not the respondents voted. These data essentially eliminate the potential for social desirability bias by checking governmental records on whether the person actually turned out to vote. While there are potential minor issues with how accurate the voter validation processes are, these are highly reliable data showing whether almost all of these respondents voted. Table 6.3 shows clear results that are essentially the same as the 2021 data self-reported data. Patriotism has a strong and consistent positive correlation with validated voter turnout in 2012.

Figure 6.2 shows that the size of the effect of patriotism on voter turnout is similar to the ANES 2012 data as it is to the 2021 data. All things being equal, around 45% of those who say they hate America are predicted to have turned out to vote in the 2012 election. On the other hand, those who say they love America had a predicted 78% likelihood of voting in 2012 based on the Model 3 of Table 6.3. The consistency of these effect sizes is remarkable, considering the candidates and political environment were so different in 2012 and 2020. The 2012 election was conducted with two relatively moderate candidates and a stable economy.

Table 6.3 Determinants of presidential validated voter turnout in 2012

Variable	*1*	*S.E*	*2*	*S.E*	*3*	*S.E*
Patriotism	0.560***	0.115	0.538***	0.113	0.381**	0.126
Ideological			0.428***	0.084	0.369***	0.093
Party ID			0.035	0.035	0.020	0.041
Black					0.637*	0.249
Hispanic					–0.109	0.210
Female					0.332	0.171
Age					0.124***	0.028
Education					0.204*	0.090
Income					0.061***	0.013
Intercept	–1.561**	0.535	–1.950***	0.523	–3.686***	0.696
N	1677		1660		1342	
chi2	23.673***		55.756***		96.042***	

Note Cells represent unstandardized coefficients and standard errors for a logistic regression model for determinants of validated voter turnout in the 2012 Presidential elections. Data from 2012 ANES, weighted

+p < .10, *p < .05, **p < .01, ***p < .001

The 2020 presidential election was conducted during the pandemic, the George Floyd protests, President Trump's unique communication style and actions, and many societal changes. Nevertheless, in both elections, patriotism had a similarly strong influence on the likelihood of voting.

Of course, it is beneficial to replicate these results with as many surveys as possible. The 2016 ANES also validated voter turnout. Its measure of patriotism, however, is less desirable than the 2012 data. It measured patriotism with the question that asked, "how good or bad do you feel when you see the American flag" on a one to seven scale from Extremely Bad (1) to Extremely Good (7). This is not the preferred measure of patriotism because feeling good about seeing an inanimate object like a flag is not exactly the same as feeling gratitude and love for a country. Some people could not care about patriotic symbology but still love the country.

Interestingly, however, this data shows similar results to the other two surveys using this subpar measure of patriotism. Table 6.4 shows lower

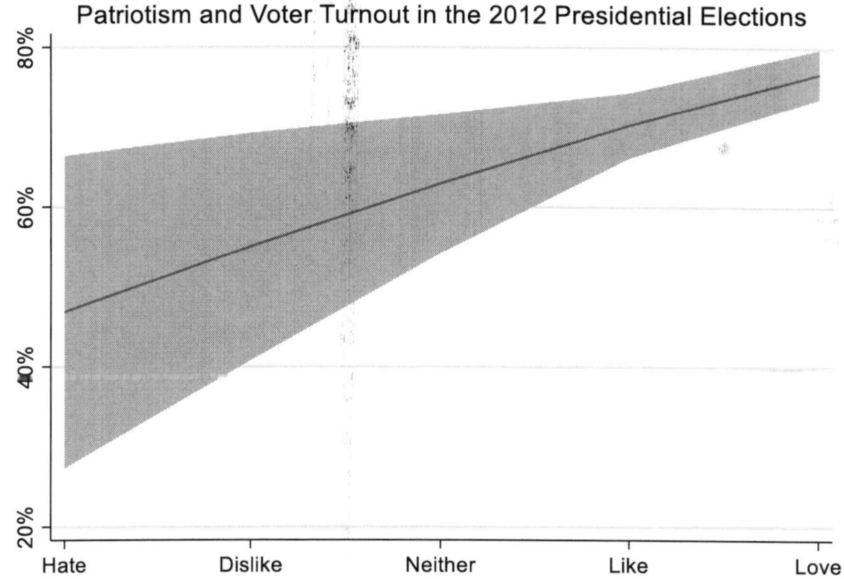

Fig. 6.2 The predicted probabilities of validated voting in the 2012 Presidential elections, calculated from Model 3 in Table 6.3

validated voter turnout for the less patriotic while controlling for the other determinants of turnout. A statistically significant positive relationship exists between holding pro-American attitudes and voting. These validated data provide an accurate behavioral measure of the benefits of patriotism. In Model 3 of Table 6.4, we see that the standard error grows in relation to the coefficient beyond standard levels of statistical significance. This may be due to a lack of effect once another important variable—such as age—is controlled for, or it is a function of this subpar measure of patriotism used in this data. Other significant predictors, such as ideological, age, education, and income, are well-known in the literature.

In sum, patriotism correlates with greater voter turnout. These results confirm Prediction 1 and support the idea that feelings of civic duty are essential in the cost-benefit analysis of the decision to vote across three electoral environments with two measures of patriotism and three electoral environments. In the next section, I examine the impact of patriotism on other forms of political participation.

Table 6.4 Determinants of presidential validated voter turnout in 2016

	1	*S.E*	*2*	*S.E*	*3*	*S.E*
Flag	0.152***	0.034	0.173***	0.044	0.056	0.049
Ideological			0.219***	0.055	0.176**	0.060
Party ID			−0.030	0.026	−0.039	0.031
Black					−0.038	0.208
Hispanic					−0.058	0.201
Male					−0.343**	0.115
Age					0.029***	0.004
Education					0.246***	0.058
Income					0.045***	0.008
cons	0.003	0.209	−0.101	0.261	−1.873***	0.370
N	3645		2874		2665	
chi2	20.144***		27.471***		161.595***	

Note Cells represent unstandardized coefficients and standard errors for a logistic regression model for determinants of validated voter turnout in the 2016 Presidential elections. Data from 2012 ANES, weighted

+p < .10, *p < .05, **p < .01, ***p < .001

Results for Political Participation

The 2012 ANES had unusually robust data measuring various types of political activities that allowed testing of the relationship between patriotism and political participation beyond voting. Respondents were asked in the last four years if they had done any of the following actions: attended a protest or march, attended a board meeting, signed an internet petition, signed a paper petition, donated money to a political organization, called into a radio/T.V. about a political issue, sent a message on Facebook/Twitter about a political issue, written a letter to newspaper or magazine about a political issue, contacted a U.S. Representative or Senator. Table 6.5 shows the bivariate pairwise correlation between patriotism and these political activities.

The results in Table 6.5 show that some political activities that challenge the system negatively correlate with patriotism, but those working

Table 6.5 Bivariate correlation between patriotism and political activities in 2012

	Patriotism
Patriotism	1.00
Protest or March	−0.04***
	(0.00)
Board meeting	0.05***
	(0.00)
Internet petition	−0.03*
	(0.03)
Paper petition	0.01
	(0.28)
Donate to Political Organization	0.01
	(0.31)
Call Radio or T.V. about Politics	−0.01
	(0.66)
Facebook or Twitter posts about politics	−0.03*
	(0.02)
Write a letter to a politician	0.00
	(0.73)
Contact Congressperson	0.04**
	(0.00)

Note Cells represent pairwise correlations for patriotism and various political activities in the last four years. Data from 2012 ANES, weighted. *P*-values in parentheses

$+p < 0.10$, $*p < 0.05$, $**p < 0.01$, $***p < 0.001$

within the system are positively related to patriotism. Several showed no correlation. For example, attending a protest or march is negatively correlated with patriotism, while attending a board meeting is positively correlated. Other activities, such as donating to political organizations or calling television and radio shows about a political issue, do not correlate with patriotism. In all, this data shows mixed results for political participation and patriotism.

One standard method used in political science to assess political participation is adding the number of acts of political participation the respondent engaged in. This measures the breadth of political activity and is a useful proxy variable for showing how politicized someone's actions are. Table 6.6 shows a negative binomial regression model.[1] of a dependent variable that summarizes the various actions listed in Table 6.5. It shows that across three model specifications, patriotism has no statistical relationship with the number of political acts that someone participates in in the four years that proceed 2012. Notice that there is no statistically significant relationship even in bivariate Model 1. This is more confirmatory evidence that patriotism and general acts of political participation are not related because socialization processes have not connected these individual acts with the need to sacrifice for the greater good, in contrast with voter turnout, which is often associated with doing one's duty to society.

Table 6.5 shows an interesting result with a negative correlation between acts of protest and patriotism, which matches Prediction 2. To more fully test this relationship, I created a logistic regression model for whether or not someone attended a protest, march, rally, or demonstration in the last four years. Across multiple model specifications, Table 6.7 shows that patriotism negatively correlates with protest politics. This may be expected as those engaged in more conflictual forms of political activity are probably angrier than members of society as a whole. Deeply embedded in protest politics is the idea that national government will not allow change to happen unless forced to. If that is how you envisage politics, it does not seem to flow directly into an idea that nation at large is something you need to express gratitude for. Of course, while it is possible to be patriotic and engage in protest politics, these results show that, probabilistically, those who are less patriotic are more likely to protest.

[1] The likelihood-ratio chi-square test that the dispersion parameter alpha equals zero is statistically significant, signifying that a negative binomial regression model is preferable.

Table 6.6 Determinants of number of acts of political participation in 2012

Variable	*Coef*	*S.E*				
Patriotism	0.005	0.011	0.001	0.011	–0.006	0.012
Ideological			0.264***	0.018	0.197***	0.018
Partisanship			–0.039*	0.017	–0.021	0.017
Media Attention			0.031***	0.004	0.027***	0.004
Age					0.002	0.006
Female					–0.022	0.033
Income					0.010***	0.002
Education					0.262***	0.016
Black					–0.018	0.046
Hispanic					–0.105*	0.048
Intercept	0.409***	0.017	–0.144**	0.054	–1.015***	0.083
lnalpha	–0.087*	0.040	–0.228***	0.043	–0.502***	0.051
N	5491		5472		4946	
chi2	0.214		291.253***		675.526***	

Note Cells represent unstandardized coefficients and standard errors for a negative binomial regression model for determinants of a number of acts of political participation in 2012. Data from 2012 ANES, weighted

+p < .10, *p < .05, **p < .01, ***p < .001

Table 6.7 Determinants of participation in protest, march, rally, or demonstration

Variable	*Coef*	*S.E*				
Patriotism	−0.102**	0.034	−0.134***	0.035	−0.100*	0.039
Ideological			0.381***	0.058	0.395***	0.064
Partisanship			−0.015	0.057	−0.023	0.062
Media Attention			0.078***	0.014	0.087***	0.015
Age					−0.043*	0.020
Female					−0.324**	0.120
Income					−0.008	0.008
Education					0.366***	0.058
Black					0.239	0.163
Hispanic					0.532***	0.156
Intercept	−2.697***	0.056	−3.970***	0.194	−4.822***	0.308
N	5523		5503		4969	
chi2	8.299**		94.342***		155.946***	

Note Cells represent unstandardized coefficients and standard errors for a logistic regression model for determinants of participation in a protest, march, rally, or demonstration in the last four years. Data from 2012 ANES, weighted
+$p < .10$, *$p < .05$, **$p < .01$, ***$p < .001$

Conclusion

This chapter shows that voter turnout across multiple elections correlates with patriotism. This correlation is robust across multiple model specifications and ways of operationalizing patriotism. The consistent correlation between patriotism and turning out to vote—including in data where the voter turnout has been validated—is strong evidence of the contractual theory of patriotism. Note also that this correlation is robust to models that include well-known predictors of voter turnout, such as age, which may also correlate with patriotism. Turnout has been a paradigmatic example of the type of behavior in politics where free-riding is common. From Downs (1957) onwards, the question has not been why people do not vote but why they bother. This research provides a cogent explanation that people are willing to incur the costs of voting because they have been socialized to believe that it is their civic duty to repay America for what it has given them.

Importantly, I also find that more patriotic people conceptualize voter turnout as a duty rather than a choice, which is robust to multiple model specifications. As specified in Chapter 2, the cost–benefit analysis is often used to describe a voter's decision to turnout or not rest on the willingness to incur costs. Because patriotic people view it as a duty they must fulfill because of what society has given them, they are more willing to incur the cost of voting. Since voter turnout is universally held to be something beneficial for citizenship, this is one clear area in which civic education designed to promote patriotism could lead to a greater societal good. If civic education instills in citizens a type of patriotism that ameliorates potential negatives, greater turnout alone is perhaps a sufficient benefit in civic education. Although it is debated how voter turnout may affect electoral outcomes, it is certainly plausible that very close elections may be affected by a rise in turnout. Also, critiques that those who do not turn out should not vote do not appreciate the myriad ways voters apply low information rationality and can make correct voting choices.

This chapter also demonstrates that other forms of political participation are not correlated with patriotism. This means that patriotism will not boost other potentially socially beneficial actions we want democratic citizens to engage in. When conceptualizing the impact of patriotism, it is important to consider what it will and will not affect. Since these other forms of partisan or confrontational political participation have not been advocated as a civic duty, most citizens probably will not connect these actions with general patriotism. Many other stimuli can boost someone's willingness to engage in partisan activities or protests, but whether someone likes or dislikes the country will not likely influence the decision to incur the cost to engage in these political activities. As stated previously, it is highly plausible that if someone is angry at America and dislikes or hates it generally, they would be motivated to engage in confrontational political activity, at least as much as someone who does it because of some concern toward improving the nation that they love. In other words, we could expect those angry at America to be just as likely to participate in these types of political activities; as such, we will not see a correlation with patriotism.

In the next chapter, I expand on this general logic of incurring costs through a contractual relationship with the country by examining diffuse support in America and its relationship with patriotism.

References

Chapman, Emilee Booth. 2019. "The Distinctive Value of Elections and the Case for Compulsory Voting." *American Journal of Political Science* 63 (1): 101–112.

Downs, Anthony. 1957. *An Economic Theory of Democracy*. New York: Harper.

Gronke, Paul, Eva Galanes-Rosenbaum, Peter A. Miller, and Daniel Toffey 2008. "Convenience Voting." *Annual Review Political Science* 11 (1): 437–55.

LeRoux, Kelly. 2007. "Nonprofits as Civic Intermediaries: The Role of Community-based Organizations in Promoting Political Participation." *Urban Affairs Review* 42 (3): 410–422.

Lever, Annabelle. 2010. "Compulsory Voting: A Critical Perspective." *British Journal of Political Science* 40 (4): 897–915.

Richey, Sean. 2008. "Voting By Mail: Political Participation and Institutional Reform in Oregon." *Social Science Quarterly* 39 (4): 902–915.

Silver, Laura. 2022. *Most Americans Say It is Very Important to Vote to Be a Good Member of Society*. Pew Research Center, November 4. https://pewrsr.ch/3NCp5yg.

Weinschenk, Aaron C., and Christopher T. Dawes. 2022. "Civic Education in High School and Voter Turnout in Adulthood." *British Journal of Political Science* 52 (2): 934–948.

White, Brent T. 2008. "Ritual, Emotion, and Political Belief: The Search for the Constitutional Limit to Patriotic Education in Public Schools." *Ga. L. Rev.* 43 (1): 447.

CHAPTER 7

Patriotism and Diffuse Support

Abstract "Diffuse support" refers to a general endorsement of the political system rather than approval of specific leaders or policies. Chapter Seven demonstrates how patriotic citizens display higher levels of political trust, external political efficacy, and commitment to democratic principles. Using novel survey data, the chapter shows that people who love their country also tend to hold more positive attitudes toward its institutions—while still acknowledging its flaws. This finding implies that patriotism can be an important buffer against democratic backsliding, as it fosters confidence in core governing structures.

Keywords Diffuse Support · Political Trust · Political Efficacy · Democracy · System Legitimacy · Democratic Stability

This chapter examines the relationship between patriotism and support for the democratic system broadly. The political science literature describes this generalized support for a political system as diffuse support (Easton 1965). The key distinction is that diffuse support does not concern support for a particular party or politician, such as presidential approval in the United States; it is instead support for the governmental system as a whole. The idea is that there is an overarching feeling of contentment and appreciation for the governmental system that can be described as diffuse

S. Richey, *Patriotism and Citizenship*,
https://doi.org/10.1007/978-3-031-89885-3_7

support. Diffuse support does not mean that all governmental actions are approved and supported. It merely suggests that the person generally supports the broad outlines of the governmental system as a whole. In comparative politics, it has been shown that societies with diffuse support are much less likely to undergo coups, civil wars, internal strife, and so on (see, e.g., Muller et al. 1982).

My general theoretical model is that having love for America will more likely allow a citizen to have a general psychological perspective that is supportive of the political system in a broad manner, which is akin to diffuse support. The key point with diffuse support is that although anyone can have disagreements and unhappiness over policy choices or candidates that win elections, one has generalized support for the system as a whole and is willing to give this system the benefit of the doubt on most mundane issues. If one does not love the country, they will be less likely to offer this initial positive starting point whereby the citizen is willing to listen to the government's suggestions on matters. Diffuse support is necessary for smooth governance and the solving of collective action problems.

The fact that 10% of the society does not like or even hates the country—as shown in Chapter 3—suggests that this is a potential problem for the United States. It is hard to imagine someone expressing hatred for the country but feeling they can trust the government to do what is right most of the time, listen to people like them, or be satisfied with the state of the electoral system. As such, patriotism should positively affect these three crucial concepts for successful democratic societies. The empirical tests below support this thesis strongly across multiple model specifications and two sets of survey data on all three dependent variables I use to measure diffuse support.

Importance of Diffuse Support

The importance of diffuse support for democratic societies cannot be overstated. The crucial alliance between the citizens and the government facilitates working together to solve societal problems (Charron and Lapuente 2010). Diffuse support is a broadly considered term engaged with a general feeling that the citizens are connected and willing to contribute to this society. Diffuse support means that the citizen feels that the government is working on their behalf, and they feel allegiance toward it. Societies that lack diffuse support have great difficulty managing social crises because their citizens will distrust them, feel that they are not listened to, and are generally unsatisfied.

Each of the issues above relates to three central concepts in political science: political trust, external efficacy, and satisfaction with democracy. In the research below, I show that patriotism has a clear and consistent positive correlation with all three of these foundational factors that make up diffuse support when grouped together. I show that across multiple surveys conducted at different times in different societal situations, patriotism strongly influences political trust, external efficacy, and satisfaction with democracy. The correlation between patriotism and these factors is often the strongest among many other covariates in the regression models below. When we think about the benefits of patriotism, greater political trust, external efficacy, and satisfaction with democracy, are some of the most important elements in securing a stable, thriving democratic system.

Measuring Diffuse Support

I measure below diffuse support with survey questions on political trust, external efficacy, and satisfaction with democracy. These measures are standard in the political science literature for diffuse support and have been correlated with many positive social outcomes. For example, Hetherington (1998) analyzes how political trust supports support the system. Morris and Klesner (2010) show an interesting bi-causal relationship between political corruption and political trust, whereby societies with more political corruption led to citizens having less political trust. However, those societies with less political trust have actors more willing to disobey social norms of collective good and engage in acts of corruption. Thus, political trust leads to greater political corruption, while acts of political corruption lower the public's trust in government. For this research, however, what is important is that political trust has a profound impact on governmental performance through aspects such as corruption.

Iyengar (1980) provides longitudinal evidence that external efficacy is a superior measure of diffuse support to political trust. Believing that a politician will listen to you is a clear example of someone having enough engagement and support of the system to be willing to participate in politics. It takes a base level of efficacy for one to be willing to engage in the costly activity of participation, and what this research is investigating is whether patriotism is part of the causal processes that allow someone to become more efficacious and, after that, more participatory. Iyengar

(1980) does show that political trust correlates with regime support. The key distinction is that political trust is bound up in a winners-and-losers effect whereby those voting for the current president tend to trust the government more, and those whose presidential candidate lost the previous election tend to have less political trust. On the other hand, efficacy does not seem to oscillate based on the winners and losers of the previous election.

Perhaps the key reason that diffuse support is important is the potential for democratic backsliding. A disturbing trend in the twenty-first century is that the aggregate level of democracy worldwide has decreased (Diamond 2022). We know that democracies provide citizens a much better quality of life (Persson and Guido 2006). If satisfaction with democracy continues to decrease, the potential for even greater levels of democratic backsliding increases. Orviska, Caplanova, and Hudson (2014) show that satisfaction with democracy greatly impacts citizens' well-being. It is important to note that democratic backsliding does not just happen in new democracies. Many well-developed established democracies have seen levels of democratic backsliding that would not have seemed plausible 15 years ago. Poland, Hungary, and Turkey are three examples of democracies that were once seen as successful but have now slid backward into what is often called illiberal democracies (Öktem and Akkoyunlu 2016). Once democracy is conceptualized as a continuum rather than a dichotomous variable, diffuse support becomes crucial because any change on the continuum toward less democracy can have profound negative consequences for members of those societies. If patriotism is shown to correlate with satisfaction for democracy, it is potentially one way to shore up support for the institutions that are necessary to prevent democratic backsliding.

I use survey data from 2021 and 2012 ANES data described previously to determine the correlation between patriotism and diffuse support. Political trust is measured with a question asking whether you trust the government in Washington to do the right thing most of the time, on a one to five scale. Political efficacy is measured as external efficacy because patriotism is conceived of as the love of the country. While internal efficacy is important for political participation, it concerns whether that individual feels they have the skills necessary to influence politics. Conversely, external efficacy, which I test in the models below, concerns whether the system will allow the person to influence politics and is much more related to patriotism. It is measured with a question on an ordinal one to five scales whether politicians listen to a person like them. Finally, satisfaction with democracy is also measured on a one to five scale, asking how much satisfaction with democracy as practiced in the United States the respondent feels. The key independent variable is the previously described patriotism variable, which is a one to five scale varying from hate, dislike, neither, like, or love of America. All three dependent variables are ordinal, so I use ordered logistic regression modeling below to match the distribution of these dependent variables.

Political Trust

Table 7.1 shows that being patriotic correlates with more political trust from survey data from 2021. The model for predicting political trust shows that while controlling for other factors, a statistically significant positive relationship remains between holding patriotic attitudes and political trust. Political trust has been shown to profoundly impact supporting the government's use of resources for important goals (Hetherington 2005). If these Americans with negative views of their nation do not trust it, they may not cooperate with it in achieving goals that require sacrifice, such as agreeing to pay taxes for social programs. We also find that the impact of the control variables matches closely with prior research. A liberal ideology, more generalized trust, education, and age positively correlate with political trust, while being Hispanic negatively correlates with it. The other control variables did not have a statistically significant impact, but the coefficients' direction matched the findings from prior research.

Table 7.2 shows the same clear effect of patriotism correlating positively with political trust in all specified models. This is a large effect that correlates positively across all three specifications. Of note is that although the circumstances between 2021 and 2012 involved profound changes in American politics, the same correlates hold in this case, as generalized trust correlates positively with political trust in 2012, and so does having a liberal ideology. Of note is that when Obama was president, black and Hispanic respondents had greater political trust than those who were not black and Hispanic in Model 3. Also of interest is that age negatively impacts political trust during this period, which is the reverse of what was found in 2021. Both samples and all model specifications show that patriotism correlates positively with political trust.

Table 7.1 Determinants of political trust in 2021

Variable	*1*	*S.E*	*2*	*S.E*	*3*	*S.E*
Patriotism	0.684***	0.084	0.741***	0.095	0.672***	0.100
Generalized trust			0.788***	0.108	0.825***	0.111
Ideology			0.196***	0.052	0.184***	0.053
Hispanic					–0.717*	0.342
Black					0.536*	0.247
Education					0.226*	0.091
Income					–0.033	0.030
Age					0.108*	0.055
Female					0.045	0.166
Cutpoint 1	2.791***	0.545	6.489***	0.775	0.977	1.170
Cutpoint 2	5.148***	0.579	9.117***	0.827	3.700**	1.182
Cutpoint 3	6.849***	0.603	10.947***	0.858	5.578***	1.192
Cutpoint 4	11.094***	1.164	15.271***	1.322	9.938***	1.554
N	552		552		551	
chi2	70.481***		152.138***		175.526***	

Note Cells represent unstandardized coefficients and standard errors for ordered logistic regression models for determinants of how often the respondent trusts the government in Washington to do the right thing. Data from 2021, weighted.
+ $p < 0.10$, * $p < 0.05$, ** $p < 0.01$, *** $p < 0.001$

Political Efficacy

Table 7.3 shows that the less patriotic also feel less efficacious in 2021. A large statistically significant linear relationship exists between patriotic beliefs and external political efficacy. This research sheds new light on why some do not believe the system will respond to them. It shows that patriotism is a beneficial foundation for political efficacy, which we know from prior research sparks greater civic involvement and other positive aspects of the democratic citizenry. The control variables also track closely with their theoretical expectations, as found in prior research. Generalized trust in this specification negatively correlates with external efficacy. Greater age and having a liberal ideology correlate positively with political efficacy. The other control variables did not have a statistically significant effect.

Table 7.4 shows that in the 2012 ANES survey data, patriotism also correlates positively in all three models with political efficacy. The replication of these positive correlations from patriotism on political efficacy in 2012, an era with much different politics than 2021, provides a great deal of confidence that this correlation is robust to political conditions.

Table 7.2 Determinants of political trust in 2012

Variable	*1*	*S.E*	*2*	*S.E*	*3*	*S.E*
Patriotism	0.118*	0.059	0.128*	0.060	0.203**	0.064
Generalized trust			0.177***	0.042	0.320***	0.049
Ideology			0.174***	0.026	0.145***	0.029
Hispanic					0.889***	0.117
Black					0.878***	0.120
Education					−0.061	0.040
Income					−0.000	0.006
Age					−0.025*	0.012
Female					0.099	0.079
Cutpoint 1	−2.260***	0.278	−2.447***	0.305	−1.750***	0.346
Cutpoint 2	1.379***	0.274	1.244***	0.301	2.075***	0.343
Cutpoint 3	2.152***	0.277	2.028***	0.301	2.872***	0.344
Cutpoint 4	4.725***	0.324	4.612***	0.342	5.597***	0.398
N	5531		5523		4988	
chi2	4.011*		66.358***		193.337***	

Note Cells represent unstandardized coefficients and standard errors for ordered logistic regression models for determinants of how often the respondent trusts the government in Washington to do the right thing. Data from 2012 ANES, weighted.
+ $p < 0.10$, * $p < 0.05$, ** $p < 0.01$, *** $p < 0.001$

This finding is important because having greater political efficacy is known to promote political participation and engagement in politics (see meta-analysis by Oser et al. 2022). While this research does not demonstrate a causal relationship between political efficacy and patriotism, the consistent correlation across multiple model specifications and political eras shows these concepts are intertwined. The only other findings are that in 2012 being black, female, and of greater age correlated with greater political efficacy.

Satisfaction with Democracy

I also find a statistically significant positive linear impact on satisfaction with democracy in Table 7.5 for the 2021 data. This suggests that those lacking patriotism are less satisfied with the governmental system used in the United States. These negative attitudes are interesting because dissatisfaction with democracy may lead to feelings that correlate with support for insurrection or undemocratic systems. For the control variables, we

Table 7.3 Determinants of political efficacy in 2021

Variable	*1*	*S.E*	*2*	*S.E*	*3*	*S.E*
Patriotism	0.626***	0.082	0.752***	0.093	0.626***	0.097
Generalized trust			–0.428***	0.100	–0.396***	0.104
Ideology			0.253***	0.051	0.270***	0.053
Hispanic					–0.555	0.336
Black					0.003	0.243
Education					0.110	0.091
Income					0.013	0.029
Age					0.226***	0.054
Female					0.056	0.164
Cutpoint 1	1.228*	0.544	1.955*	0.862	1.711	1.147
Cutpoint 2	2.412***	0.536	3.201***	0.857	2.964**	1.143
Cutpoint 3	3.046***	0.540	3.887***	0.859	3.649**	1.145
Cutpoint 4	4.747***	0.563	5.708***	0.878	5.538***	1.162
N	552		552		551	
chi2	61.630***		112.942***		135.636***	

Note Cells represent unstandardized coefficients and standard errors for ordered logistic regression models to determine how efficacious the respondent is about the government. Data from 2021, weighted.

+ $p < 0.10$, * $p < 0.05$, ** $p < 0.01$, *** $p < 0.001$

find that greater trust decreased satisfaction with democracy, while no other variable had a significant relationship.

Table 7.6 shows that patriotism had a strong positive relationship with satisfaction for democracy in 2012. Across all three measurements, patriotism strongly correlates with being satisfied with democracy, as conducted in the United States. As was said previously, the fact that these different political conditions where different factors are influencing the way that democracy is practiced in the United States in 2012 versus 2021 shows that patriotism has had a long, robust correlation with satisfaction with democracy. This relationship is not determined by contextual factors within the election but is based on a broader impact of patriotism and its relationship with opinions about the practice of democracy. Additional correlates with satisfaction with democracy in 2012 are a positive relationship between generalized trust, being Hispanic and black and a liberal ideology.

Table 7.4 Determinants of political efficacy in 2012

Variable	*1*	*S.E*	*2*	*S.E*	*3*	*S.E*
Patriotism	0.404***	0.055	0.396***	0.057	0.337***	0.062
Generalized trust			–0.007	0.037	–0.001	0.043
Ideology			0.029	0.024	0.037	0.025
Hispanic					0.166	0.112
Black					0.592***	0.126
Education					0.051	0.034
Income					0.007	0.005
Age					0.051***	0.011
Female					0.251***	0.069
Cutpoint 1	–0.730**	0.257	–0.664*	0.271	–0.131	0.314
Cutpoint 2	0.114	0.254	0.179	0.266	0.743*	0.307
Cutpoint 3	1.369***	0.255	1.433***	0.266	2.031***	0.309
Cutpoint 4	2.559***	0.259	2.624***	0.271	3.231***	0.314
N	5533		5524		4986	
chi2	54.119***		58.380***		118.780***	

Note Cells represent unstandardized coefficients and standard errors for ordered logistic regression models to determine how efficacious the respondent is about the government. Data from 2012 ANES, weighted

+ $p < 0.10$, *$p < 0.05$, **$p < 0.01$, ***$p < 0.001$

Table 7.5 Determinants of satisfaction with democracy in 2021

Variable	*1*	*S.E*	*2*	*S.E*	*3*	*S.E*
Patriotism	0.845***	0.094	0.845***	0.094	0.834***	0.100
Generalized trust	–0.485***	0.100	–0.485***	0.100	–0.548***	0.104
Ideology	–0.070	0.050	–0.070	0.050	–0.070	0.052
Hispanic					–0.624	0.325
Black					0.460	0.244
Education					–0.112	0.089
Income					0.017	0.028
Age					0.027	0.052
Female					0.158	0.162
Cutpoint 1	2.008*	0.843	2.008*	0.843	0.626	1.093
Cutpoint 2	3.838***	0.856	3.838***	0.856	2.490*	1.099
Cutpoint 3	4.526***	0.862	4.526***	0.862	3.180**	1.102
Cutpoint 4	7.732***	0.903	7.732***	0.903	6.411***	1.129
N	552		552		551	
chi2	154.609***		154.609***		165.124***	

Note Cells represent unstandardized coefficients and standard errors for ordered logistic regression models for determinants of satisfaction with democracy. Data from 2021, weighted.
+ $p < 0.10$, * $p < 0.05$, ** $p < 0.01$, *** $p < 0.001$

Table 7.6 Determinants of satisfaction with democracy in 2012

Variable	*1*	*S.E*	*2*	*S.E*	*3*	*S.E*
Patriotism	0.546***	0.058	0.563***	0.060	0.569***	0.065
Generalized trust			0.143***	0.041	0.195***	0.046
Ideology			–0.169***	0.026	–0.149***	0.028
Hispanic					0.672***	0.118
Black					0.877***	0.119
Education					0.016	0.037
Income					0.004	0.005
Age					0.012	0.011
Female					0.052	0.075
Cutpoint 1	–0.142	0.255	–0.371	0.270	0.262	0.317
Cutpoint 2	1.797***	0.262	1.590***	0.277	2.263***	0.324
Cutpoint 3	4.571***	0.278	4.401***	0.290	5.152***	0.341
N	5505		5496		4969	
chi2	89.686***		154.772***		226.351***	

Note Cells represent unstandardized coefficients and standard errors for ordered logistic regression models for determinants of satisfaction with democracy. Data from 2012 ANES, weighted.
+ $p < 0.10$, * $p < 0.05$, ** $p < 0.01$, *** $p < 0.001$

Conclusion

There is a strong correlation between patriotism and three common measurements of diffuse support. Patriotism has a consistent correlation with all three sub-measurements of diffuse support. It is clear from these strong empirical findings that patriotism is a key component of diffuse support. If this is a causal relationship and not merely a spurious correlation, then patriotism's effect on diffuse support would be an important reason to promote it through public schooling due to the vast benefits that diffuse support has in making society more successful. For societies to interact successfully and efficiently with their citizenry, they need diffuse support.

Unnecessary suspicion, distrust, and unwillingness to engage and appreciate the values of democracy will lead to suspicion and inefficient cooperation with the government on needed societal goals. Key to this formulation is political trust. Political trust is incredibly important in democratic societies, and the clear correlation demonstrated empirically by this research provides one pathway by which political trust could be increased if patriotism could be increased.

Additionally, we know that political efficacy greatly impacts the willingness to participate and become engaged in the political world. If one does not believe that politicians will listen to people like them, they probably will not spend much time on politics. We see clearly in this chapter that patriotism correlates with external efficacy. This again provides another pathway by which patriotism augments democratic society.

Finally, there has been much angst and consternation over democratic backsliding among political elites (Jee et al. 2022). They worry that the gains over democracy in the twentieth century will be lost in the twenty-first century. This research shows that patriotism is a key correlate of satisfaction with democracy. As such, patriotism may be one of the few avenues by which we can hope to prevent greater democratic backsliding. In sum, across three common measures of diffuse support, we see a consistent positive correlation with patriotism.

The last few chapters demonstrated theoretically relevant and important correlations between patriotism and socially beneficial aspects of a democratic society. The next couple of chapters examine well-known and often articulated potential problems with patriotism. Specifically, the next two chapters look at the influence of patriotism on political judgment and xenophobia.

References

Charron, Nicholas, and Victor Lapuente. 2010. "Does Democracy Produce Quality of Government?" *European Journal of Political Research* 49 (4): 443–470.

Diamond, Larry. 2022. "Democracy's Arc: From Resurgent to Imperiled." *Journal of Democracy* 33 (1): 163–179.

Easton, David. 1965. *A Systems Analysis of Political Life*. New York: Wiley.

Hetherington, Marc J. 1998. "The Political Relevance of Political Trust." *American Political Science Review* 92 (4): 791–808.

Hetherington, Marc J. 2005. *Why Trust Matters: Declining Political Trust and the Demise of American Liberalism*. Princeton, NJ: Princeton University Press.

Iyengar, Shanto. 1980. "Subjective Political Efficacy as a Measure of Diffuse Support." *Public Opinion Quarterly* 44 (2): 249–256.

Jee, Haemin, Hans Lueders, and Rachel Myrick. 2022. "Towards a Unified Approach to Research on Democratic Backsliding." *Democratization* 29 (4): 754–767.

Morris, Stephen D., and Joseph L. Klesner. 2010. "Corruption and Trust: Theoretical Considerations and Evidence From Mexico." *Comparative Political Studies* 43 (10): 1258–1285.

Muller, Edward N., Thomas O. Jukam, and Mitchell A. Seligson. 1982. "Diffuse Political Support and Antisystem Political Behavior: A Comparative Analysis." *American Journal of Political Science* 26 (2): 240–264. https://doi.org/10.2307/2111038.

Öktem, Kerem, and Karabekir Akkoyunlu. 2016. "Exit from Democracy: Illiberal Governance in Turkey and Beyond." *Southeast European and Black Sea Studies* 16 (4): 469–480.

Orviska, Marta, Anetta Caplanova, and John Hudson. 2014. "The Impact of Democracy on Well-being." *Social Indicators Research* 115 (1): 493–508.

Oser, Jennifer, Amit Grinson, Shelley Boulianne, and Eran Halperin. 2022. "How Political Efficacy Relates to Online and Offline Political Participation: A Multilevel Meta-analysis." *Political Communication* 39 (5): 607–633.

Persson, Torsten, and Guido Tabellini. 2006. "Democracy and Development: The Devil in the Details." *American Economic Review* 96 (2): 319–324.

CHAPTER 8

Patriotism and Political Judgment

Abstract Does patriotism blind citizens to national problems or sharpen their critical thinking about the country's future? Chapter Eight answers this by measuring political judgment across several domains, including openness to criticism, economic forecasting, and conspiracy beliefs. The data indicate that patriotism does not hinder critical reflection; patriotic individuals remain capable of identifying problems in the nation. Moreover, they are less prone to conspiratorial mindsets and more accurate at predicting outcomes vital to national welfare. These findings challenge assumptions that patriotism necessarily reduces objective analysis.

Keywords Political Judgment · Critical Reflection · Conspiracy Beliefs · Public Opinion · Economic Perceptions · Objectivity

In the next two chapters, I examine two of the most described potential problems with patriotism: irrational support of the nation and xenophobia. As we have seen in Chapter 2, one of the most vexing issues for critics of patriotism is the potential of citizens to lose their ability for critical judgment. A constant refrain amongst these critics is that once citizens are patriotic, they can no longer critique their nation (Keller 2014). Indeed, worries over propaganda in authoritarian countries involve almost exclusively the promotion of patriotism to obscure legitimate critiques

S. Richey, *Patriotism and Citizenship*,
https://doi.org/10.1007/978-3-031-89885-3_8

of the regime (Snyder 2017). The worry is that once people love their nation, they will be unwilling to ascertain its problems and, therefore, unable to fix them. Being able to delineate problems in society clearly allows that society to begin investments to fix those problems. If patriotism prevents citizens from analyzing their nation, this would be a legitimate source of worry about its presence.

Additionally, one of the key justifications and goals of the modern education system derives from Dewey's (1916) conception of how the role of public education should promote a better democratic citizenry. Dewey (1916) argues that mass public education is beneficial because it will create citizens with analytical abilities to discern the superior course of action and preferable candidates. Democracies require citizen input, and a more enlightened citizenry should be able to provide better input, leading to more optimal outcomes. If patriotism limits critical thinking skills because these citizens are so in love with their nation that they will not criticize it, then education will undermine one of its chief justifications and goals by promoting patriotism. A major goal of promoting a mass public education system was to make critical thinkers who could find societal problems. Patriotic education, if it has this unintended outcome of making citizens less critical, would undermine the very goal of public education. Thus, whether patriotism limits critical analysis and makes worse political judgments is a crucial question for whether patriotism should be promoted in society.

Up to this point, however, this topic has not received the empirical analysis necessary to discern whether patriotism has the implied effect on delimiting critical analysis. I utilize the concept of political judgment to measure the analytical abilities of citizens. I empirically test whether patriotism leads to worse judgments as predicted. Chapter 2 showed there are theoretical reasons to expect that patriotism will positively impact analytical abilities and political judgment in some situations. It is necessary, then, to test the impact of patriotism on political judgment, which I measure with the ability to recognize problems with America, the level of conspiracy theory beliefs, and the ability to ascertain objective economic conditions. In this chapter, I also explain the importance of political judgment in a democracy and then investigate patriotism's relationship to three important metrics of political judgment.

Democracy and Political Judgment

To consider political judgment, it is crucial to recognize the difficult tasks that citizens in a democracy are asked to undertake. The world is incredibly complex, with multiple contentious and potentially deceitful actors trying to sway decision-making. The vast limits on time in human cognition combined with the sheer scope of information it takes to decide wisely creates massive cognitive requirements that people must perform to be good democratic citizens. This work is almost always unpaid labor. Berlin (1996) accurately describes the cognitive difficulties as "integrating a vast amalgam of constantly changing, multicolored, evanescent, perpetually overlapping data, too many, too swift, too intermingled to be caught and pinned down and labeled like so many individual butterflies" (Berlin 1996, 28). It is incredibly difficult for the average citizen to devote the time and energy required to make a rational decision.

Political Science has made tremendous progress in explaining the democratic dilemma (Lupia and McCubbins 1998), which is that while citizens cannot make supremely rational decisions, democracy is the most successful system in human history. Democracies succeed more the other systems across almost any measurable dimension, including giving their citizens better health (Bollyky et al. 2019), wealth (Acemoglu et al. 2019), safety (Lin 2007), more education (Dahlum and Knutsen 2017), and on and on. How does democracy succeed when citizens are blatantly incompetent? Three main explanations revolve around heuristic decision-making (e.g., Popkin 1991, Lupia 1994), aggregation of errors (e.g., Page and Shapiro 1992), and the beneficial impact of social decision-making (Huckfeldt 2001). These ideas are incredibly sophisticated explanations of why democracies succeed even though most citizens are unable or unwilling to devote the time and energy to make good decisions.

Even though these three indirect processes explain how democracies overcome mass incompetence, it is clear in all these explanations that if citizens had better political judgment, it would lead to even better societal outcomes. In other words, there is nothing in these explanations as to why democracy performs well that forecloses the potential for it to perform even better if citizens make better decisions. Thus, finding any explanation that alters citizens' decision-making in either a positive or a negative direction is crucial. Since patriotism has been described as something that worsens critical decision-making because it limits the ability of citizens to admit that problems exist, it is crucial to analyze empirically whether their patriotism harms political judgment.

Since direct tests of rationality are not possible, I will examine political judgment and its relationship to patriotism by examining the prior theoretical critiques of patriotism and the underlying presuppositions of those critiques. First, many of the critiques of patriotism suggest that patriotic people would be unable to find flaws in their country, so I will examine the relationship between patriotism and finding flaws in America. Finding flaws in the country is crucial because it is the first step in fixing them. Second, I will examine conspiracy theory beliefs, which are pernicious and commonplace in the modern world. Finally, I will look at retrospective and prospective economic opinions as these are crucial for voting behavior and assessing the state of the nation.

These three measures will be used to ascertain the relationship of patriotism to political judgment.

Patriotism and Discerning Problems with America

The 2012 ANES asks respondents what the most important problem in the country is. Respondents can select no problem exists as an option. I will create a dichotomous variable to measure whether the respondent could discern even one problem with their nation. An advantage of this approach is that it does not impose any ideological constraints on what is legitimate to recognize as a problem. Here, merely mentioning that there is a problem proves that they are not blind to the potential for America to have problems. If those who are patriotic can list problems at the same level as those who are not patriotic, it will show that patriotism does not limit the ability of citizens to recognize problems with America.

Figure 8.1 shows the point estimate and 95% confidence intervals of the percentage of respondents expressing at least one major problem with the United States using data from 2012. The results show that patriotic people were just as likely to denote a major problem with America as those who hate the country. Almost the same percentage of those who hate America and those who love America could list one major problem with the country (38%). Indeed, all five levels of patriotism showed around the same level of listing problems, and there is no statistically significant difference between all five categories. Also of note is that in 2012 every category of patriotism had under 40%, that had even had one major problem with the nation. This suggests that patriotism has no impact on whether someone has a major problem with the country.

Since the political philosophers who criticize patriotism have based most of this criticism on the idea that patriotic people become uncritical of their country's problems, this empirical evidence strongly rejects this assertion. In this data, patriotic people are just as likely to have a major problem with their nation as those who are not patriotic. Interestingly, 62% of those who hate America could not list a problem with it. One wonders why they hate America when they do not have a major problem with it. There must be another reason other than societal problems why these respondents say they hated America, and this suggests that having problems with the nation is orthogonal to patriotism or the lack of patriotism. These data imply that political judgment is not related to loving the country. Whether one ascertains major problems in a country does not determine whether one loves their nation or not. This suggests

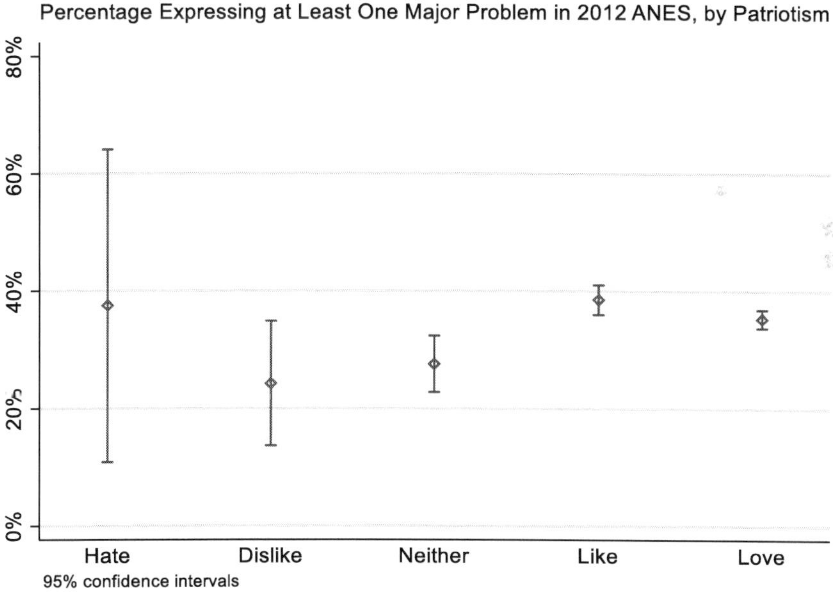

Fig. 8.1 This graph shows the point estimate and 95% confidence intervals of the percentage of respondents expressing at least one major problem with the United States. Data from 2012

that public education that promotes patriotism will not create a nation of obedient uncritical followers.

Results for Conspiracy Theories

Another issue where patriotism potentially benefits political judgment is with anti-governmental conspiracy theories. Conspiracy theories are more common than is typically assumed (Oliver and Wood 2014). Since almost all conspiracy theories are anti-governmental in the sense that they assume that there is a conspiracy of elites working within the government to foster some nefarious scheme, loving the nation potentially limits the level of belief that a cabal runs the nation. It is possible that patriotism benefits political judgment by curtailing conspiracy theory beliefs.

I will test this with 2021 data that asks about conspiracy ideation, a validated psychometric scale measuring a general tendency to believe in anti-governmental conspiracies (Brotherton et al. 2013). The conspiracies that comprise this scale are:

- The government permits or perpetrates acts of terrorism on its own soil, disguising its involvement
- Groups of scientists manipulate, fabricate, or suppress evidence in order to deceive the public
- Technology with mind-control capacities is used on people without their knowledge
- The government is involved in the murder of innocent citizens and/or wellknown public figures, and keeps this a secret
- A small, secret group of people is responsible for making all major world decisions, such as going to war
- The spread of certain viruses and/or diseases is the result of the deliberate, concealed efforts of some organization
- The power held by heads of state is second to that of small unknown groups who really control world politics

These were measured on a scale of Definitely not true (1), Probably not true (2), Not sure/cannot decide (3), Probably true (4), and Definitely true (5). To verify compliance with the survey, one item of this scale was a manipulation check which asked respondents to select option 3, and 100% of respondents did so, suggesting that this sample had a high compliance rate. I created an additive scale of these items to measure general conspiracy ideation. The Cronbach's alpha of this scale was 0.91, suggesting strong reliability.

Table 8.1 shows that patriotism has a strong negative correlation across all three model specifications. These results clearly show that patriotism correlates with less conspiracy ideation, and this relationship is robust to including relevant covariates in the model. The ordinary least squares regression models for determinants of conspiracy ideation show that it is negatively related to a liberal ideology and age but is more common among black respondents. These findings generally match the previous literature on conspiracy ideation. Interestingly, Trump voters are not more likely to subscribe to these conspiracy ideations as Trump often espouses conspiracy theories.

Figure 8.2 shows the predicted level and 95% confidence intervals of belief in conspiracy ideation from Table 8.1 Model 3. I took the scale in Table 8.1 and divided it by the number of included conspiracy theories to allow for more readability. Moving from hating America to loving America would make someone drop around one level on the scale. This equates to the median person, all things being held constant, to a change

Table 8.1 Determinants of conspiracy ideation in 2021

Variable	*1*	*S.E*	*2*	*S.E*	*3*	*S.E*
Patriotism	−1.367***	0.381	−1.799***	0.396	−1.362***	0.404
Republican			−2.734*	1.184	−2.205	1.160
Trump voter			1.059	1.129	1.773	1.172
Ideology			−1.210***	0.317	−1.061**	0.328
Black					2.100*	0.919
Female					1.187	0.785
Age					−0.525*	0.241
Hispanic					1.094	1.459
Education					−0.747	0.484
Income					−0.086	0.143
Intercept	24.698***	2.671	32.965***	3.453	30.149***	4.484
N	552		552		551	
r2	0.038		0.103		0.174	

Note Cells represent unstandardized coefficients and standard errors for ordinary least squares regression models for determinants of conspiracy ideation. Data weighted from 2021
+ $p < 0.10$, * $p < 0.05$, ** $p < 0.01$, *** $p < 0.001$

from not knowing whether these conspiracies are true to thinking they are probably not true.

Assuming that this is a causal relationship, this would be a massive improvement for society if the median person were to believe the conspiracy theories were probably not true rather than not knowing whether they are true or not; it would greatly facilitate the defeat of conspiracy theories which are often transmitted through interpersonal communication (Chadwick et al. 2023). In social network theory, each person is a potential tree node with many subsequent branches. If the person probably does not think the conspiracy theory is true, they will be less likely to start a new set of branches and be less likely to add to communicating this conspiracy theory belief interpersonally.

The 2012 ANES did not have such broad-based measures of conspiracy theories but focused on two common conspiracy theories that were politically salient in its time: birtherism and trutherism. These are the

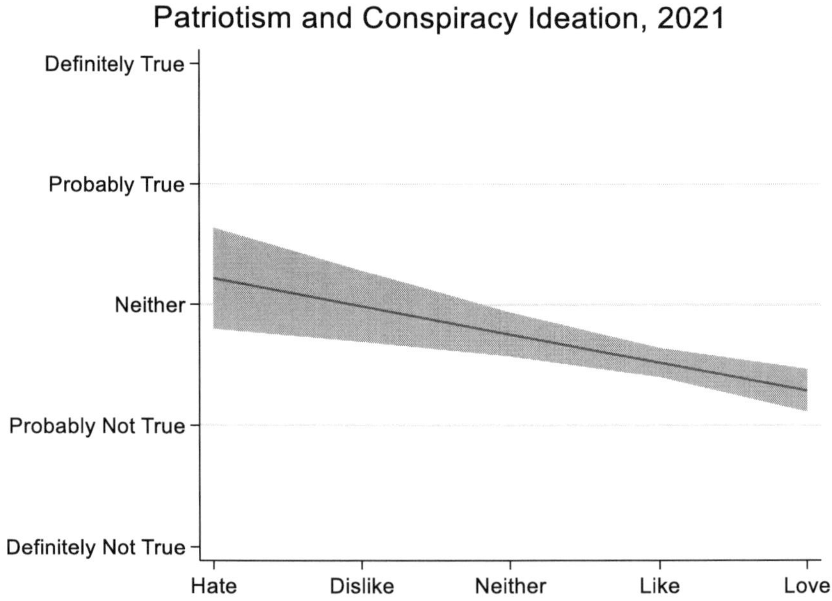

Fig. 8.2 This graph shows the predicted level and 95% confidence intervals of belief in conspiracy ideation. See text for details of the conspiracy ideation psychology scale used—data from 2021

beliefs that Barack Obama was not born in the United States and, therefore, unable to legally become president and the belief that George W. Bush knew of or even perpetuated the 9/11 attacks. These thoroughly debunked anti-governmental conspiracies were commonly believed in these periods and will act with a valid measure of conspiracy ideation in 2012. Table 8.2 shows the results for a bivariate probit regression model for determinants of whether the respondent believes in both the birtherism and trutherism conspiracy theories. It shows that patriotism correlates with less belief in these conspiracy theories. Patriotism in all three models correlates with less belief in trutherism. Of note is that the bivariate correlation in Model 1 between patriotism and birtherism is not significant, but once controlled variables are included in Models 2 and 3, it becomes significant and negatively signed. The other control variables match what we would expect based on the previous literature on the correlates of conspiracy theory beliefs. In sum, the results from 2012 matched the 2021 results, which is that patriotic people hold fewer conspiracy theory beliefs.

Figure 8.3 shows the predicted level and 95% confidence intervals of belief in birtherism and trutherism based on model 3 from Table 8.2. The graph's Y axis shows the probability that the respondent simultaneously believes in trutherism and birtherism. Around 25% of those who hate America believe in both conspiracy theories. Those who love America, conversely, have around 10% believe in both conspiracy theories. Moving from those who hate America to those who love America shows a 15 percentage point reduction in believing in both conspiracy theories. Interestingly, even 10% of those who say they love America believe a president intentionally sponsored the 9/11 attacks and that another president was lying about his birth certificate and whether he was born in the United States. Nevertheless, the general trend of this data is clear that patriotic people are less likely to believe in conspiracy theory beliefs.

Results for Economic Outcomes

Another way I investigate political judgment is for the respondent to describe the state of America and see if these descriptions match empirical reality. It could be that patriotism makes the respondent more likely to say positive descriptions of the reality than is warranted by data. Conversely, those lacking patriotism may be more likely to describe positive conditions negatively since they dislike the country. Motivated reasoning

Table 8.2 Determinants of believing in birtherism and trutherism in 2012

Variable	*Coef*	*S.E*	*Coef*	*S.E*	*Coef*	*S.E*
Birther						
Patriotism	0.026	0.028	−0.092**	0.030	−0.086**	0.033
Ideology			0.167***	0.019	0.156***	0.020
Party ID			0.189***	0.012	0.205***	0.014
Age					0.011	0.007
Female					0.049	0.044
Income					−0.011***	0.003
Education					−0.201***	0.022
Hispanic					−0.076	0.064
Black					−0.220**	0.073
Intercept	−0.871***	0.128	−1.804***	0.144	−1.190***	0.170
Truther						
Patriotism	−0.172***	0.025	−0.151***	0.026	−0.100***	0.028
Ideology			−0.050**	0.016	−0.066***	0.017
Party ID			−0.021*	0.010	0.012	0.012
Age					−0.028***	0.006
Female					0.013	0.038
Income					−0.010***	0.003
Education					−0.112***	0.018
Hispanic					0.265***	0.053
Black					0.141**	0.054
Intercept	0.513***	0.116	0.697***	0.123	1.000***	0.145
athrho	0.114***	0.024	0.205***	0.027	0.184***	0.029
N	5261		5250		4809	
chi2	48.493***		802.392***		970.253***	

Note Cells represent unstandardized coefficients and standard errors for bivariate probit regression models for determinants of whether the respondent believes in the birtherism and trutherism conspiracy theories. Data from 2012 ANES
+p<.10, *p<.05, **p<.01, ***p<.001

implies that positive or negative emotions will color the objective reality's analysis (Lodge and Taber 2013). I measured this by examining both retrospective and prospective economic beliefs.

In 2012 and 2021, I examined the respondent's description of the economic change in the 12 months preceding the survey date. As shown in Tables 8.3 and 8.4, patriotism has a clear, consistent positive correlation with the likelihood that the respondent correctly identified the state of the economy in 2021 and 2012 and respectively. These correlations were consistently significant and positive across all model specifications.

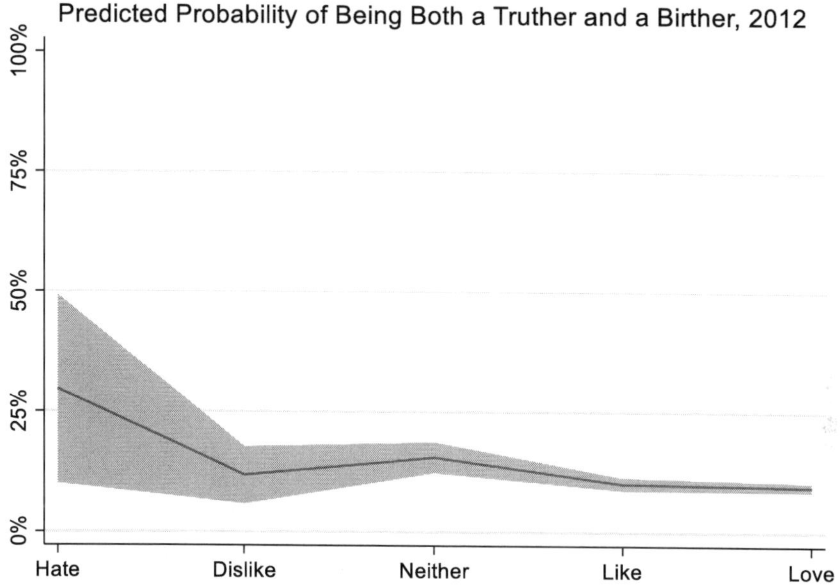

Fig. 8.3 This graph shows the predicted level and 95% confidence intervals of belief in both birtherism and trutherism. Data from 2012

This is strong evidence that across two samples in different states of the economy, patriotism correlates with being more likely to say correctly that the economy is positive.

Figures 8.4 and 8.5 show the predicted level and 95% confidence intervals of correctly assessing the economic levels in the preceding 12 months calculated from the results shown in Model 3 in both tables. Those tables show that those who love America are around 10 to 15 percentage points more likely to be correct on the state of the economy than those who hate America. The theory stated in Chapter 2 is not that patriotism makes someone more likely to be correct but that it makes them less likely to engage in negatively motivated reasoning to assert that a positive situation is negative incorrectly. If the state of the economy is, in fact, positive, people who dislike the country will engage in motivated reasoning plausibly to deny that positive state. Here we see that the same motivated reasoning coincidentally results in a correct outcome. Thus, it is not necessarily negatively impactful on decision-making to love one's country because the economy changes every year, cycling through positive and

Table 8.3 Determinants of correctly knowing the state of the economy in 2021

Variable	*1*	*S.E*	*2*	*S.E*	*3*	*S.E*
Patriotism	0.220*	0.106	0.511***	0.117	0.321*	0.129
Republican			−0.355	0.538	−0.188	0.558
Trump voter			−0.275	0.506	−0.375	0.542
Ideology			0.433***	0.099	0.546***	0.109
Black					0.182	0.340
Female					−0.904***	0.236
Age					0.346***	0.079
Hispanic					−0.130	0.456
Education					−0.063	0.131
Income					0.077	0.041
Intercept	−2.762***	0.729	−6.942***	1.092	−6.474***	1.519
N	552.000		552.000		551.000	
chi2	4.534*		55.704***		93.213***	

Note Cells represent unstandardized coefficients and standard errors for logistic regression models for determinants of whether the respondent correctly knew the state of the economy in the preceding twelve months. Data from 2021, weighted

+p<.10, *p<.05, **p<.01, ***p<.001

Table 8.4 Determinants of correctly knowing the state of the economy in 2012

Variable	*1*	*S.E*	*2*	*S.E*	*3*	*S.E*
Patriotism	0.025	0.042	0.166***	0.047	0.114*	0.053
Ideology			−0.290***	0.028	−0.256***	0.031
Party ID			−0.351***	0.019	−0.405***	0.024
Age					0.002	0.011
Female					−0.445***	0.070
Income					0.035***	0.005
Education					0.218***	0.033
Hispanic					−0.186	0.098
Black					0.273**	0.092
Intercept	−0.868***	0.194	0.747***	0.223	0.061	0.270
N	5541		5520		4990	
chi2	0.354		955.717***		1117.720***	

Note Cells represent unstandardized coefficients and standard errors for logistic regression models for determinants of whether the respondent correctly knew the state of the economy in the preceding twelve months. Data from 2012

+ $p < 0.10$, *$p < 0.05$, **$p < 0.01$, ***$p < 0.001$

negative outcomes. The clear, consistent results in Tables 8.3 and 8.4 confirm the theory that patriotism is correlated with a correct outcome when situations are positive.

In 2012, the ANES survey also asked the respondents to predict how the economy would change in the next 12 months, which was 2013. Table 8.5 shows logistic regression models for determinants of whether the respondent correctly predicted the state of the economy in 2013. All three models' specifications show that patriotism positively correlates with correctly predicting the economy. Prospective economic voting is crucial for voters because they must consider when they vote not only how the economy has been but also how it might likely become. Understanding the overall trends in the economy is often more important than understanding the current economic state. For example, historically, 2013 was not actually a strong year in the United States economy, but its direction signified a rapid improvement from a previously lower state created

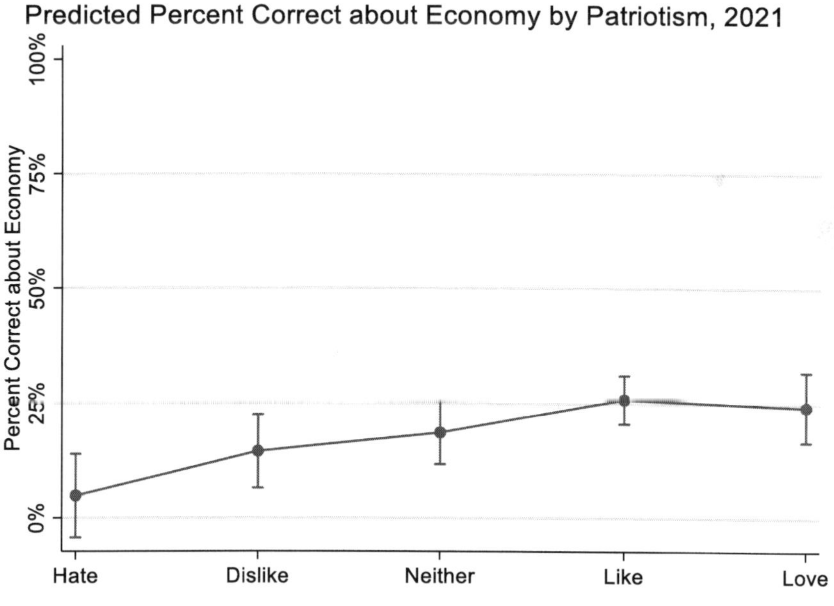

Fig. 8.4 This graph shows the predicted level and 95% confidence intervals of correctly assessing the economic levels in the preceding 12 months. Data from 2021

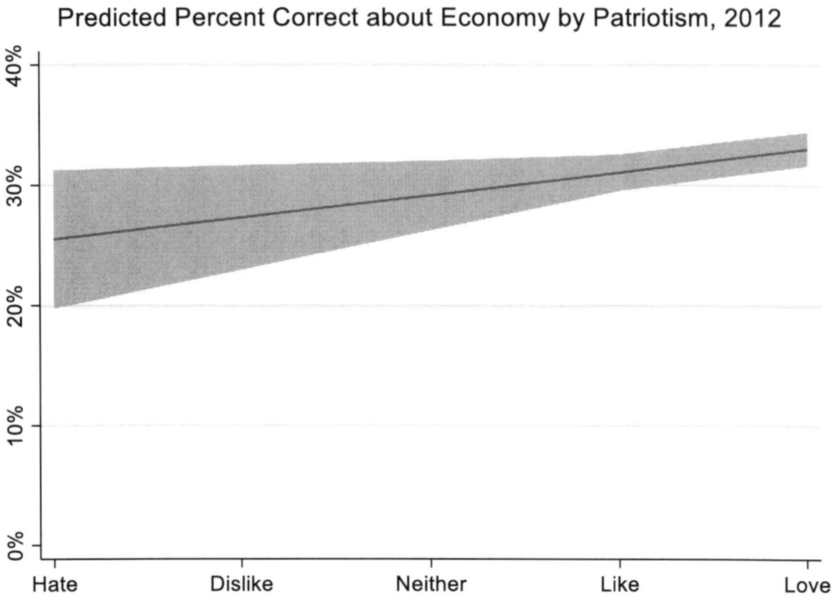

Fig. 8.5 This graph shows the predicted level and 95% confidence intervals of correctly assessing the economic levels in the preceding 12 months. Data from 2012

by the Great Recession. Table 8.5 shows that patriotism correlates with being more correct prospectively on the economy in all three models, which signifies that patriotic people have better political judgment.

Figure 8.6 shows the predicted level and 95% confidence intervals of correctly predicting the economic levels in the next 12 months, calculated from Table 8.5 Model 3. It shows around a 20 percentage point differential between those who hate America and love America in being correct about what will happen with the 2013 economy. Around 90% of those who love America could correctly predict that the economy would improve, while only 70% of those who hate America were correct. Of course, both groups had a majority that was correct in the economy's direction as it was clear that we were leaving the Great Recession by 2012, and things continued to improve in 2013. However, more important than the aggregate level of correct prediction is that patriotism correlates with a massive improvement in being correct prospectively on the economy.

Table 8.5 Determinants of Correctly Predicting the Economy in 2013

Variable	*1*	*S.E*	*2*	*S.E*	*3*	*S.E*
Patriotism	0.117*	0.054	0.166***	0.047	0.295***	0.061
Ideology			–0.290***	0.028	–0.181***	0.041
Party ID			–0.351***	0.019	–0.169***	0.028
Age					–0.029*	0.014
Female					0.056	0.086
Income					0.010	0.006
Education					0.094*	0.042
Hispanic					0.338*	0.132
Black					0.754***	0.164
Intercept	1.320***	0.250	0.747***	0.223	1.595***	0.316
N	5441		5520		4907	
chi2	4.474*		955.717***		262.628***	

Note Cells represent unstandardized coefficients and standard errors for logistic regression models for determinants of whether the respondent correctly predicted the state of the economy in 2013. Data from 2012

+p<.10, *p<.05, **p<.01, ***p<.001

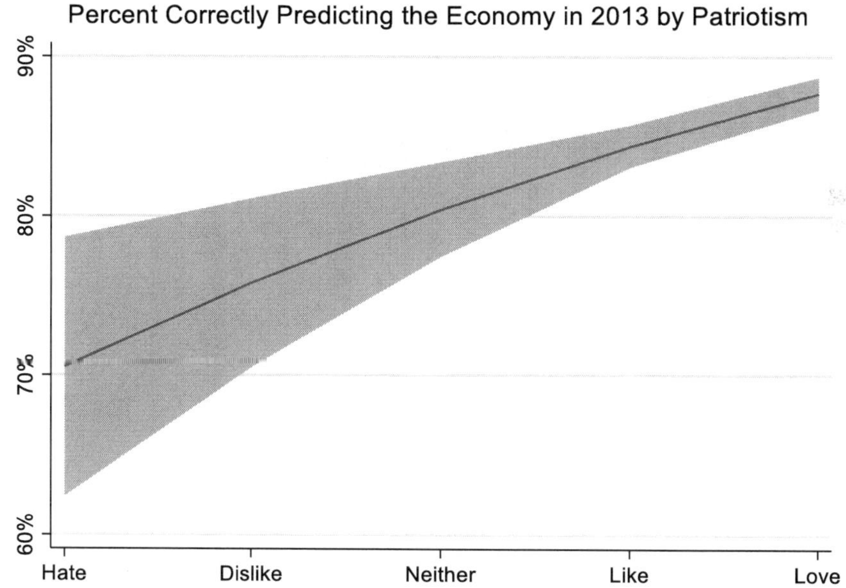

Fig. 8.6 This graph shows the predicted level and 95% confidence intervals of correctly predicting the economic levels in the next 12 months. Data from 2012

Conclusion

This chapter brings strong empirical evidence that worries over patriotism's deleterious effects on political judgment are unfounded. The evidence clearly shows that patriotic people are just as likely to complain about problems in the country as those who are unpatriotic. By demonstrating their ability to critique the country's problems, these patriots belie any concern that they are uncritical in their analysis of the situation in their nation. Critiquing your own country is crucial for political progress because an unwillingness to admit a problem will likely forgo a chance to improve it. While citizens must retain the critical capacity to discern societal problems, patriotism does not interfere with these capacities.

In addition to the ability to discern problems in their country, this chapter also demonstrates two very important ways in which patriotism improves political judgment. First, it was demonstrated that patriotism correlates with less conspiracy ideation and with two specific conspiracy beliefs that were popular in the time that they were measured. As conspiracy theories are a particularly pernicious problem in the information age, where they are commonly spread through social media, patriotism's ability to diminish belief in conspiracy theories greatly benefits society. Conspiracy theories are particularly insidious because experts typically debunk them. However, the people who believe in conspiracy theories are inherently suspicious of these elite experts, who they often envision as part of the very cabal oppressing them. Thus, patriotism's ability to prevent someone from going down the rabbit hole of conspiracy theory beliefs argues strongly in its favor and shows one way that patriotism benefits political judgment.

Additionally, it was shown that patriotic people are more likely to assess economic conditions correctly when those conditions are, in fact, positive for the nation. Capitalist economies oscillate through business cycles that are both positive and negative. In some years, the economic conditions improve while others remain the same and can also be negative. One crucial role of voters in a democracy is to be able to assess the state of the economy through both retrospective and prospective voting. While patriotism is often associated with a "rose-colored glasses" effect, where patriotic individuals view their nation in an overly positive light, the data show that unpatriotic individuals similarly engage in motivated reasoning, displaying excessive negativity toward the country's economic conditions they dislike. This is highly plausible as Nir (2011) shows strong evidence of the prevalence of motivated reasoning in various aspects of public opinion. The assumption made by some critics is that patriotism leads to irrational optimism, but I find that lacking patriotism also shows irrational pessimism when the economic conditions are, in fact, positive. Thus, being patriotic is not inherently any more likely to be incorrect when assessing economic conditions than someone who is unpatriotic; it is just that the direction of the mistake is different. This is not inherently an area where patriotism benefits society, but it shows that those who lack patriotism can also be incorrect in positive economic conditions.

In the next chapter, I examine another commonly described problem with patriotism, xenophobia.

References

Acemoglu, Daron, Suresh Naidu, Pascual Restrepo, and James A. Robinson. 2019. "Democracy Does Cause Growth." *Journal of Political Economy* 127 (1): 47–100.

Berlin, Isaiah. 1996. "On Political Judgment." *New York Review of Books* 43 (15): 26–30.

Bollyky, Thomas J., Tara Templin, Matthew Cohen, Diana Schoder, Joseph L. Dieleman, and Simon Wigley. 2019. "The Relationships between Democratic Experience, Adult Health, and Cause-specific Mortality in 170 Countries between 1980 and 2016: An Observational Analysis." *The Lancet* 393 (10181): 1628–1640.

Brotherton, Robert, Christopher C. French, and Alan D. Pickering. 2013. "Measuring Belief in Conspiracy Theories: The Generic Conspiracist Beliefs Scale." *Frontiers in Psychology* 4: 279.

Chadwick, Andrew, Cristian Vaccari, and Natalie-Anne. Hall. 2023. "What Explains the Spread of Misinformation in Online Personal Messaging Networks? Exploring the Role of Conflict Avoidance." *Digital Journalism*. https://doi.org/10.1080/21670811.2023.2206038.

Dahlum, Sirianne, and Carl Henrik Knutsen. 2017. "Do Democracies Provide Better Education? Revisiting the Democracy–Human Capital Link." *World Development* 94 (1): 186–199.

Dewey, John. 1916. *Democracy and Education: An Introduction to the Philosophy of Education*. New York: Macmillan.

Huckfeldt, Robert. 2001. "The Social Communication of Political Expertise." *American Journal of Political Science* 45 (2): 425–438.

Keller, Simon. 2014. "The Case Against Patriotism." In *The Ethics of Patriotism: A Debate* edited by John Kleinig, Simon Keller, and Igor Primoratz. Germany: Wiley.

Lin, Ming-Jen. 2007. "Does Democracy Increase Crime? The Evidence from International Data." *Journal of Comparative Economics* 35 (3): 467–483.

Lodge, Milton, and Charles Taber. 2013. *The Rationalizing Voter*. New York: Cambridge University Press.

Lupia, Arthur. 1994. "Shortcuts Versus Encyclopedias: Information and Voting Behavior in California Insurance Reform Elections." *American Political Science Review* 88: 63–76.

Lupia, Arthur, and Mathew D. McCubbins. 1998. *The Democratic Dilemma: Can Citizens Learn What They Need to Know?* New York: Cambridge University Press.

Nir, Lilach. 2011. "Motivated Reasoning and Public Opinion Perception." *Public Opinion Quarterly* 75 (3): 504–32.

Page, Benjamin I., and Robert Y. Shapiro. 1992. *The Rational Public: Fifty Years of Trends in American's Policy Preferences*. Chicago: The University of Chicago Press.

Popkin, Samuel. 1991. *The Reasoning Voter: Communication and Persuasion in Presidential Campaigns*. Chicago: The University of Chicago Press.

Oliver, J. Eric., and Thomas J. Wood. 2014. "Conspiracy Theories and the Paranoid Style(s) of Mass Opinion." *American Journal of Political Science* 4 (4): 952–966.

Snyder, Timothy. 2017. *On Tyranny: Twenty Lessons from the Twentieth Century*. New York: Tim Duggan Books.

CHAPTER 9

Patriotism and Authoritarianism, Racism, Bigotry, and Xenophobia

Abstract Chapter Nine tackles one of the most contentious issues surrounding patriotism: whether it fosters exclusionary attitudes or hostility toward outgroups. Contrary to popular worries, the data show that patriotism, measured by love of country, is not strongly correlated with authoritarianism, racism, or xenophobia once other psychological traits are accounted for. While bigotry certainly exists in American society, it appears to stem more from factors such as authoritarian worldviews and social dominance orientation, rather than patriotic attachment per se.

Keywords Authoritarianism · Racism · Xenophobia · Bigotry · Outgroup Attitudes · Social Dominance Orientation

In this chapter, I detail empirical research that compares levels of patriotism with various forms of anti-out-group and discriminatory attitudes. Through decades of research examining ingroup outgroup attitudes, a classic formulation is that the more someone loves their ingroup, the more likely they will be to have hostility and animus toward outgroups (Tajfel 1974). A common critique of patriotism is that it will engender a similar process whereby loving one's nation will activate animus toward those seen as not fitting into the dominant group of that nation. The idea is that the more one loves America, the more likely one will be to

S. Richey, *Patriotism and Citizenship*,
https://doi.org/10.1007/978-3-031-89885-3_9

be hostile toward those viewed as not belonging to the American mainstream. Despite all the positive relationships described empirically in the previous chapters for patriotism, these outcomes may not be worthy of an increase in outgroup animus. Thus, we must investigate whether patriotism has the predicted relationships with various forms of discriminatory and bigoted beliefs to fully adjudicate its influence on citizenship in the United States.

Specifically, I investigate whether patriotism correlates with an authoritarian personality, racism, bigotry, and xenophobia. Measuring these concepts has been debated throughout various academic literatures, and I describe below how I measure these concepts. But, the consistent finding below is that patriots are not more likely to hold discriminatory attitudes than unpatriotic ones. This matches classic research, which has found that nationalism is the concept that is often mistaken for patriotism and simultaneously corresponds with various forms of discriminatory and bigoted beliefs. I now examine the potential relationships between patriotism and several correlated yet distinct common forms of bigotry and discrimination in America.

Patriotism and Authoritarianism, Racism, Bigotry, and Xenophobia

The chief insight that critics of patriotism have is that when one loves their group, they tend to dislike those not in their group. Critics commonly suggest that loving America produces outgroup animus to anyone deemed not fitting into preconceived conceptions of what an American is (Willis-Esqueda et al. 2017). Due to the profound negative impact that discriminatory attitudes have on the lives of marginalized populations, these critics suggest patriotism is, therefore, something that should not be promoted in public schooling or society at large (Kateb 2006).

Generally speaking, this conception is known as social identity theory (see Hogg and Abrams 1988 for a review of this literature). Famously, Tajfel, Billig, Bundy, and Flament (1971) show that even minimally constructed groups randomly assigned in a laboratory setting still produce ingroup favoritism and simultaneously outgroup animus. These are disturbing findings because this effect happens even though these randomly assigned lab groups have no importance in the lives of those who are participants in the experiment (Tajfel 1982). The implication is that if these minimally constructed groups provide enough impetus to hate the outgroup, more socially relevant groups will almost certainly have outgroup animus (Tajfel and Turner 1979).

Crucially, however, for this research, Ellemers, Spears, and Doosje (2002) find that this outgroup animus is situational based on the context of the identities and intergroup relations. It is not clear that the groups that are considered in this formulation around bigotry and patriotism, such as the country of America and a racial group, are in direct conflict in the same way that laboratory groups are divided up specifically to conflict with each other because one is a nation and the other is a racial or ethnic category.

In their classic research on this topic, Elkins and de Figueiredo (2003) show how nationalism is about comparing your nation with other nations, and patriotism is about showing loving gratitude for what the national government and general societal systems have provided for you. Once this distinction is made, it is easy to see why nationalism would correlate with bigotry because it is about saying that your nation or group is better than another nation or group. Patriotism has no such comparison; it is simply about your relationship with your nation and may not necessarily correlate with other attitudes related to sub-national groups. Simply put, the research below replicates these findings with different data and discriminatory attitudes. Patriots are not bigots.

In the next sections, I detail how to measure the difficult to measure concepts of the authoritarian personality, racism, bigotry, and xenophobia in the American context.

Data

Measuring the Authoritarian Personality with SCA

One of the most consistent findings in social science is that authoritarianism correlates with all manner of negative outcomes for a democratic society, including various forms of prejudice (Adorno et al. 1950). This consistent finding dates to the 1940s (Fromm 1941) and has been shown in many groups (Altman 1996). Revealingly, this animosity extends to groups that do not exist, which suggests that these feelings of outgroup animosity derive from psychological propensities to punish weaker members of society and are not necessarily derived from realistic conflict with those groups. Another key point is that the authoritarian personality is not the person who wants to rule society, such as an authoritarian leader. In fact, it is the opposite; authoritarian personalities want to be ruled by a powerful leader who will simultaneously protect them by smashing undesirables in society. These attributes show why authoritarian personalities have greater prejudice.

One of the chief debates is how to measure authoritarianism. At first, it was measured with an F scale in Adorno, Frenkel-Brunswik, Levinson, and Sanford (1950). However, the F scale had various psychometric errors, leading it to conflate authoritarianism with other factors (Camilleri 1959). The RWA scale is another proposed psychometric scale to measure authoritarianism (Altman 1981). A critique of this scale is that it intertwines conservative right-wing ideology with the measurement of an underlying propensity to submit to a powerful ruler who will punish social deviance.

From its earliest conception authoritarianism has been conceived of as something that derives from childhood. This leads to the creation of the SCA scale, which measures social conformity through questions that measure attitudes toward optimal child rearing (Feldman 2003). This scale has shown repeatedly to load on a single factor with well-implied psychometric properties and is free of ideological content, avoiding the troubles of the RWA scale. Because of these advantageous features, I use SCA to measure authoritarianism. In the ANES 2012 data, it is measured as follows:

Please tell me which one you think is more important for a child to have:

- Independence or respect for elders
- curiosity or good manners
- obedience or self-reliance
- being considerate or well behaved

I use principal component analysis to extract one component with an eigenvalue well above 1. The eigenvectors load as the theory would expect. No other eigenvalue is above 1.

Measuring Racism with the Symbolic Racism Scale

Due to social desirability bias, measuring racism through surveys is notoriously difficult. Socially desirable behaviors such as attending church or voting have often been shown to be vastly overstated in survey research. This implies that people will not want to admit they have socially undesirable attitudes such as racism. Due to these difficulties, researchers proposed an alternative measurement system, symbolic racism or racial resentment[1] (Henry and Sears 2002).

This scale included in the ANES 2012 has become the standard measurement of the modern version of less overt racism. It is measured by asking, "Do you agree strongly, agree somewhat, neither agree nor disagree, disagree somewhat or disagree strongly" with each of the following statements:

- Irish, Italians, Jewish, and many other minorities overcame prejudice and worked their way up. Blacks should do the same without any special favors.
- Generations of slavery and discrimination have created conditions that make it difficult for blacks to work their way out of the lower class.\
- Over the past few years, blacks have gotten less than they deserve.
- It's really a matter of some people not trying hard enough; if blacks would only try harder they could be just as well off as whites.

The second and third statements are reverse-coded. I use a principal component analysis to extract one component with an eigenvalue over 2. The eigenvectors load as the theory would expect. No other eigenvalue is above 1.

Measuring Bigotry with Attitudes Toward Gays and Lesbians

Although there are nearly limitless types of bigotries against various groups, I focus on a common and pernicious one: attitudes toward gays and lesbians. This is socially relevant, and an important measure of a commonplace bigotry in the politics of the United States. To measure

[1] For simplicity, I will use the term symbolic racism moving forward, although it is interchangeable with racial resentment or modern racism.

attitudes toward gays and lesbians, I use a measure that ranks feelings of warmth or coldness to particular social groups called a feeling thermometer. Feeling thermometers measure the level of support or antipathy toward groups on a zero to 100 scale with a higher rating equating to more support. There is a question that asked whether the respondent is gay or lesbian, which will allow me to remove those respondents because this exercise examines the outgroup, so removing gays and lesbians for an attitude toward gays and lesbians is important.

Measuring Xenophobia with Attitudes Toward Muslims and Immigration

As with bigotry above, xenophobia is difficult to measure because there are so many groups that anyone could be against. Taking the strategy above of using socially relevant and politically important groups as a proxy measure for xenophobia, I focus on anti-Muslim sentiment and antipathy toward immigration as proxy variables. Of course, there are various reasons that one may oppose immigration, but in combination with other measures in this chapter, it will be another significant test on a politically salient topic. Muslim sentiment is measured with a thermometer variable on attitudes toward Muslims. Immigration is measured with a sentiment out of a one to five scale of whether you support decreasing or increasing immigration into the United States.

Results

Table 9.1 shows that patriotism does not correlate with the SCA scale across three model specifications.[2] This has large downstream implications for various antisocial behaviors correlated with authoritarian personalities. Previous literature has documented many undesirable characteristics that correlate with authoritarianism (Altemeyer 1996). Crude stereotypes of overly patriotic Americans often depict them as akin to authoritarian personalities (see description in Abadi 2018), but this research shows that patriotic people are no more likely to be authoritarian than non-patriotic people. For simplicity, I will not describe the control variables, which largely match the prior literature, such as having more education correlates with less authoritarianism.

Table 9.2 shows the correlations of patriotism with symbolic racism for white respondents in the 2012 ANES. The results here are interesting because, in the bivariate correlation, white patriots do correlate with slightly more symbolic racism. However, once ideology or Republican Party identification is controlled for, this correlation dissipates. In Model 3, we see that a statistically insignificant correlation exists once socioeconomic demographics are controlled for. Due to the profound importance of ideology and party identification to political beliefs, this suggests that a spurious relationship may exist between white patriotism and symbolic racism. As shown in Chapter 2, those with very liberal ideologies have much less patriotism. Simultaneously these results show that liberals have less symbolic racism.

This is a classic example of a spurious relationship, whereby the seeming correlation between two variables is explained by a greater preponderance in the independent variable of a third causal variable

[2] I also ran models with national identity included for the 2021 data that I collected and described in Chapter 4 and entered this new variable into the same basic model and specification used in the manuscript. It was measured with a question used in prior research on this topic (see Huddy and Khatib 2007, 63). *National Identity* is derived from a question that asks, "How important is being an American to you personally?". It was coded as Not at all important (1), A little important (2), Somewhat important (3), Very important (4), and Extremely important (5). I kept the same control variables in these models for the reasons described in the manuscript. All models show that the results do not change and that patriotism retains a positive correlation with democratic support, satisfaction with democracy, and political trust. And either no relationship or positive with out-group hostility, as measured in the manuscript with a thermometer of feelings towards gays and lesbians, Muslims, and attitudes about immigration. See Appendix Table A2–A7.

Table 9.1 Determinates of an authoritarian personality 2012

Variable	*1*	*S.E*	*2*	*S.E*	*3*	*S.E*
Patriotism	0.041	0.035	0.001	0.032	0.058	0.035
Ideology			0.255***	0.021	0.198***	0.019
Republican			−0.210***	0.059	0.107	0.061
Black					0.645***	0.071
Hispanic					0.383***	0.076
Age					0.001	0.008
Income					−0.008*	0.003
Female					0.095*	0.047
Education					−0.357***	0.023
Intercept	−0.217	0.162	−1.032***	0.167	−0.209	0.186
N	5086		5086		4644	
r2	0.001		0.053		0.197	

Note Cells represent unstandardized coefficients and standard errors for ordinary least squares regression models for determinants of scoring higher on the SCA authoritarian personality scale. Data from 2012 American National Election Studies (ANES), weighted. + $p < 0.10$, * $p < 0.05$, ** $p < 0.01$, *** $p < 0.001$

Table 9.2 Determinates of symbolic racism for white respondents 2012

Variable	*1*	*S.E*	*2*	*S.E*	*3*	*S.E*
Patriotism	0.167***	0.048	0.028	0.041	0.032	0.044
Ideology			0.336***	0.025	0.312***	0.026
Republican			0.436***	0.068	0.511***	0.071
Age					−0.002	0.009
Income					0.002	0.004
Hispanic					−0.047	0.097
Female					0.016	0.056
Education					−0.254***	0.027
Intercept	−0.417	0.225	−1.433***	0.202	−0.645**	0.220
N	4050		4050		3731	
r2	0.006		0.184		0.227	

Note Cells represent unstandardized coefficients and standard errors for ordinary least squares regression models for determinants of scoring higher on the symbolic racism scale for white respondents. Data from 2012 ANES, weighted

+ $p < 0.10$, * $p < 0.05$, ** $p < 0.01$, *** $p < 0.001$

causing the dependent variable. Certainly, Models 2 and 3 are more accurate descriptions of the potential determinants of symbolic racism for white respondents than Model 1. Thus, although Model 1 presents some evidence of slightly higher levels of symbolic racism in white patriots, this is plausibly a spurious relationship shown by the lack of significance in Models 2 and 3.

Tables 9.3 and 9.4 show unstandardized coefficients and standard errors for ordinary least squares regression models for determinants of thermometer feelings toward Gays and Lesbians. I also find that patriotism is not correlated with worse feelings toward gays and lesbians. These results show that negative feelings toward gays and lesbians are not more common with those who love America. Patriotism does not correlate with cooler feelings in the three models.

Next, I examine the tests of xenophobia. Tables 9.5 and 9.6 show unstandardized coefficients and standard errors for ordinary least squares regression models for determinants of thermometer feelings toward Muslims. I find that having patriotism does not correlate with anti-Muslim sentiment. This shows that Muslim sentiment is not lower for those who love America. Patriots are not more or less likely to express

Table 9.3 Thermometer feelings toward Gays and Lesbians 2021

Variable	*1*	*S.E*	*2*	*S.E*	*3*	*S.E*
Patriotism	–2.186	2.139	1.307	1.962	3.458	1.814
Generalized trust			7.897***	1.946	7.044***	1.910
Trump voter			–6.407	5.050	–6.711	4.807
Ideology			6.987***	1.353	6.245***	1.256
Hispanic					–3.455	4.058
Black					–6.363	4.747
Education					4.439**	1.630
Income					–0.755	0.587
Age					–4.327***	1.020
Female					4.685	3.067
Intercept	81.292***	15.077	7.429	17.142	5.622	15.368
N	552		552		551	
chi2						

Note Cells represent unstandardized coefficients and standard errors for ordinary least squares regression models for determinants of thermometer feelings toward Gays and Lesbians. Data from 2021, weighted

+ $p < 0.10$, * $p < 0.05$, ** $p < 0.01$, *** $p < 0.001$

Table 9.4 Thermometer Feelings Toward Gays and Lesbians 2012

Variable	*1*	*S.E*	*2*	*S.E*	*3*	*S.E*
Patriotism	–0.055	0.555	1.413**	0.525	2.054***	0.558
Generalized trust			2.867***	0.380	3.031***	0.415
Ideology			–5.943***	0.307	–5.361***	0.316
Republican			–4.982***	0.891	–5.659***	0.958
Hispanic					2.717**	1.042
Black					–0.597	1.026
Education					1.900***	0.352
Income					0.135**	0.050
Age					–0.925***	0.115
Female					8.646***	0.722
Intercept	51.365***	2.570	62.708***	2.727	51.577***	3.034
N	5135		5130		4682	
chi2						

Note Cells represent unstandardized coefficients and standard errors for ordinary least squares regression models for determinants of thermometer feelings toward Gays and Lesbians. Self-professed Gays and Lesbians were excluded from data analysis; see text for details. Data from 2012 ANES, weighted + $p < 0.10$, * $p < 0.05$, ** $p < 0.01$, *** $p < 0.001$

negative feelings in a feeling thermometer for Muslims. This shows that normatively undesired proprieties are not more associated with patriots, despite common wisdom that they would be more xenophobic.

Tables 9.7 and 9.8 show that in the bivariate correlation, patriotism correlates with a slight decrease in support for immigration. However, similar to the symbolic racism scale above, I also find that patriotism is not correlated with opposition to immigration in models 2 and 3 once ideology, party I.D., or demographics are controlled for. These results in Tables 9.7 and 9.8 show that opposition to immigration does not follow from being patriotic in four of the six tested models. It is important to note again that a much more realistic description of the determinants of immigration would certainly include ideology in contemporary America. Thus, it seems like another example of a spurious correlation.

Table 9.5 Thermometer feelings toward muslims 2021

Variable	*1*	*S.E*	*2*	*S.E*	*3*	*S.E*
Patriotism	−3.326	1.781	−1.428	1.810	0.583	1.681
Generalized trust			8.948***	1.938	8.288***	1.868
Trump voter			−10.170*	4.347	−8.815*	4.226
Ideology			3.861***	1.080	3.389**	1.031
Hispanic					−5.280	4.630
Black					−1.447	4.153
Education					4.593**	1.659
Income					−0.961	0.536
Age					−3.919***	0.958
Female					0.803	2.937
Intercept	84.671***	12.345	31.775*	13.758	35.807*	16.101
N	552		552		551	
chi2						

Note Cells represent unstandardized coefficients and standard errors for ordinary least squares regression models for determinants of thermometer feelings toward Muslims Data from 2021, weighted

+ $p < 0.10$, *$p < 0.05$, **$p < 0.01$, ***$p < 0.001$

Table 9.6 Thermometer feelings toward muslims 2012

Variable	*1*	*S.E*	*2*	*S.E*	*3*	*S.E*
Patriotism	0.396	0.491	1.476**	0.480	2.072***	0.511
Generalized trust			1.991***	0.343	3.080***	0.377
Ideology			−2.937***	0.277	−2.599***	0.288
Republican			−7.104***	0.813	−4.962***	0.879
Hispanic					2.164*	0.925
Black					10.921***	0.949
Education					1.944***	0.318
Income					0.023	0.046
Age					−0.752***	0.106
Female					4.012***	0.657
Intercept	43.173***	2.279	46.887***	2.471	33.524***	2.745
N	4911		4904		4435	
chi2						

Note Cells represent unstandardized coefficients and standard errors for ordinary least squares regression models for determinants of thermometer feelings toward Muslims. Self-professed adherents of non-Christian religions were excluded from data analysis; see text for details. Data from 2012 ANES, weighted

+ $p < 0.10$, * $p < 0.05$, ** $p < 0.01$, *** $p < 0.001$

Table 9.7 Support for immigration 2021

Variable	*1*	*S.E*	*2*	*S.E*	*3*	*S.E*
Patriotism	−0.457**	0.142	−0.162	0.163	−0.105	0.164
Generalized trust			0.303	0.155	0.201	0.154
Trump voter			−0.461	0.314	−0.627	0.340
Ideology			0.584***	0.094	0.588***	0.094
Hispanic					−0.935*	0.369
Black					−0.401	0.317
Education					0.321*	0.134
Income					0.021	0.040
Age					−0.092	0.072
Female					−0.132	0.242
Cutpoint 1	−4.770***	1.038	−0.017	1.297	−1.238	1.556
Cutpoint 2	−3.821***	1.017	1.106	1.290	−0.041	1.574
Cutpoint 3	−1.670	0.994	3.761**	1.323	2.767	1.626
Cutpoint 4	−0.269	0.993	5.321***	1.303	4.369**	1.608
N	552		552		551	
chi2	10.355**		91.660***		113.779***	

Note Cells represent unstandardized coefficients and standard errors for ordered logistic regression models for determinants of supporting more immigration. Data from 2021, weighted
+ $p < 0.10$, * $p < 0.05$, ** $p < 0.01$, *** $p < 0.001$

Table 9.8 Support for immigration 2012

Variable	*1*	*S.E*	*2*	*S.E*	*3*	*S.E*
Patriotism	−0.101**	0.037	−0.068	0.037	−0.021	0.041
Generalized trust			0.229***	0.027	0.250***	0.031
Republican			−0.213***	0.064	−0.129	0.071
Ideology			−0.205***	0.022	−0.195***	0.023
Hispanic					0.809***	0.077
Black					0.443***	0.075
Education					0.229***	0.026
Income					0.009*	0.004
Age					−0.041***	0.008
Female					−0.156**	0.053
Cutpoint 1	−1.726***	0.172	−1.844***	0.194	−0.889***	0.222
Cutpoint 2	−0.762***	0.171	−0.852***	0.193	0.147	0.222
Cutpoint 3	1.325***	0.172	1.304***	0.194	2.373***	0.225
Cutpoint 4	2.599***	0.180	2.598***	0.200	3.733***	0.232
N	5449		5439		4928	
chi2	7.604**		254.106***		522.565***	

Note Cells represent unstandardized coefficients and standard errors for determinants of supporting more immigration. Data from 2012 ANES, weighted
+ $p < 0.10$, * $p < 0.05$, ** $p < 0.01$, *** $p < 0.001$

Conclusion

The results of this chapter primarily show that patriots are not more likely to have greater authoritarian personality, racism, bigotry, or xenophobia than those who are unpatriotic. While it is impossible to measure all types of discriminatory beliefs, the issues measured in this chapter are profoundly important in American politics. Racism, anti-gay and lesbian beliefs, attitudes toward Muslims, and immigration are all some of the most salient topics in America. If someone does not have these beliefs, it is probably safe to assume they are not bigots generally. Further, showing that patriotism does not correlate with one of the main psychological drivers of bigotry, the authoritarian personality, implies that many other types of outgroup animus will also not correlate with patriotism.

It is important to note that bivariate correlations show that patriotism alone has a slight correlation with an increase in symbolic racism and a decrease in support for immigration. However, these correlations disappear once other variables, such as ideology, are included. It is highly plausible that the lower levels of symbolic racism and greater support of immigration for those who are very liberal while simultaneously lower levels of patriotism amongst those who are very liberal produce these spurious correlations. In sum, the empirical results generally suggest patriotism will not lead someone to be more likely to hold higher levels of outgroup animus.

This research empirically demonstrates and augments what has previously been found by showing that these null findings apply across multiple political settings and marginalized groups. One of the chief reasons patriotism has been avoided in modern education is the worry that it will spark discriminatory attitudes toward outgroups (Brighouse 2006). However, this chapter shows that these critiques are unfounded and that patriotism could be promoted without a negative impact on political and civil society.

In the next chapter, I apply these ideas to the local level of governance to see if similar relationships can be found with patriotism toward one's municipality. This novel concept tests whether loving one's city will encourage them to be involved in politics, civic engagement, trusting government, and willing to engage in sacrifice for collective action. The following chapter essentially replicates the findings of the last few chapters at the level of local patriotism.

References

Abadi, Mark. 2018. "I've Been to 25 Countries, and these are the 7 Worst Stereotypes I've Heard about Americans." *Business Insider*. Accessed at https://www.businessinsider.com/stereotypes-of-americans-usa-2018-6

Adorno, Theodor W., Else Frenkel-Brunswik, Daniel J. Levinson, and Nevitt Sanford. 1950. *The Authoritarian Personality*. Harper & Brothers.

Altemeyer, Bob. 1996. *The Authoritarian Specter*. Harvard University Press.

Altman, Irwin. 1981. *The Environment and Social Behavior: Privacy, Personal Space, Territory, and Crowding. Monterey*, CA: Brooks/Cole Publishing Company.

Altman, Irwin. 1996. "Higher Education and Psychology in the Millennium." *American Psychologist* 51 (4): 371–378.

Brighouse, Harry. 2006. *On Education*. New York, NY: Routledge Press.

Camilleri, Santo F. 1959. "A Factor Analysis of the F-Scale." *Social Forces* 37 (4): 316–323.

Ellemers, Naomi, Russell Spears, and Bertjan Doosje. 2002. "Self and Social Identity." *Annual Review of Psychology* 53 (1): 161–186.

Elkins, Zachary, P. de Rui José, and Figueiredo. 2003. "Are Patriots Bigots? An Inquiry into the Vices of Ingroup Pride." *American Journal of Political Science* 47 (1): 171–188.

Feldman, Stanley. 2003. "Enforcing Social Conformity: A Theory of Authoritarianism." *Political Psychology* 24 (1): 41–74.

Fromm, Erich. 1941. *Escape from Freedom*. Rinehart.

Henry, Patrick J., and David O. Sears. 2002. "The Symbolic Racism 2000 Scale." *Political Psychology* 23 (2): 253–283.

Hogg, Michael A., and Dominic Abrams. 1988. *Social Identifications: A Social Psychology of Intergroup Relations and Group Processes*. Routledge.

Huddy, Leonie, and Nadia Khatib. 2007. "American Patriotism, National Identity, and Political Involvement." *American Journal of Political Science* 51 (1): 63–77.

Kateb, George. 2006. *Patriotism and Other Mistakes*. Yale University Press.

Tajfel, Henri. 1974. "Social Identity and Intergroup Behaviour." *Social Science Information* 13 (2): 65–93.

Tajfel, Henri. 1982. "Social Psychology of Intergroup Relations." *Annual Review of Psychology* 33 (1): 139.

Tajfel, Henri, Michael G. Billig, R.P. Bundy, and Claude Flament. 1971. "Social Categorization and Intergroup Behaviour." *European Journal of Social Psychology* 1 (2): 149–178.

Tajfel, Henri, and John C. Turner. 1979. "An Integrative Theory of Intergroup Conflict." In *The Social Psychology of Intergroup Relations*, pp. 33–47, Monterey, CA: Brooks/Cole.

Willis-Esqueda, Cynthia, Rosa Hazel Delgado, and Karina Pedroza. 2017. "Patriotism and the Impact on Perceived Threat and Immigration Attitudes." *Journal of Social Psychology* 157 (1): 114–125.

CHAPTER 10

Local Patriotism

Abstract Expanding the concept of patriotism to the municipal level, this chapter explores how love of one's town or city affects civic life and local politics. Drawing on preregistered survey data and experimental manipulations, it finds that local patriotism significantly heightens participation in community events, local elections, and grassroots initiatives. Respondents primed with local pride are more willing to donate resources to improve local infrastructure or social services, suggesting that place-based attachment can reinforce collective action at smaller scales as well.

Keywords Local Patriotism · Municipal Politics · Community Engagement · Civic Participation · Experimental Research · Place-Based Identity

Do citizens love their towns[1] the way they love their nations[2]? If so, what impact does this local patriotism have on citizens' attitudes and behaviors in local politics? Patriotism has almost exclusively been viewed

[1] I use the terms town, city, and municipality interchangeably.

[2] This chapter is mostly derived and reprinted with permission from Richey (2023).

S. Richey, *Patriotism and Citizenship*,
https://doi.org/10.1007/978-3-031-89885-3_10

as a national concept.[3] In this chapter, I posit that people hold similarly strong feelings toward their municipal area. Such feelings explain much about their participation in local politics, civic participation, trust in the local government, and willingness to sacrifice for the town. Based on my contractual theory of national-level patriotism from Chapter 2, I developed a theory of how local patriotism can influence behavior and attitudes, such as motivating participation in local politics. Empirically, I also show that local patriotism is a distinct form of attachment from previously measured concepts, such as national patriotism, and therefore needs to be studied.

Derived from the contractual theory of patriotism, I also expect citizens with a greater love of their town to be willing to carry the cost of engaging in politics and civic activities. Conversely, if someone dislikes or even hates their town, they will have diminished feelings of civic duty. Such sentiments are necessary to explain any rational actor's decision to participate in political activity that requires sacrifice (Riker and Ordeshook 1968). Hundreds of studies have examined attitudes and behaviors in local activities and civic participation (e.g., Titus 1981), but none have conceptualized local patriotism as an explanatory factor. The persuasive empirical results below show that local patriotism is an important omitted variable in our understanding of local politics.

Since Aristotle, we have known that daily interactions in the *agora* (a local place of assembly, such as a marketplace) are crucial for understanding how people relate to their political world (see, e.g., Aristotle 1988, vii, II, 2). Local interactions are the best chance for citizens to express themselves politically (DeSantis and Hill 2004) because the nature of mass politics dilutes one person's impact on national politics to the point of being ineffectual (Berry et al. 1993). However, depending on the town's size (Oliver 2000), an individual may affect political outcomes at the local level (Lassen and Serritzlew 2011).

Nevertheless, participation in town politics and civic participation requires a willingness to get involved. The local level is where an impact may be more likely, but it is also the level where political participation is the least prevalent (Oliver et al. 2012). Low participation in town politics often leads to domination by a concerted minority mobilized by direct

[3] For example, Huddy and Khatib (2007, 63) state that "(t)here is broad agreement on the meaning of patriotism as 'a deeply felt an affective attachment to the *nation*'" (emphasis added).

self-interest (see an example from housing policy in Einstein et al. 2018). As such, low participation levels may make outcomes unrepresentative of the general populace's will in the town (Fung 2006). Thus, understanding why people get involved in town politics is a crucial question for political science.

This topic is vital to study because local government is a critical factor in determining the quality of life (Young and Kaczmarek 2000). Still, many citizens ignore it by focusing on national politics or ignoring politics altogether. Local politics are well known to have a tremendous impact on citizens' well-being (Cárcaba et al. 2017). Criminal justice, education, housing, and public health policies are mainly administered by the local government. A voluminous literature finds that an involved, committed citizenry will improve the local area and simultaneously improve many of the outcomes for the citizens themselves (see, e.g., Aldrich 2012). A possible explanation for the lack of local political involvement may be a lack of willingness to sacrifice to achieve the town's goals because residents do not feel attached to the city (see Yang and Callahan 2007). Generally, I posit that local patriotism should correlate with greater willingness to incur costs to help the town.

To investigate the impact of local patriotism, I preregistered two survey questionnaires, experimental protocols, and theoretical predictions.[4] Using novel survey[5] data matched to nationally representative data for gender, age, and race, I show that people have feelings of love, indifference, or hate toward their municipality. I also find a strong positive correlation between loving one's municipality and participation in local politics, civic participation, and trust in local government. The survey results are augmented by the clear causality provided by two survey experiments with real cash consequences. The survey experiments show that priming feelings toward one's town strongly motivates the willingness to make a financial sacrifice to solve local collective action problems.

In both experiments, participants were asked to identify the biggest problem facing their town. They were then asked to donate their $1

[4] These preregistration materials are available at https://bit.ly/3cfF2Jd

[5] I obtained voluntary and informed consent from participants at the beginning of each survey questionnaire. Participants were told that they were taking part in a research study. This research did not intervene in political processes. Respondents were paid $1 to complete the survey, which took on average 5 minutes to complete. This payment equates to about $12 per hour.

payment for taking the survey to help address that specific problem. The treatment groups were asked to think about their feelings of love and/or hate toward the town, while the control group was only asked to donate to help the town's problem. The treatment group was much more likely to donate than the control groups in both experiments. This outcome shows the power of local patriotism in motivating behavior. These participants signed up to take the survey for money, yet thinking about their feelings toward their town led many more respondents to donate that money willingly. The survey experiments show that these results are not merely some form of social desirability bias or survey wording response bias.

This chapter continues as follows: I examine how local patriotism has been conceptualized in the literature, examine how national patriotism has affected political attitudes and behaviors, and state several theories about how local patriotism can be influential. I then describe my preregistered predictions; detail the experimental procedures, data, and methodology; describe the results, and conclude with a discussion of the findings.

Conceptualizing Local Patriotism

While no prior research in political science considers the impact of local patriotism on political participation, civic participation, trust in local government, and collective action, similar concepts have been investigated. There is literature on local patriotism in the field of history examines local uprisings in the past—particularly the 1700s and 1800s—whereby townsfolk opposed the nation-state, showing that they care more about their locality than their nation (e.g., Ashton 2010). More directly, a few articles have examined how Europeans view their region compared to their nationality in human geography. For example, researchers have investigated how Spain's Basque region citizens are more likely to be proud of being Basque than being Spanish (Melich 1986). Also, Gnatiuk (2017) examined local patriotism in Ukraine and compared it with national patriotism among Ukrainians. However, none of these studies examined the impact of local patriotism on political attitudes or behaviors.

The sociological literature has a long-running debate on a concept that is similar to local patriotism termed community attachment (Cuba and Hummon 1993). Different scholars define Community attachment differently, but it is essentially how close one feels to the local community

(DeHoog et al. 1990). This relates in many ways to how I conceptualize local patriotism, but the key insights from this literature concern what creates it rather than what it creates. In other words, these sociologists examine community attachment as a dependent variable, not an independent variable, as I do local patriotism in this paper (e.g., Kasarda and Janowitz 1974). The main factors that they find that predict community attachment are having close knit social ties in the town and length of residency (Buttel, Martinson, and Wilkening 1979).

In sum, while some research has examined elements of local patriotism, the predictions that arise from this research has not been tested directly. As such, I now examine the research on national patriotism and how it affects attitudes and behaviors, and I use this information to delineate the possible effects of local patriotism on attitudes and behaviors at the local level.

Patriotism at the National Level

The extensive literature on how national-level patriotism affects national-level politics serves as a helpful starting point to understand how local patriotism may affect local politics. The literature on patriotism almost universally assumes that this concept concerns the love of the nation-state. Crucial to this research, the above chapters consistently found that national patriotism correlates with participation in national-level politics, such as voter in Chapter 3. This finding leads to the expectation that local patriotism will also correlate with participation in local politics.

Local patriotism is related to constructive patriotism in that its focus is on helping the town. It is not related to nationalistic or blind patriotism because it is measured below with a question that asks if the respondent loves, likes, neither/nor dislikes, or hates their town. The question used below does not ask about opinions of the town's superiority or general relationship with other towns because the underlying concept of local patriotism is not conceptualized in this research as having anything to do with superiority. The underlying concept of local patriotism is also related to constitutional patriotism because anyone who moves to the town could develop a love for it. The uniqueness of this measure of local patriotism is that it is used in this research for the first time to measure the impact of these concepts at the local level on critical political phenomena.

These streams of research conclude that patriotism is not to be confused with nationalistic or xenophobic belligerence toward outgroups and minorities, and it features a willingness to sacrifice to solve the nation's problems. These forms of patriotism motivate political participation, civic participation, and trust without necessarily devolving into nationalism (Gangl et al. 2016). Extending these ideas to the local level, local patriotism should not cause hostility toward surrounding towns or subgroups in the town but should engender a willingness to bear the costs required to participate in and engage with one's town for its betterment. Using this understanding of how patriotism interacts with politics at the national level, I now present several ideas about how local patriotism can shape citizens' participation with local politics.

Local Patriotism and Citizens' Attitudes and Behaviors

The first research question is: What influence does local patriotism have on local political participation? The early research into political participation demonstrated that civic duty is crucial to understanding the cost–benefit analysis for civic participation and political participation. The fundamental logic explicated in Downs should hold for local participation and participation in national politics. Simply put, one person typically does not make much of a difference, and the cost of involvement almost always outweighs the plausible possibility of achieving a political goal. Whether attending a meeting, donating to a candidate, or emailing a City Council member, one additional action from an individual is not likely to determine a change in public policy or electoral results.

However, the cost–benefit analysis for citizens who love their town and want to improve it is different than those how do not love the town. For those who love their town, sacrifice includes the instrumental benefit and the psychological benefit of helping improve the town they love (Riker and Ordeshook 1968). These benefits likely outweigh the cost of participation for many individuals who express local patriotism. Thus, knowing the foundation for the psychological desire to help the town is crucial for understanding political participation. I posit that local patriotism is a profound motivator that alters the cost–benefit analysis of participation, with greater patriotism equating to greater participation. Thus, I present prediction 1:

Prediction 1. Local patriotism correlates with greater participation in local politics.

The second research question is: What influence does local patriotism have on civic participation? Patriotism may correlate with civic participation for an intuitive and straightforward reason: The more people care about their town, the more they will volunteer in activities that promote its improvement. At their core, almost all civic participation activities hinge on improving the local situation. Citizens who care more about the local community should engage with it more often. Furthermore, those who dislike or hate their town would be less likely to sacrifice their time and effort to engage in voluntary and other civic activities to benefit that town. Thus, prediction 2 is the following:

Prediction 2. Local patriotism correlates with greater civic participation.

The third research question asks how local patriotism influences trust in local government. Decades of studies have shown that the relationship between political trust and attitudes toward government is complex. It is difficult to discern whether people like the government and therefore trust it or trust the government and subsequently like it. Correlational survey analysis does not go far in untangling the intertwined causal relationships of trust and affection. While noting the lack of causation, I expect that local patriotism should significantly correlate with political trust because it is doubtful that people would like the city's government that they could not trust.

Furthermore, while the survey evidence provided below cannot identify causation directly, it is essential to know that this relationship exists. Many public health campaigns, for example, demonstrate the unique role of trust in getting community members to cooperate with public health officials. If we can find a way to boost local patriotism, we may find an avenue to increase trust in local political institutions and compliance in these campaigns that require cooperation with the town. Based on these ideas, prediction 3 is as follows:

Prediction 3. Local patriotism correlates with greater trust in local government.

The fourth research question centers on the influence that local patriotism has on solving collective action problems. These problems are well-known social traps that feature a large amount of free-riding from individuals unwilling to sacrifice for the greater good (Olson 1965). Local patriotism potentially offers a solution to social traps that are created by collective action problems. The simple idea is that if people love their town, they will be more willing to trust that others will not cheat in the iterated prisoner's dilemmas that give rise to social traps (Rothstein 2005). Further, a greater love of town may inspire people to be more likely to sacrifice short-term self-interest for the town's benefit. With greater local patriotism, we should see a process similar to what is often referred to as a patriotic act by those who sacrificed for their nation. Thus, prediction 4 is the following:

Prediction 4. People primed with local patriotism are more likely to contribute to solving local problems.

Experimental Procedures

To examine whether local patriotism affects the willingness to sacrifice for the town, I conducted two survey experiments similar to the one in Chapter 5. Experiment 1 was conducted on the same sample from which the survey data were derived in October 2020. Experiment 2 was from a different online sample, with slightly different stimuli explained below in April 2021. In both experiments, participants were first asked to write what they considered is the biggest problem facing their town. For example, in Experiment 1, approximately 15% indicated that traffic was the biggest problem in their town, while another 12% identified crime as the biggest problem. The central idea of both experiments was to test whether inducing local patriotism influences the desire to sacrifice for the town by donating money to help solve its biggest problem.

In Experiment 1, the treatment group was primed to consider their feelings of love and hate toward the town. If, after considering their feelings about the town, this group is more likely to donate to help solve town problems, a causal relationship would be revealed between local patriotism and the willingness to sacrifice to solve collective action problems. In this case, the sacrifice is the participant's money earned from filling out the survey. Note that while $1 may not seem like a substantial sacrifice, it was sufficient to motivate the respondent in the Prolific sample to fill out the survey and indicative of an extensive enough reward to motivate effort.

> You are making $1 for taking this survey. **Thinking about your feelings of love and hate toward your town,** would you like to donate this $1 to help your town solve the problem that you just listed above? If so, please click Yes, Donate $1 below. If not, please click No, Do Not Donate $1.
> You are making $1 for taking this survey. Would you like to donate this $1 to help your town solve the problem that you just listed above? If so, please click Yes, Donate $1 below. If not, please click No, Do Not Donate $1.

In Experiment 2, a third of the sample was randomly assigned to be asked to think about their feelings of love toward the town. Another third of the sample was randomly assigned to be asked to think about their feelings of hate toward the town. The control group was asked for the same donation but without the stimulus to prime their feelings of love or hate toward the town. All three groups were then asked to donate the money ($1) that they had earned by taking the survey. The two treatments and control stimuli are respectively listed below:

> You are making $1 for taking this survey. **Thinking about your feelings of love toward your town,** would you like to donate this $1 to help your town solve the problem that you just listed above? If so, please click Yes, Donate $1 below. If not, please click No, Do Not Donate $1.
> You are making $1 for taking this survey. **Thinking about your feelings of hate toward your town,** would you like to donate this $1 to help your town solve the problem that you just listed above? If so, please click Yes, Donate $1 below. If not, please click No, Do Not Donate $1.
> You are making $1 for taking this survey. Would you like to donate this $1 to help your town solve the problem that you just listed above? If so, please click Yes, Donate $1 below. If not, please click No, Do Not Donate $1.

Randomization produced balance across a broad set of pretest variables. The experiments used deception, which was revealed after the survey was completed. The respondents were told that the money was not donated to the town and that they could donate it themselves.[6]

Data and Methods

The data analysis was conducted using preregistered survey questionnaires with survey experiments. The first sample included 500 US citizens who Prolific recruited. The survey was conducted online, and respondents were matched to nationally representative age, gender, and race Census data. The respondents were paid $1 for completion.[7] A total of 524 respondents started the survey, but only 468 finished it. Incomplete surveys were excluded from the analysis. I included one manipulation check to ensure that the participant read the survey (Kane and Barabas 2019). All respondents responded correctly to the instruction, "Please select 3 from the responses below."

The second survey used in Experiment 2 was sampled about six months later than the first using the same online methodology and survey company, Prolific. However, this online convenience sample was not matched to nationally representative benchmark data. The point of the second survey was to replicate Experiment 1 at a different time with a different sample.

Dependent Variables

I followed past researchers in measuring political participation on a scale of possible activities. The logic of using such a scale is that there are many ways to participate in politics. Simply measuring voter turnout, for example, is not sufficient to measure the diversity of ways in which the public can be involved in politics. Further, because people can participate with larger or smaller amounts of time, it is best to weight participation by active involvement. *Local Political Participation* was measured with an additive scale of expressed activity in the following political activities: never (0), once or twice (1), or more than twice (2). Survey participants

[6] Specifically, they were told, "Unfortunately, we are not able to find a place to donate the $1 to solve the problem in your town, but you can donate it yourself if you like."

[7] AAPOR (2021) describes this type of sample as "respondents were not randomly selected from among the total population, but rather from among those who took the initiative or agreed to volunteer to be a respondent".

were asked to mark how often they have engaged in the following local political activities: sent an email or letter to a local politician, commented on social media about local politics, discussed local politics with friends or family, volunteered for a local election campaign, donated money to a local campaign, and attended a meeting/event on a local political issue. Each question specified that it was about local politics, not to confuse the respondent that this might be a about a national-level political issue or person. For example, the question on sending an email or letter to a local politician, was worded as "Sent an email or letter to a local politician."

As with political participation, there are also many ways to be involved civically. As such, I also use a scale to measure civic participation weighted by the level of participation. *Civic participation* was adapted from an additive scale of expressed civic activity suggested by the National Research Council (2014). It is measured with agreement with the statements that the respondents have not done this (0), have done it a little (1), or have done it a lot (2). The participants were asked, "Have you ever spent time participating in any activity below in the last 12 months?" The list of activities included involvement with a church or religious group; parent-teacher association; neighborhood organization/ homeowners association; youth sports; Boy Scouts/Girls Scouts or similar youth groups; Rotary, Masons, Elks or Moose Lodge, Lions, Kiwanis, or similar group; Chamber of Commerce or local business group; cleaning-up litter project or similar beautification group; and other community group not listed.

I adapted a question for local political trust from the American National Election Studies (ANES) study that has been frequently used to measure national-level political trust (ANES 2016). *Local Political Trust* was measured with the question, "Now speaking of the municipality that you listed above, how often do you trust the local government to do the right thing?" Answers were coded as always (4), most of the time (3), about half the time (2), sometimes (1), and never (0).

Collective Action Problem Solving was measured with a question about participants' willingness to donate the fee they earned for completing the survey to help the town solve an important problem. Responses were coded as 1 if a participant chose to donate and 0 if they did not.

Local Patriotism Variable

The 2012 ANES included a question on patriotism at the national level, which I adapted for the local level by asking, "Now speaking of the municipality that you listed before, how do you feel about the town you live in?" Responses were coded as follows: hate it (–2), dislike it (–1), neither like nor dislike it (0), like it (1), or love it (2). Interestingly, not many demographic factors correlated with local patriotism, although it seemed to increase with greater age and income.

I have no way to verify the content validity of the wording of this local patriotism question, which centers on a novel concept. While it is not easy to assess content validity, the question does have face validity in that it is plausible that respondents can reasonably assess their feelings toward their town. And although it is measured with a single question and not a scale of questions, it is intended to measure local patriotism generally. Single-item measures also have some psychometric advantages. For example, having a single item reduces the common method variance problem, a type of systematic error shared among similarly measured variables.[8] Due to the shared common understanding of the terms like, dislike, love, and hate, the question should be able to determine the level of local patriotism for this sample and test my hypotheses.

Figure 10.1 shows a skew in the distribution toward more positive feelings about the town. Indeed, the modal category indicates that around half of the sample liked their town. However, it is essential to note that a full 25% did not express any positive feelings toward their town, and 3% hated their town. This outcome confirms that local patriotism exists; real feelings of love and hate are distributed across a nationally representative sample toward their town. As such, it brings into focus the need to study such feelings and their implications for participation in town politics, civic participation, trust in local government, and a willingness to sacrifice for collective action problems.

This is important to show because, while we may not expect every person to have similar ideas of love or hate toward their town, the distribution of this unmeasured variable is currently unmeasured and, thus, unknown. Intuitively, because each town is unique and can have broad variations in the quality of life and provisions of resources, there will

[8] I hope to in the future work to further validate this measure and potentially develop a multiple-item scale of local patriotism.

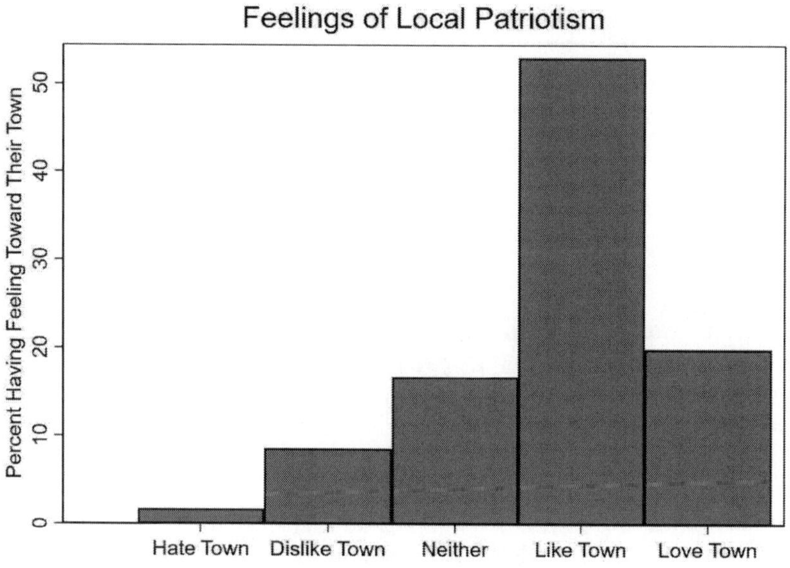

Fig. 10.1 This bar graph shows the distribution of local patriotism

be wide variations in attitudes toward it. Importantly, negative experiences with a town can also range widely, encompassing challenges such as corruption and conflicts with police.

The Tiebout model suggests that people can move if they do not like their town, and having such a choice works as a form of pressure on towns to provide a better quality of life (Tiebout 1956). However, newer research suggests that people are closely tied to their communities and do not move as freely as the Tiebout model suggests, even if they do not like it (Boadway and Tremblay 2012). Consequently, some residents may love their town while others hate it, and a group exists between these extremes.

I also expect that there are underlying psychological propensities to express patriotism and that these tendencies will be positively correlated with the expression of patriotism at the national and local level. Beyond psychological propensities, various factors have likely socialized the respondent to have stronger or weaker patriotic feelings, and the distinction between national and local governments will not necessarily erase the effects of socialization.

However, while several reasons support the expectation that national and local patriotism will be positively correlated, citizens can distinguish between local and national governments. Their patriotism may, therefore, differ across these distinct levels. Since there is only one federal government but 37,000 municipalities in the United States, I expect a much broader variation in attitudes toward towns than the national government.

Figure 10.2 shows a scatterplot of national patriotism measured on the same 5-point scale from hate to love of America as the local patriotism variable. Figure 10.2 is jittered so that the dots are viewable, showing a correlation between local and national patriotism. Pairwise correlations show that these two variables correlate at 0.340 with a *p*-value of less than 0.001. While a significant positive correlation does exist, plenty of people in the sample felt differently about the nation and their town. This difference is apparent from the number of people who, for example, love America but hate their town.

In the regression models below, I controlled for national patriotism to address the underlying psychological propensities and political socialization processes that influence general opinion toward the government. This allows me to isolate the unique effect of local patriotism on the dependent variables.

Control Variables

I control for national patriotism to separate the general psychological propensity and the political socialization of a generalized tendency to like government. The models below show local patriotism's separate and unique impact by including national patriotism in their regression models. The question for national patriotism was taken from the 2012 ANES and was worded as "Now speaking of the United States of America, how do you feel about it?" Responses were coded as follows: hate it (–2), dislike it (–1), neither like nor dislike it (0), like it (1), or love it (2).

Similarly, I wanted to control for general tendencies to trust the government and other people to accurately measure the impact of local patriotism on trust in the local government. For interpersonal trust, I used the ANES question, "Generally speaking, how often can you trust other people?" Responses were coded as follows: always (4), most of the time (3), about half the time (2), once in a while (1), and never (0).

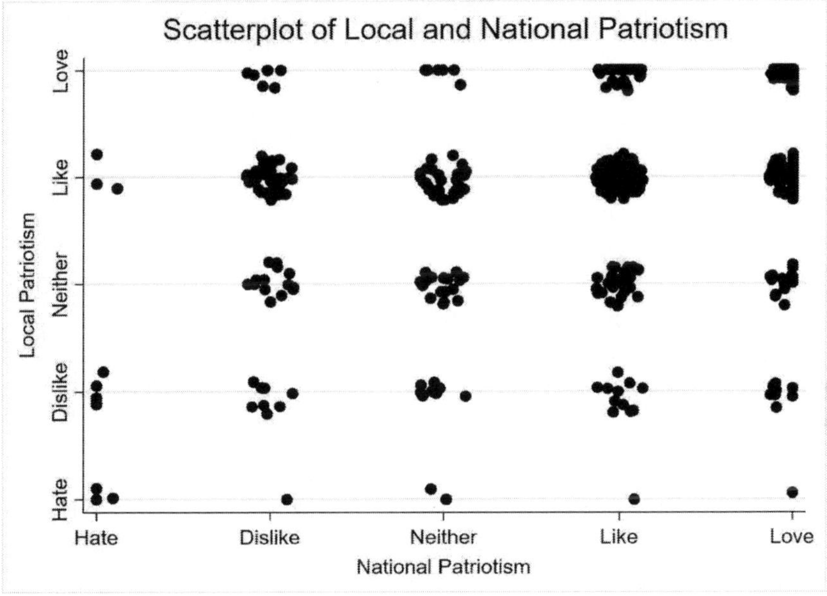

Fig. 10.2 This scatterplot shows the relationship of local patriotism and national patriotism

The question about trusting the national government was also from the ANES: "Now speaking of the United States of America, how often do you trust the federal government in Washington DC to do the right thing?" Responses were coded using the same scale as for interpersonal trust.

For the political participation and civic participation models, I wanted to control for a general desire to participate in politics and care about political actions. First, I measured voting in the 2020 presidential elections by asking, "Whom do you plan to vote for in the 2020 Presidential elections?" I coded responses as 1 for those who answered they did not plan to vote and 0 for those who said they planned to vote. Additionally, I control for interest in politics with the question, "How closely are you following politics?" Responses were coded as follows: very closely (3), somewhat closely (2), not too closely (1), or not at all (0).

I also controlled for *Education*, *Age*, *Income*, and whether the respondent was *Black*, *Hispanic*, or *Female* because socioeconomic status variables have been shown to have a massive impact on individuals' political participation, civic participation, and trust in government (Verba, Schlozman, and Brady 1995). Additionally, I controlled for how long the respondent resided in the town because longer experiences with a town could plausibly lead to greater trust and attachment (Kang and Kwak 2003). The variable *Residency Tenure* was measured in years.

Methods

Local Political Participation and *Civic participation* were count variables that indicated the number of activities a respondent was involved in. I used a Poisson regression model to analyze these dependent variables statistically. *Trust in Local Government* was measured with an ordinal variable, and I used an ordered logistic regression model for its analysis. The decision to donate or not to the town in the experiments was a dichotomous variable, and I used a logistic regression model to measure the effect of assignment to treatment. For all these models, the modeling choice was robust to alternative specifications, such as pairwise correlations and ordinary least squares regression models.

I use data from the first survey for the correlational analysis testing predictions 1, 2, 3, 4, and 5 below because of the validity derived from it being matched to nationally representative data. For this reason, I omit correlational analysis from the second convenience sample below. However, analysis shows that the same correlations predicted by predictions 3, 4, and 5 are obtained in this convenience sample; although the p-value for Local Participation is above 0.05, it is signed in the expected positive direction. Additionally, in survey 2, Local Patriotism showed a similar distribution as Figure and has a pairwise correlation with National Patriotism at 0.3243 with a p-value < 0.001.

Results

Prediction 1

Prediction 1 is that local patriotism correlates with greater participation in local politics. Table 10.1 shows a strong positive correlation between local patriotism and political participation across multiple specifications. A strong effect is apparent in Model 1, which controls for national patriotism. It diminishes in Models 2 and 3, although it remains statistically significant and positive. Model 3 shows that the predicted number of participatory acts for those who hate their town is around 4, while those who love their town are predicted to do 5.13 acts.[9] This equates to about one-third of a standard deviation increase in the dependent variable when going from the lowest level of local patriotism to the highest while controlling for the other variables in the model. These results confirm that local patriotism correlates with participation in local politics. Hundreds of studies of political participation have been conducted without considering local patriotism as a correlating factor. This finding shows that local patriotism is a large variable bias that has been omitted in prior research.

The control variables match prior research expectations over what influences political participation. Having more interest in politics, the length of residency in the town, greater education and income, and being female raised the propensity to participate in politics, while not voting in national elections correlates with less participation in local politics. The other control variables were not statistically significant.

Table 10.1 Determinants of participation in local politics

Variable	*1*	*S.E*	*2*	*S.E*	*3*	*S.E*
Local patriotism	0.127***	0.026	0.104***	0.027	0.057*	0.027
National patriotism	0.061**	0.021	0.063**	0.022	0.057**	0.022
Nonvoter					−0.502***	0.123
Interest					0.300***	0.033
Residency tenure					0.009***	0.001
Hispanic			−0.085	0.100	−0.108	0.101
Black			−0.178**	0.069	−0.065	0.070
Education			0.121***	0.023	0.101***	0.023
Income			−0.008	0.008	−0.014	0.008
Age			0.002	0.015	−0.044**	0.015
Female			0.069	0.044	0.112*	0.045
Intercept	1.456***	0.032	1.055***	0.170	0.226	0.202
N	457		457		457	
chi2	26.563***		68.476***		242.699***	

Note Cells represent unstandardized coefficients and standard errors for Poisson regression models for determinants of participation in local politics.
+ $p < 0.10$, * $p < 0.05$, ** $p < 0.01$, *** $p < 0.001$

[9] This was measured using the margins command in Stata 16.

Prediction 2

Prediction 2 is that local patriotism correlates with greater civic participation. Table 10.2 shows that local patriotism strongly and positively correlates with civic participation across three model specifications. By controlling for national patriotism, I show the unique impact of local patriotism on civic participation. Models 1 and 2 show a strong significant positive correlation at a p-value of less than 0.05, and in Model 3, the *p*-value rises to 0.063. For model 3 in Table 10.2, the predicted number of weighted acts of civic participation for those who hate their town is 1.79, while those who love their town are predicted to do 2.42 weighted acts. This equates to about one-fifth of a standard deviation increase in the dependent variable when going from the lowest level of local patriotism to the highest while controlling for the other variables in the model.

Table 10.2 Determinants of civic participation

Variable	*1*	*S.E*	*2*	*S.E*	*3*	*S.E*
Local patriotism	0.155***	0.040	0.115**	0.041	0.075 +	0.041
National patriotism	0.286***	0.035	0.326***	0.037	0.310***	0.037
Nonvoter					–0.213	0.171
Interest					0.129**	0.048
Residency tenure					0.010***	0.002
Hispanic			–0.110	0.150	–0.123	0.151
Black			0.215*	0.092	0.281**	0.094
Education			0.227***	0.034	0.224***	0.035
Income			0.028*	0.012	0.023	0.012
Age			–0.098***	0.023	-0.122***	0.023
Female			–0.054	0.066	–0.004	0.067
Intercept	0.311***	0.059	–0.099	0.257	–0.587	0.306
N	458		458		458	
chi2	115.362***		218.604***		263.001***	

Note Cells represent unstandardized coefficients and standard errors for Poisson regression models for determinants of civic participation

+ $p < 0.10$, * $p < 0.05$, ** $p < 0.01$, *** $p < 0.001$

The control variables match expectations from prior research over what is influencing civic participation. Having more interest in politics, the length of residency in the town, greater education, and being Black correlates with civic participation, while age correlates with lower likelihood of participating in local politics. The other control variables were not statistically significant.

Prediction 3

Prediction 3 is that local patriotism correlates with greater trust in local government. As predicted, local patriotism has a strong correlation with trust in local government. Across all three model specifications, there is a large, statistically significant positive correlation with trust in local government. The *p*-value in all three model specifications is less than 0.001. The control variables in the model were changed to include interpersonal and national trust in government. As expected, both interpersonal trust and national political trust lead to large positive correlations with trust in local government. The other variables matched their predicted outcomes based on the relationships that were found in prior research. For Model 3 in Table 10.3, the predicted level of trust for those who hate their town is 2.45, while those who love their town are predicted to have an average level of trust at 3.67. This equates to about one standard deviation increase in the dependent variable when going from the lowest level of local patriotism to the highest while controlling for the other variables in the model.

The control variables do not significantly impact trust in local government. Having more interpersonal and national-level political trust correlates with more trust in local government, while age correlates with lower trust. The other control variables were not statistically significant.

Prediction 4

Prediction 4 was that local patriotism would correlate with a greater willingness to solve local collective action problems. Specifically, this prediction was measured by the respondent being willing to donate their payment for completing the survey ($1) to solve a problem that they identified about their town. This was tested with two survey experiments.

In Experiment 1, the treatment group was prompted to consider their feelings of love and hate toward the town; 18% said they would donate

Table 10.3 Determinants of trust in local government

Variable	*1*	*S.E*	*2*	*S.E*	*3*	*S.E*
Local patriotism	0.841***	0.107	0.814***	0.108	0.721***	0.113
National patriotism	0.297***	0.084	0.271**	0.089	0.091	0.100
National trust					0.503***	0.119
Interpersonal trust					0.967***	0.127
Residency tenure					–0.002	0.006
Hispanic			–0.548	0.359	–0.542	0.380
Black			–0.357	0.250	–0.077	0.254
Education			0.205*	0.091	0.167	0.094
Income			0.040	0.033	0.012	0.034
Age			–0.023	0.059	–0.037	0.062
Female			–0.451*	0.176	–0.370*	0.181
Cut point 1	–1.998***	0.190	–2.619***	0.656	0.860	0.770
Cut point 2	0.179	0.134	–0.371	0.633	3.388***	0.776
Cut point 3	1.454***	0.147	0.950	0.632	4.879***	0.788
Cut point 4	4.559***	0.293	4.122***	0.682	8.483***	0.873
N	467		467		466	
chi2	100.751***		124.193***		215.325***	

Note Cells represent unstandardized coefficients and standard errors for ordered logistic regression models for determinants of trust in local government
+ $p < 0.10$, *$p < 0.05$, **$p < 0.01$, ***$p < 0.001$

the money to help their town. In the control group, which received no prompts about feelings, only 3% said they would donate the $1 to the town. The six-fold difference between the treatment and control groups is significant at a 0.001 level[10] (Fig. 10.3).

This result shows that stimulating feelings of local patriotism by having the respondents think of their feelings toward the town generated a willingness to incur costs to solve collective problems. When thinking about their feelings toward their town, one in six of the treatment group respondents were willing to incur an actual monetary cost to help the town.

[10] Please see Appendix Table 6 for logistic regression results which features a bi-variate model and a model with a control valuable that was not balanced across both conditions, *Nonvoter*.

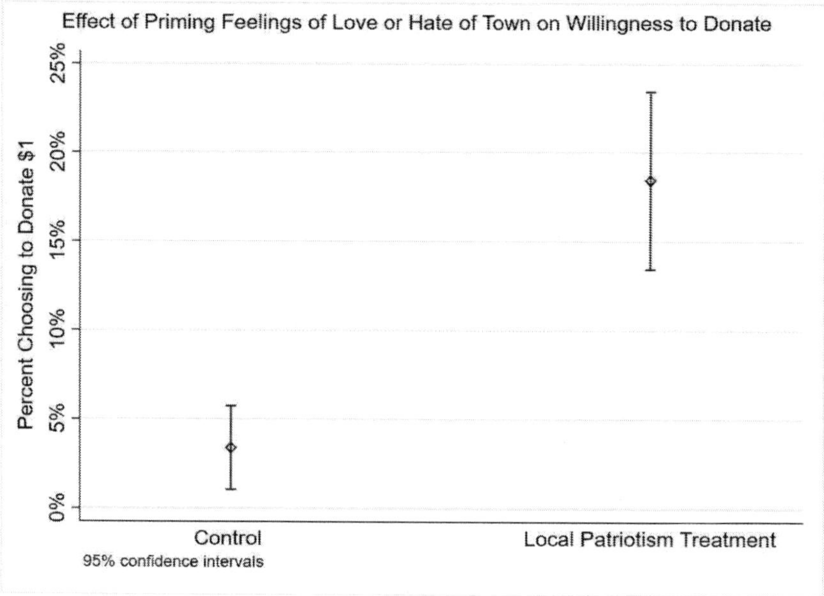

Fig. 10.3 This box plot shows the mean and 95% confidence intervals of the willingness to donate to help solve the town's biggest problem for the treatment and control groups

Without being spurred to think about their feelings toward their town, only one in 30 participants in the control group was willing to sacrifice for the town. This outcome demonstrates that local patriotism is a powerful motivator for solving collective action problems.[11]

Experiment 2, Fig. 10.4 shows that no one in the control group was willing to pay the $1 they received for the survey to help their town's

[11] To consider how the treatment effects vary by how people felt about their town, I divided the sample into groups that either liked (4) or loved their town (4), or those who had no opinion (3), disliked (2) or hated their town (1). There were 128 participants in the Less Local Patriotism Group and 340 participants in the More Local Patriotism Group. The results of box plots shown in Appendix Figures 2 and 3 show that the treatment effect is similar for both groups. Interestingly, no one in the Less Local Patriotism Group donated to help the town's problem in the control condition, but around 14% donated when stimulated with local patriotism. This suggests that even people who have a basic dislike of the town can be motivated through patriotic appeals.

problem. In the treatment group that stimulated a love of the town, we see that 8% were willing to donate to the town. The difference between these two conditions is statistically significant, with a p-value < 0.001. This confirms prediction 6 and replicates the finding in Experiment 1.

Interestingly, the stimuli which provoked hate of town also saw 5% of its participants willing to donate their $1 in earnings to help the town. This is also statistically significantly different from the control group, with a p-value < 0.001. Of note is that the difference between the treatment conditions stimulating feelings of hate of town and love in town is not statistically significant. This suggests that stimulating any feelings toward the town will generate more willingness to sacrifice to resolve collective action problems. Perhaps engendering emotions toward the town in and of itself is motivating sacrifice when compared to a control group in which no emotions were stimulated.

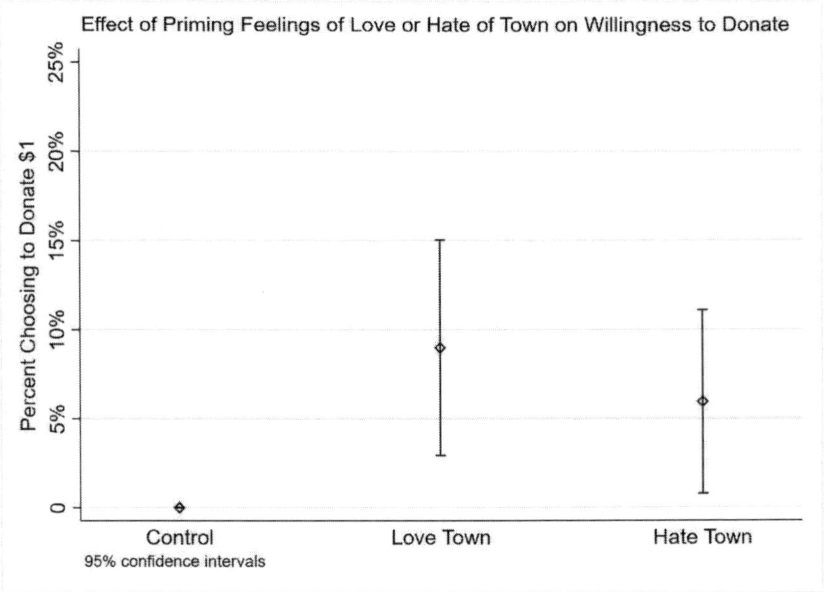

Fig. 10.4 This box plot shows the mean and 95% confidence intervals of the willingness to donate to help solve the town's biggest problem for the treatment and control groups

These results clearly show that if you can prime local patriotism, it may lead to more willingness to sacrifice for the town. There are several ways to prime patriotism, but perhaps the chief way is incentivizing a willingness to work with the town. Richey finds that experiments done in Japanese towns show that incentivizing working with the town could increase trust in the town. This finding suggests that a similar incentive process can engender local patriotism by facilitating working with the town.

Conclusion

I find that local patriotism exists; people do have feelings of love or hate for their town. The distributions of national patriotism and local patriotism are correlated, but not strongly. Thus, an underlying psychological predisposition or political socialization process that predicts someone expressing a positive attitude toward government does not entirely explain the phenomenon of local patriotism. One or more factors distinguish people's feelings toward local government from those toward the national government. Even after controlling for national patriotism, I found that local patriotism matters greatly in local politics. A robust and clear correlation was apparent between local patriotism and political participation in local politics, civic participation, and local government trust. The correlations were robust to multiple model specifications and data analysis. Although causality cannot be obtained for predictions 3, 4, and 5 from cross-sectional survey data, these pre-registered strong results show that these relationships need much more study. Crucially, I show that local patriotism is a distinct concept from previous measures of attachment, such as national patriotism, and therefore, needs to be studied.

I also conducted two survey experiments that showed that priming feelings toward one's town is a powerful motivator of sacrifice to solve local collective action problems. In the first experiment, stimuli that elicited feelings of love or hate toward the town encouraged a six-fold increase in the number of participants willing to donate their payment to solve a town problem. Exposure to treatment increased donation rates from 3 to 18%. The second experiment found that the stimulating feelings of love of town led 8% of participants to donate their fee while stimulating feelings of hate led to 5%. These conditions were statistically significantly different from a control group that did not stimulate feelings toward the town. These results show that more work in political science is needed to understand how feelings toward the local area affect local politics.

Local patriotism has been mostly ignored in the political science literature on participation in local politics and civic participation, but these results clearly show that it should not be. These findings help elucidate the role of civic education in promoting positive images of the town. The common concerns about patriotic education becoming nationalistic, xenophobic, and jingoistic are not applicable to local patriotism (see MacMullen 2012) because there are typically no local military disputes or harsh xenophobic relationships with nearby towns. The clear findings of this research, including the survey experiments, show that one of the best ways to mobilize political action at the local level is to engender feelings of local patriotism.

Future research can examine how these results are moderated and mediated by local context, such as town size; it is true that this is not an expected finding. One interesting finding was that prompting hate of the town elicited more donations. I expected that priming hate of the town would have the opposite reaction or potentially have no reaction in terms of promoting donating to help the most prominent problem in the town. Perhaps getting the participant to think about their dislike of the town also makes them think about prominent problems in the town, thereby eliciting more willingness to donate money to help these problems, which are now top of mind. This is a possibility that future researchers should investigate. Future research would also benefit by analyzing these potential subdivisions of local patriotism that are similar to those found in national patriotism. The literature has made several distinctions between the multiple forms of patriotism. This includes detailed literature on constructive patriotism, blind patriotism, nationalistic patriotism, and constitutional patriotism. These might also exist at the local level.

References

AAPOR. 2021. "Report on Online Panels—AAPOR." Available at: ¡https://www.aapor.org/EducationResources/Reports/Report-on-Online-Panels.aspx¿. Accessed 16 November 2021.

Aldrich, Daniel P. 2012. *Building Resilience: Social Capital in Post-Disaster Recovery*. Chicago: University of Chicago Press.

ANES. 2016. *Users Guide and Codebook for the ANES 2012 Time Series Voter Validation Supplemental Data*. Ann Arbor, MI and Palo Alto, CA: The University of Michigan and Stanford University.

Aristotle. 1988. *The Politics*, trans. Jowett, Benjamin; ed. Stephen Everson. Cambridge: Cambridge University Press.

Ashton, Paul. 2010. "'The Spirit of Local Patriotism': Progress and Populism in Sydney's Northern Suburbs in the 1920s." *Journal of Australian Studies* 34 (2): 163–177.

Berry, Jeffrey M., Kent E. Portney, and Ken Thomson. 1993. *The Rebirth of Urban Democracy*. Washington, DC: Brookings Institution Press.

Boadway, Robin, and Jean-Francois Tremblay. 2012. "Reassessment of the Tiebout Model." *Journal of Public Economics* 96 (11–12): 1063–1078.

Buttel, Fredrick H., Oscar B. Martinson, and E.A. Wilkening. 1979. "Size of Place and Community Attachment: A Reconsideration." *Social Indicators Research* 6: 475–485.

Cárcaba, Ana, Eduardo González, Juan Ventura, and Rubén Arrondo. 2017. "How Does Good Governance Relate to Quality of Life?" *Sustainability Journal* 9 (4): 1–16.

Cuba, Lee, and David M. Hummon. 1993. "A Place to Call Home: Identification with Dwelling, Community, and Region." *The Sociological Quarterly* 34: 111–131.

DeHoog, Ruth H., David Lowery, and William E. Lyons. 1990. "Citizen Satisfaction with Local Governance: A Test of Individual, Jurisdictional, and City-specific Explanations." *Journal of Politics* 52 (3): 807–837.

DeSantis, Victor S., and David Hill. 2004. "Citizen Participation in Local Politics: Evidence from New England Town Meetings." *State & Local Government Review* 36 (3): 166–173.

Einstein, Katherine Levine, Maxwell Palmer, and David M. Glick. 2018. "Who Participates in Local Government? Evidence from Meeting Minutes." *Perspectives on Politics* 17 (1): 1–19.

Fung, Archon. 2006. *Empowered Participation: Reinventing Urban Democracy*. Princeton, NJ: Princeton University Press.

Gangl, Katharina, Benno Torgler, and Erich Kirchler. 2016. "Patriotism's Impact on Cooperation with the State: An Experimental Study on Tax Compliance." *Political Psychology* 37 (6): 867–881.

Gnatiuk, Oleksiy. 2017. "National and Local Patriotism in Spatial Dimension: Case of Podolia, Ukraine." *Human Geography Journal* 21 (2): 75–79.

Huddy, Leonie, and Nadia Khatib. 2007. "American Patriotism, National Identity, and Political Involvement." *American Journal of Political Science* 51 (1): 63–77.

Kane, John V., and Jason Barabas. 2019. "No Harm in Checking: Using Factual Manipulation Checks to Assess Attentiveness in Experiments." *American Journal of Political Science* 63 (1): 234–249.

Kang, Naewon, and Nojin Kwak. 2003. "A Multilevel Approach to Civic Participation: Individual Length of Residence, Neighborhood Residential Stability, and Their Interactive Effects with Media Use." *Communication Research* 30 (1): 80–106.

Kasarda, John D., and Morris Janowitz. 1974. "Community Attachment in Mass Society." *American Sociological Review* 39 (8): 328–339.

Lassen, David Dreyer, and Soren Serritzlew. 2011. "Jurisdiction Size and Local Democracy: Evidence on Internal Political Efficacy from Large-scale Municipal Reform." *American Political Science Review* 105 (2): 238–258.

MacMullen, Ian. 2012. "Doing Without Love: Civic Motivation, Affection, and Identification." *Journal of Politics* 76 (1): 73–85.

Melich, Anna. 1986. "The Nature of Regional and National Identity in Catalonia. Problems of Measuring Multiple Identities." *European Journal of Political Research* 14 (1–2): 149–169.

Oliver, J. Eric. 2000. "City Size and Civic Involvement in Metropolitan America." *American Political Science Review* 94 (2): 361–373.

Oliver, J. Eric., Shang E. Ha, and Zachary Callen. 2012. *Local Elections and the Politics of Small-Scale Democracy*. Princeton, NJ: Princeton University Press.

Olson, Mancur. 1965. *The Logic of Collective Action*. Cambridge, MA: Harvard University Press.

National Research Council. 2014. *Civic Engagement and Social Cohesion: Measuring Dimensions of Social Capital to Inform Policy*. Washington, DC: The National Academies Press. https://doi.org/10.17226/18831.

Richey, Sean. 2023. "The Influence of Local Patriotism on Participation in Local Politics, Civic Participation, Trust in Local Government and Collective Action." *American Politics Research* 51 (3): 357–372. https://doi.org/10.1177/1532673X221125449.

Riker, William, and Peter Ordeshook. 1968. "A Theory of the Calculus of Voting." *American Political Science Review* 62 (1): 25–42.

Rothstein, Bo. 2005. *Social Traps and the Problem of Trust*. Cambridge, UK: Cambridge University Press.

Tiebout, Charles. 1956. "A Pure Theory of Local Expenditures." *Journal of Political Economy* 64 (5): 416–424.

Titus, A. Constandina. 1981. "Shaping Attitudes towards Local Government: Factors That Influence Political Trust and Efficacy." *Urban Interest* 3 (2): 37–45.

Verba, Sidney, Kay Lehman Schlozman, and Henry E. Brady. 1995. *Voice and Equality: Civic Voluntarism in American Politics*. Cambridge, MA: Harvard University Press.

Yang, Kaifeng, and Kathe Callahan. 2007. "Citizen Involvement Efforts and Bureaucratic Responsiveness: Participatory Values, Stakeholder Pressures, and Administrative Practicality." *Public Administration Review* 67 (2): 249–264.

Young, Craig, and Sylwia Kaczmarek. 2000. "Local Government, Local Economic Development and Quality of Life in Poland." *GeoJournal* 50 (2/3): 225–34.

CHAPTER 11

Conclusion

Abstract The final chapter summarizes the empirical findings and theoretical contributions. It revisits the central question of whether patriotism ultimately benefits or harms democratic societies. The evidence underscores the constructive role of patriotism in spurring voter turnout, civic engagement, and diffuse support, without systematically engendering bigotry. The chapter closes by offering policy considerations (e.g., civic education reforms) for cultivating healthy patriotic attitudes, while cautioning against conflating patriotism with nationalism or authoritarian sentiment. Possible directions for future research are also proposed.

Keywords Policy Implications · Civic Education · Democratic Health · Normative Citizenship · Future Research · Summary

In this chapter, I conclude by summarizing the arguments and results. I also suggest new ways patriotism can be fruitfully analyzed by future researchers and examine some policy proposals to make citizens more patriotic. I created and tested a novel contractual theory of patriotism in this book. The processes described by this theory are like a contract in that citizens repay America based on gratitude for what they have been given. In any contract, a giving party provides a good or service, and a receiving party pays for what they have been given. Modern liberal

S. Richey, *Patriotism and Citizenship*,
https://doi.org/10.1007/978-3-031-89885-3_11

democratic nations provide citizens with rights, freedoms, and basic safety and infrastructure so that the citizens can often live thriving, happy lives. In exchange for these tremendously important gifts, many citizens feel grateful and, with it, an obligation to repay it by engaging in acts that help it. These sacrificial acts help the greater good by resolving collective action problems, a central problem of politics.

To test my theory, observational data is combined with experimental evidence to show that patriotism correlates with greater civic engagement, voter turnout, and a specific behavioral measure—clicking on a link to donate blood. I find that patriotism correlates with a willingness to sacrifice for the nation's good, as predicted. While some research shows that parts of this relationship, for example, patriotism, have been shown to correlate with not cheating on taxes (Konrad and Qari 2012), these relationships have been ignored by prior literature.

In addition to these directly and indirectly measured behaviors, I examine attitudes toward the government specifically through diffuse support, which I operationalized as political trust, external political advocacy, and satisfaction with democracy. Again, as predicted by the theory, I find that patriotism positively correlates with all three measurements of diffuse support. These topics were studied because they are both theoretically relevant to patriotism and are important topics that have generated a large amount of prior research. In sum, patriotism positively correlates with some of the most important aspects of citizenship.

Additionally, I found that two common complaints about patriotism are not found in the data. Some critics of patriotism suggest that it impairs citizens' ability to think critically about their government's actions. I theorized that patriotism benefits decision-making in situations in which America does something positive. The research in Chapter 8 shows that in situations where America's economy was improving, patriotic people were more likely to predict this improvement correctly. I do not theorize that this comes from greater rationality or insight, but rather, it derives mechanically due to their general positive assessments of America. In contrast to what was predicted by many critics of patriotism, I also find that patriotic people are no less likely to denote problems with the nation.

I also examined another common complaint about patriotism: it facilitates greater discriminatory attitudes toward marginalized subpopulations. The evidence presented in Chapter 9 shows a general picture that patriotic people are not higher in authoritarian personality, symbolic racism, bigotry, or xenophobia. Together, this research shows that patriotism has many positives and few negatives for citizenship.

I extended this research to local patriotism, a novel concept I developed to explain how similar processes may influence local politics. The idea is that some people love their town and this will create a similar likelihood of resolving collective action problems at the local level. I tested it with similar experimental research and survey data. I find strong evidence that local patriotism influences the likelihood of engaging in collective action-solving at the local level and correlates with many of the same beneficial properties as national-level patriotism for national politics. Among these are greater political participation, civic engagement, trust in local government, and a willingness to pay money to help solve a town's problem. The insights from national-level patriotism showed that the general mechanisms could be applied at other levels and greatly strengthen the theory because it was tested at another level of governance.

Given the demonstrated benefits of patriotism on civic engagement and political participation, it is crucial to consider how these insights can be translated into educational practices. Schools and educational institutions play a pivotal role in shaping future citizens' understanding of their responsibilities and rights. Therefore, fostering patriotism should be a priority in civic education curricula. Policymakers and educators can design programs that emphasize patriotism as a reciprocal social contract, as detailed in this manuscript, to motivate students to contribute positively to democratic society.

In the next section, I will discuss future areas of research that can expand on this work of this book to investigate these topics more fully.

Future Areas of Research on Patriotism

Impact of Nationalism on Citizenship

This research offers a useful correction to much of the theoretical literature on patriotism, as patriotism must be separated from nationalism (sometimes called blind patriotism). Some research shows that nationalism has multiple types and is understood differentially by citizens. For example, using survey data from 34 nations, Davidov (2009) shows that patriotism can be distinguished from nationalism by their ability to be critical of their country. Unpacking these concepts may allow us to show that nationalistic Americans also have different political and social beliefs and behaviors in areas other than discrimination and similar concepts.

It may also have deleterious effects on cognition and political judgment in that it may negate critical analysis. People with nationalistic cognition values also probably can find no fault with the United States, and this, too, needs more research. There are two reasons by which we can expect political judgment to be affected by nationalism. First, they could be making the same mistake that the critics of patriotism are making: They may see any criticism as being inversely proportional to the love of the country—secondly, the extensive literature on manifest destiny and our civil religion (Bellah 1967). Nationalistic people may have quasi-metaphysical belief in the divine blessing of America, which would imply national infallibility because God has ordained this country's destiny.

It may also be that nationalism correlates with socially desirable properties, such as greater participation or volunteering in addition to cultural chauvinism. There has not been enough empirical research on nationalism in other areas to demonstrate these potential impacts, although nationalism has not been found to correlate with volunteerism (Richey 2011). It would benefit future researchers to conduct similar research on the impact to citizenship from nationalism as was conducted in this book on patriotism.

Unpatriotic Americans: Causes and Impacts

One innovation of the research in this book is to take seriously the 5 to 10% of Americans who do not like America. Unpatriotic Americans have been essentially ignored in academic research, and a useful extension of this book is to examine the causes and other potential impacts of lacking patriotism that have been examined in this book. These would be citizens who do not like their country and are quite different from the constructive patriots described in Huddy and Khatib (2007). These anti-Americanists are angry at America's action and have little affection for it. To fully understand the impact of patriotism, we should also focus on these anti-Americanists. Thus, the prior research has not fully investigated patriotism because it has not focused on the minority who are not patriotic.

Maintaining eternal vigilance over the nation's actions is crucial, and those who always oppose a nation make the same cognitive error as blindly supportive nationalists. For example, Barack Obama, speaking about European anti-Americanism, though his words are just as applicable in America, says, "Instead of recognizing the good that America so often does in the world, there have been times where (anti-Americanists) choose to blame America for much of what is bad" (Obama 2009). Obama clearly states the theme of America achieving both good and bad, but anti-Americanists are deterministically blaming the United States and refusing to acknowledge the benefit of America's actions. A future contribution could be to define and model unpatriotic cognition systems based on deterministically negative views of America. Future research would also benefit by taking their complaints seriously by examining what causes them to dislike their own country and how this may affect many political behaviors and beliefs.

Patriotism and Cognition

Additionally, the relationship between cognition and patriotism needs further work in future research. To fully understand the impact of patriotism, researchers should model the different ways patriotism alters judgment. The chief problem revolves around the importance of decision science to understand the impact of patriotism. The problem with nationalistic feelings or blind patriotism is that it is deterministic and does not leave the potential for error open. Determinism will only be correct in the unlikely case that all important actions are either positive or negative. We know from decision science that the most correct decision-making is probabilistic, which recognizes the inherent diversity in most things (Heitele 1975). In other words, the crucial question is not whether the United States is always right or consistently wrong but how often it acts beneficially or not. The starting assumption should be that there have been good and bad, or correct and incorrect, actions.

With topics as complex as the actions of a large nation, it would be nearly impossible for the United States to have always acted negatively or positively, however defined. That is because the thousands of actions the United States takes each year create too many possible decisions for all of them to be disagreeable or agreeable to anyone. The relationship between probabilistic thinking and patriotism is unknown, and it would be beneficial for future researchers to delve into these topics with more specific tests of cognition and judgment.

I now turn to potential ways to promote patriotism based on my contractual theory of patriotism.

Potential Ways to Increase Patriotism Through Civic Participation

Since the book found that patriotism is generally beneficial for a democratic society and features little downside, it is important to think about potential ways to increase patriotism. Based on my contractual theory of patriotism, I posit that civic participation mainly increases patriotism because of the exposure that this would promote to the beneficial work that the government does. Specifically, pedagogical work on promoting civic participation through service learning and how that may relate to collective action is worth investigating. As civic participation has been thought to be decreasing in the United States over the last 50 years (see Putnam 2000), it may have impacted patriotism, which would possibly have down-the-line impacts on public opinion, strength of partisanship, and vote choice. The findings in Chapter 8 show that the concern that service-learning or other programs promoting civic participation are wrong to imply that greater participation leads to a loss of critical abilities and greater blind patriotism. The results suggest that the stimulation of civic participation will benefit citizenship if it promotes greater patriotism and should be promoted.

Of all the potential ways to increase patriotism, the most straightforward one is through service-learning projects in education. At its core, distrust of government resolves around the feeling that the government is run by people who will not listen to it, which is another way of saying external efficacy. Comparatively, the United States has less corruption and higher efficiency in its bureaucracy than most governments (see, e.g., Transparency International 2022). Additionally, survey data suggests that most people are happy with their interactions with government workers (Wang et al. 2021). One would assume then that the more citizens get off their phones and out into the streets working with government officials on beneficial volunteer projects, their likelihood to have efficacy and trust in government and thereby subsequently increase their feelings of appreciation for the hard work the government does every day to keep the roads, schools, trains, and planes running, with this greater appreciation for the gifts that the government has given them, my contractual theory suggests that they would be more likely to have feelings of gratitude. The most straightforward way to ensure citizens are involved with beneficial voluntary projects is to mandate them in schools through service learning projects. By giving students credit for participating in these voluntary activities, they will have beneficial interactions with the government and, on the whole, come out net positive even if they are sometimes unhappy with the experience.

I expect two things from greater civic participation: increased love and criticism for their society. Thus, civic participation should increase patriotism. These improved feelings toward others, combined with improved knowledge of society's problems, will develop a constructive patriotism that is loving and critical. At the same time, these enlightening experiences may also show that the nation is not always good or without problems and contains hypocrisies. By greater civic participation, these people will encounter realities that bust the myths that undergird and motivate blind patriotism. These experiences will then directly work to lower nationalism, which is blind to the nation's problems.

Based on research on social capital discussed above, it may be that civic participation alters patriotism. It consists of two widely validated claims about the impact of civic participation. Firstly, much literature shows that face-to-face interaction and the communal spirit gained through participation engender better feelings about society (e.g., Ikeda and Richey 2009). In this view, civic participation develops the inherent norms of reciprocity experienced when working together, which makes people feel that their neighbors will treat them fairly (Rothstein 2005). So, the first impact of patriotism from civic participation will be an increase in care for the society they worked to help. The second impact of civic participation on patriotism involves developing knowledge about societal problems. Civic participation has been widely shown to increase knowledge of politics and society's problems (see Galston 2007 for a summary). In part, many forms of civic participation are directed toward specific problems. With increased experiential knowledge of problems gained through voluntary activities, civic participation will develop critical citizens with a list of things they want changed about their society. Thus, we can expect greater interaction with civic participation to stimulate patriotism and provide one avenue to promote patriotism.

I now conclude by considering patriotism's impact on society.

Conclusion

Although modern politics features almost daily accusations of blind nationalism that are often misrepresented as patriotism or accusations that critics of America lack patriotism, academic research has not sufficiently studied this crucial concept for modern citizenship. The in-depth research on patriotism undertaken in this book shows the crucial nature of patriotism in American politics. Volunteering, voter turnout, trust in government, and conspiracy theories are almost universally considered crucial topics. The fact that patriotism correlates in a beneficial way to augment these crucial characteristics of a democratic society shows the potential benefits of patriotism. In sum, I find that various measures of sacrifice for the United States positively correlate with patriotism, which has profound importance for understanding American politics.

It is crucial to note that two of the main complaints over patriotism, which are that it affects political judgment by making someone blind to society's problems and that it promotes discriminatory attitudes, were not shown to be empirically valid in Chapters 8 and 9. Additionally, local patriotism was presented as a novel way to understand town politics. The causal mechanisms shown by the national experiment also affect local-level behaviors, such as blood donation or financial donations. This suggests that the correlations found are potentially measuring causal relationships. Although this cannot be stated with certainty, this research suggests that increasing patriotism at a minimum will support collective action problem solving, which theory has suggested is useful for these other important characteristics of democratic citizenship. In sum, patriotism is beneficial and worthwhile to promote in society.

References

Bellah, Robert N. 1967. "Civil Religion in America." *Daedalus* 96 (1): 1–21.

Davidov, Eldad. 2009. "Measurement Equivalence of Nationalism and Constructive Patriotism in the ISSP: 34 Countries in a Comparative Perspective." *Political Analysis* 17 (1): 64–82.

Galston, William A. 2007. "Civic Knowledge, Civic Education, and Civic Engagement: A Summary of Recent Research." *International Journal of Public Administration* 30 (6): 623–642.

Heitele, D. 1975. "An Epistemological View on Fundamental Stochastic Ideas." *Educational Studies in Mathematics* 6: 187–205.

Huddy, Leonie, and Nadia Khatib. 2007. "American Patriotism, National Identity, and Political Involvement." *American Journal of Political Science* 51 (1): 63–77.

Ikeda, Ken'ichi, and Sean Richey. 2009. "The Impact of Diversity in Informal Social Networks on Tolerance." *British Journal of Political Science* 39 (3): 655–668.

Konrad, Kai A., and Faizel Ismail Qari. 2012. "The Last Refuge of a Scoundrel? Patriotism and Tax Compliance." *Economics Letters* 115 (1): 12–14.

Obama, Barack. 2009. "Strasbourg Townhall Address." Lecture, Strasbourg France, April 3.

Putnam, Robert D. 2000. *Bowling Alone: The Collapse and Revival of American Community*. New York: Simon & Schuster.

Richey, Sean. 2011. "Civic Engagement and Patriotism." *Social Science Quarterly* 42 (4): 1044–1056.

Rothstein, Bo. 2005. *Social Traps and the Problem of Trust*. Cambridge UK: Cambridge University Press.

Transparency International. 2022. "Corruption Perceptions Index." Technical Report. Accessed at: https://www.transparency.org/en/cpi/2022

Wang, F., K.-N. Jun, and L. Wang. 2021. "Bureaucratic Contacts and their Impact on Citizen Satisfaction with Local Government Agencies: The Influence of Expectation." *Public Policy and Administration* 3 (1): 41–68.

Appendix

S. Richey, *Patriotism and Citizenship*,
https://doi.org/10.1007/978-3-031-89885-3

Table A1 Correlation matrix patriotism and 2012 ANES volunteering items

	Patriotism		*paprofile_ orgschool*	*paprofile_ orgyouth*	*paprofile_ orgethnic*	*paprofile_ attendpta*	*paprofile_ attendcommun*	*paprofile_ workcharity*	*paprofile_ workcommuniss*	*paprofile_ workcommbd*
Patriotism	1.00									
paprofile_ orgservice	0.06									
	(0.00)									
		1.00								
paprofile_ orgveterans	0.05									
	(0.00)									
		0.06								
paprofile_ orgrelig	0.08	(0.00)								
	(0.00)									
		0.05								
paprofile_ orgsenior	0.07	(0.01)								
	(0.00)									
		0.13								
paprofile_ orgwomen	0.04	(0.00)								
	(0.01)									
		0.04								
paprofile_ orgcivic	0.02	(0.02)								
	(0.17)									
		0.26								

	Patriotism		*paprofile_ orgschool*	*paprofile_ orgyouth*	*paprofile_ orgethnic*	*paprofile_ attendpta*	*paprofile_ attendcommun*	*paprofile_ workcharity*	*paprofile_ workcommuniss*	*paprofile_ workcommbd*
paprofile_ orgschool	–0.00	(0.00)	1.00							
	(0.83)									
		0.1[illegible]								
paprofile_ orgyouth	0.05	(0.00)	0.18	1.00						
	(0.00)		(0.00)							
		0.27								
paprofile_ orgethnic	–0.01	(0.00)	0.06	0.03	1.00					
	(0.42)		(0.00)	(0.06)						
		0.30								
paprofile_ attendpta	0.01	(0.00)	0.38	0.09	0.01	1.00				
	(0.70)		(0.00)	(0.00)	(0.38)					
paprofile_ attendcommun	0.08		0.17	0.15	0.12	0.18	1.00			
	(0.00)		(0.00)	(0.00)	(0.00)	(0.00)				
paprofile_ workcharity	0.10		0.12	0.14	0.05	0.13	0.23	1.00		
	(0.00)		(0.00)	(0.00)	(0.00)	(0.00)	(0.00)			
paprofile_ workcommuniss	0.03		0.13	0.14	0.09	0.10	0.42	0.25	1.00	
	(0.05)		(0.00)	(0.00)	(0.00)	(0.00)	(0.00)	(0.00)		

(continued)

Table A1 (continued)

	Patriotism	*paprofile_ orgschool*	*paprofile_ orgyouth*	*paprofile_ orgethnic*	*paprofile_ attendpta*	*paprofile_ attendcommun*	*paprofile_ workcharity*	*paprofile_ workcommuniss*	*paprofile_ workcommbd*
paprofile_ workcommbd	0.04	0.11	0.09	0.13	0.11	0.31	0.18	0.34	1.00
	(0.02)	(0.00)	(0.00)	(0.00)	(0.00)	(0.00)	(0.00)	(0.00)	

Note p-values in parentheses

Table A2 Attitudes towards gays and lesbians

	Coef.	*S.E*
Patriotism	2.745*	1.345
American identity	−1.525	1.050
Generalized trust	−5.534***	1.210
Ideology	5.564***	0.755
Female	7.911***	1.948
Age	−2.579***	0.661
Hispanic	−0.572	3.906
Education	2.040	1.077
Income	0.077	0.345
Black	−10.969***	2.966
Trump voter	−8.292*	3.338
Intercept	55.610***	14.878
N	550	
r2	0.344	

Table A3 Attitudes towards Muslims

	Coef.	*S.E*
Patriotism	0.989	1.471
American identity	−1.279	1.149
Trump voter	−8.310*	3.653
Generalized trust	−7.158***	1.324
Ideology	3.309***	0.826
Female	5.987**	2.132
Age	−3.160***	0.723
Hispanic	−2.907	4.274
Education	2.749*	1.178
Income	0.198	0.378
Black	−1.359	3.246
Intercept	79.356***	16.279
N	550	
r2	0.238	

Table A4 Attitudes towards immigration

	Coef.	*S.E*
Patriotism	–0.086	0.117
American identity	–0.130	0.090
Generalized trust	–0.305**	0.107
Ideology	0.615***	0.070
Female	–0.185	0.164
Age	–0.132*	0.056
Hispanic	–0.270	0.316
Education	0.266**	0.090
Income	–0.004	0.029
Black	–0.371	0.248
Trump voter	–0.439	0.283
cut1	–3.174*	1.255
cut2	–2.019	1.250
cut3	0.604	1.252
cut4	2.174	1.254
N	550	
chi2	253.589***	

Table A5 Government trust

	Coef.	*S.E*
Patriotism	0.473***	0.120
American identity	0.291**	0.094
Generalized trust	–0.850***	0.112
Ideology	0.228***	0.055
Female	–0.009	0.167
Age	0.061	0.057
Hispanic	–0.534	0.350
Education	0.230*	0.092
Income	–0.036	0.030
Black	0.545*	0.249
cut1	3.022*	1.326
cut2	5.787***	1.346
cut3	7.680***	1.359
cut4	12.069***	1.692
N	550	
chi2	186.215***	

Table A6 Efficacy

	Coef.	*S.E*
Patriotism	0.491***	0.114
American identity	0.191*	0.089
Generalized trust	–0.406***	0.104
Ideology	0.296***	0.054
Female	0.032	0.165
Age	0.199***	0.056
Hispanic	–0.560	0.344
Education	0.098	0.091
Income	0.011	0.029
Black	0.010	0.243
cut1	2.768*	1.283
cut2	4.031**	1.282
cut3	4.711***	1.286
cut4	6.614***	1.303
N	550	
chi2	139.709***	

Table A7 Democracy satisfaction

	Coef.	*S.E*
Patriotism	0.782***	0.119
American identity	0.071	0.089
Generalized trust	–0.551***	0.104
Ideology	–0.060	0.053
Female	0.146	0.163
Age	0.016	0.054
Hispanic	–0.589	0.334
Education	–0.115	0.089
Income	0.017	0.028
Black	0.462	0.244
cut1	1.083	1.241
cut2	2.947*	1.247
cut3	3.630**	1.250
cut4	6.869***	1.278
N	550	
chi2	165.309***	

Index

A

American National Election Studies (ANES), 6, 33, 43, 51, 53, 85, 90, 99, 102, 103, 105, 107, 114, 116, 117, 120, 130, 135, 145, 148, 151, 167, 168, 170

Anti-Americanism, 19, 22, 48, 50, 189

Authoritarianism, 6, 12, 13, 143, 144, 147

B

Blood donation experiment, 7, 77, 81–83, 192

C

Civic duty, 32, 92, 97–99, 104, 108, 109, 158, 162

Civic engagement, 2, 3, 5, 7, 8, 11, 20, 22, 25, 29, 64–66, 68, 77–80, 83–85, 87–89, 91, 154, 186, 187

Collective action, 4, 5, 7, 9–11, 13, 18, 21, 23, 26–30, 32, 36, 37, 68, 74, 75, 77–80, 82, 83, 89, 91, 92, 112, 154, 159, 160, 164, 165, 168, 175, 177–179, 186, 187, 190, 192

Collective action problem, 7, 9, 11, 13, 18, 23, 26, 27, 32, 74, 83, 91, 112, 159, 164, 175, 177–179, 186, 187, 192

Constitutional patriotism, 21, 161, 180

Constructive patriotism, 21, 22, 58, 61, 161, 180, 191

Contractual theory of patriotism, 9, 17, 19, 21, 23, 25, 27, 29, 31, 33, 35–37, 39, 98, 108, 158, 185, 189, 190

Cost-benefit analysis, 2, 5, 6, 28, 29, 104, 109, 162

D

Democracy, 3, 5, 8, 9, 11, 12, 17, 21, 22, 28, 29, 34, 35, 45, 95,

S. Richey, *Patriotism and Citizenship*,
https://doi.org/10.1007/978-3-031-89885-3

96, 98, 113–115, 117, 118, 120, 121, 124, 125, 138, 147, 186
Diffuse support, 7, 11, 12, 20, 34, 37, 65, 109, 111–114, 121, 186
Drift-Diffusion model, 30, 31

E

Empirical research on patriotism, 141

F

Freedom and patriotism, 75

I

Immigration and national attitudes, 2

L

Local patriotism, 8, 13, 36, 154, 157–165, 168–177, 179, 180, 187, 192
Locke, John, 24

M

MacIntyre, Alasdair, 20, 33, 37
Merry, Michael S, 4

N

National identity, 2, 22, 55
Nationalism, 2, 19–22, 55, 74, 142, 143, 162, 187, 188, 191, 192
National pride, 2

P

Patriotism and democracy, 8, 12, 22, 35, 96, 114, 118, 186
Patriotism and education, 2–4, 8, 17, 109, 124, 128, 154, 180
Patriotism and history education, 4
Patriotism in mass media, 4, 26
Pew Research Center studies on patriotism, 1
Political behavior, 3, 4, 18–20, 36, 189
Political efficacy, 3, 11, 12, 28, 34, 35, 116, 117, 121
Political ideologies, 42, 54
Political judgment, 12, 33, 37, 121, 124–128, 131, 136, 138, 188, 192
Political participation, 2, 3, 5, 7, 8, 11, 20, 28, 32, 33, 36, 64, 65, 68, 74, 91, 96, 97, 104–107, 109, 114, 117, 158, 160, 162, 166, 167, 171–173, 179, 187
Political psychology, 3
Political trust, 3, 11, 12, 19, 34, 71, 113–115, 121, 147, 163, 167, 175, 186
Populism, 2
Psychological benefits of patriotism, 5
Public opinion, 3, 4, 19, 36, 69, 70, 139, 190

R

Rational choice theory, 27
Riker, William H., 5, 27–29, 32, 158, 162

S

Social contract theory, 24, 187
Socialization of patriotism, 26, 28, 96, 99, 170
Surveys on patriotism, 3, 4, 43, 45, 48, 103, 113

T

Tacit consent (Locke), 24, 98
Text analysis in political science, 69

V

Viroli, Maurizio, 21
Voter turnout, 3, 11, 32, 36, 95–104, 106, 108, 109, 166, 186, 192

X

Xenophobia, 3, 6, 7, 12, 13, 21, 23, 35, 37, 66, 121, 123, 139, 142, 143, 146, 149, 153, 187

The manufacturer's authorised representative in the EU is Springer Nature Customer Service Centre GmbH, Europaplatz 3, 69115 Heidelberg, Germany. If you have any concerns regarding our products, please contact ProductSafety@springernature.com

Printed and bound by CPI Group (UK) Ltd, Croydon, CR0 4YY
22/06/2025
01905090-0002